Year 1
Teacher's Guide

Author: Alison Milford

William Collins' dream of knowledge for all began with the publication of his first book in 1819. A self-educated mill worker, he not only enriched millions of lives, but also founded a flourishing publishing house. Today, staying true to this spirit, Collins books are packed with inspiration, innovation and practical expertise. They place you at the centre of a world of possibility and give you exactly what you need to explore it.

Collins. Freedom to teach.

Published by Collins
An imprint of HarperCollins*Publishers*
The News Building
1 London Bridge Street
London
SE1 9GF

Browse the complete Collins catalogue at
www.collins.co.uk

British Library Cataloguing in Publication Data

A Catalogue record for this publication is available from the British Library

Publishing Managers: Tom Guy and Lizzie Catford
Project Managers: Dawn Booth and Sarah Thomas
Development editor: Jessica Marshall
Copy editor: Cassandra Fox
Cover design and artwork: Amparo Barrera
Internal design: Linda Miles and Hugh Hillyard-Parker

Printed in Great Britain by Martins the Printers

Contents

Contents

Welcome to the Treasure House Teacher's Guide for Year 1

Welcome to this Treasure House Teacher's Guide. We have created this guide, with our expert authors, to provide a framework that will support you in planning your literacy teaching across Year 1. In the 15 engaging teaching sequences it contains, we have woven together the four core dimensions of the National Curriculum for English:

- Comprehension
- Composition
- Vocabulary, Grammar and Punctuation
- Spelling.

Word reading, speaking and listening, and transcription skills are integral throughout all sequences, as this is fundamental to the development of all literacy learning.

All of these elements are covered in each of the teaching sequences, as we have always found that applied learning is by far the most effective. Our experience is that this approach allows children to practise their skills purposefully and improves retention, particularly of spelling, vocabulary, grammar and punctuation. It is also considerably more fun!

The teaching sequences can be used as the basis of your literacy planning, providing potentially 30 weeks of teaching inspiration. They feature a range of different literary genres, both fiction and non-fiction. We have also included a wide range of poetry as, in addition to featuring prominently in the National Curriculum, its comprehension and composition can have a profound impact on a child's more general reading, writing and thinking skills. The sequences and the Curriculum Coverage Charts suggest which National Curriculum objectives will be covered by each unit so that full curriculum coverage can be achieved.

We all know, however, that formative assessment provides the most effective guidance for planning. Therefore, we have designed the units to be adaptable to the needs of different classes, according to your professional judgement. The sequences can be used in any order and the activities can be adjusted, to meet the needs of your class and to fit with your broader teaching scheme. Their flexibility allows you to draw upon your own experiences, and apply your own imagination, as frequently as you wish. This is a handbook that seeks to support and enhance teachers', as well as children's, skills and creativity.

Christine Chen and **Lindsay Pickton**
Primary Education Advisors
Series Editors, Treasure House Teacher's Guides

About Treasure House

Treasure House is a comprehensive and flexible bank of print and digital resources covering the 2014 English Programme of Study.

Treasure House comprises of:

- Print Pupil Books
- Print Teacher's Guides and Anthologies
- Online digital resources hosted on Collins Connect.

Treasure House Teacher's Guides and Anthologies

There are six Treasure House Teacher's Guides and six Anthologies. Each Teacher's Guide provides 15 teaching sequences. The sequences weave together all four dimensions of the National Curriculum for English – Comprehension; Composition; Vocabulary, Grammar and Punctuation; and Spelling – into a complete unit of work. The Anthologies contain the source texts for each sequence.

Treasure House Teacher's Guides and Anthologies

Year	Teacher's Guides	Anthologies	Year	Teacher's Guides	Anthologies
1	978-0-00-813360-3	978-0-00-816044-9	4	978-0-00-813357-3	978-0-00-816047-0
2	978-0-00-813359-7	978-0-00-816045-6	5	978-0-00-813356-6	978-0-00-816048-7
3	978-0-00-813358-0	978-0-00-816046-3	6	978-0-00-813355-9	978-0-00-816049-4

Inside the Treasure House Teacher's Guides and Anthologies

The Teacher's Guides contain 15 teaching sequences. Every teaching sequence follows the same four phases:

- **Enjoy and immerse** engages children with a source text through discussion and comprehension activities.
- **Capture and organise** uses discussion, drama and writing to help children analyse the text in more depth and record ideas for written work.
- **Collaborative composition** supports group and classwork exploring the process of writing.
- **Independent writing** provides opportunities for children to construct their own texts independently.

The Anthologies contain fully illustrated, extended extracts from all the text types specified in the curriculum, including classic fiction and leading contemporary children's authors. The extracts should be used as source texts for the teaching sequences.

About Treasure House

Teacher's Guide

Source text details provide information on the Anthology texts for each sequence.

Big Picture outlines success criteria for the sequence.

Diagnostic assessment options support an effective teaching and learning cycle by assessing children's knowledge and understanding at the start of a sequence.

Cross-curricular links gives details of curriculum objectives that are covered from other areas of the National Curriculum.

Rhymes and poems

Sequence 4
Rhymes and poems

Approximate duration: Two weeks

Big Picture

Through this teaching sequence, children explore the poem, 'Cats'. By the end of the sequence, they will have written a new version of the poem, based on a different element of a cat's life and behaviour.

Phase 1: Enjoy and immerse

Children become familiar with the content, language and structure of the model text poem, 'Cats'.

Phase 2: Capture and organise

Children are supported in developing ideas for a new poem about cats.

Phase 3: Collaborate and compose

Children undertake supported writing sessions to develop their own writing based on the class poem.

Phase 4: Write independently

Children write, edit and read aloud their own poems about cats.

Main source text

Treasure House Anthology Sequence 4 text, 'Cats', Eleanor Farjeon, *The Puffin Book of Fantastic First Poems*, ISBN 978-01-41-30898-2, p.6

Extra source texts

'No Hickory No Dickory No Dock', John Agard, *The Puffin Book of Fantastic First Poems*, ISBN 978-0-14-130898-2, p.15

Background knowledge

Eleanor Farjeon (1881–1965) was a prolific English author, poet and playwright whose stories, poems and nursery rhymes for children have been universally acclaimed and are still popular today. She grew up in a large, literary, creative family, with a father and two brothers who were also writers and another brother who was a composer. Encouraged to write from an early age, she got her inspirations for her writing from everyday life around her and on her many trips away. Her most well-known work today is her children's hymn, 'Morning has broken' (1931), which is sung to an old Scottish folk tune.

Spoken outcome

To read or perform their poem on cats

Writing outcome

To write a poem about cats

Prior knowledge

Check children's knowledge and understanding of:

* cats and their behaviour
* poems with simple rhymes
* nursery rhymes (including by Eleanor Farjeon)
* poems about animals and cats.

62

Rhymes and poems

Diagnostic assessment options

Before starting the unit, you may wish to conduct an initial diagnostic assessment of the children's knowledge and understanding.

Ideas for initial diagnostic assessment options include:

* reviewing children's writing for correct sentence punctuation in poems and verses such as capital letters at the beginnings of lines
* speaking and listening activities where children listen to and identify exclamation sentences
* reviewing children's writing for their ability to understand and use compound words
* reviewing children's writing to check for the correct spelling of words with the /k/ sound spelled ck.

Cross-curricular links

KS1 Art and design

* Use drawing, painting and sculpture to develop and share their ideas, experiences and imagination.

KS1 Music

* Use their voices expressively and creatively by singing songs and speaking chants and rhymes.

KS1 Science – Animals, including humans

* Identify and name a variety of common animals including fish, amphibians, reptiles, birds and mammals.
* Identify and name a variety of common animals that are carnivores, herbivores and omnivores.

Treasure House links

* Treasure House, Year 1, Comprehension Unit 4: Rhymes and poems: 'Cats'
* Treasure House, Year 1, Composition Unit 6: Poetry: My Favourite
* Treasure House, Year 1, Punctuation Unit 1: Punctuating sentences
* Treasure House, Year 1, Spelling Unit 2: Spelling ck after a short vowel

Resources

Props and percussion instruments for drama and storytelling activities (optional); information and images of cats and their behaviour

63

Background knowledge contains contextualising information on the text type and content of the text.

Spoken outcome and **Written outcome** provide oral and written outcomes for each sequence.

Prior knowledge lists questions to help elicit what children already know.

Treasure House links lists details of relevant units in the Pupil Books and digital resources.

Anthology

Extended extracts provide quality source texts for use during the teaching sequences.

Non-fiction

Fabulous Creatures – Are They Real? by Scoular Anderson

Phoenix

A phoenix is a bird with magnificent gold and purple feathers. When it's about to die, it builds a nest of cinnamon twigs in the tallest palm tree it can find. As soon as it jumps into the nest, the sun heats it so that the nest bursts into flames and the phoenix is turned to ashes.

Is this fabulous creature real or not?

No!

The phoenix is a bird from an ancient Egyptian legend. People believed that the bird lived for a long time – between 500 and 1,000 years. It never ate anything – ever!

In the legend, as soon as the phoenix and its nest had been burnt, a small worm crawled out of the ashes. This eventually turned into another phoenix – so the bird never really died.

The word "phoenix" is Greek, meaning "palm tree" or "purple".

When someone talks about something "rising like a phoenix from the ashes", they mean it has been reborn.

Beautiful illustrations engage children with the text.

7

About Treasure House

Treasure House Pupil Books

There are four Treasure House Pupil Books for each year group, based on the four dimensions of the National Curriculum for English: Comprehension; Composition; Vocabulary, Grammar and Punctuation; and Spelling.

Treasure House Pupil Books

Year	Comprehension	Composition	Vocabulary, Grammar and Punctuation	Spelling
1	978-0-00-813348-1	978-0-00-813354-2	978-0-00-813336-8	978-0-00-813342-9
2	978-0-00-813347-4	978-0-00-813353-5	978-0-00-813335-1	978-0-00-813341-2
3	978-0-00-813346-7	978-0-00-813352-8	978-0-00-813334-4	978-0-00-813340-5
4	978-0-00-813345-0	978-0-00-813351-1	978-0-00-813333-7	978-0-00-813339-9
5	978-0-00-813344-3	978-0-00-813350-4	978-0-00-813332-0	978-0-00-813338-2
6	978-0-00-813343-6	978-0-00-813349-8	978-0-00-813331-3	978-0-00-813337-5

About Treasure House

Inside Treasure House Print Pupil Books

Comprehension

Includes high-quality, annotated text extracts covering poetry, prose, traditional tales, playscripts and non-fiction.

Pupils retrieve and record information, learn to draw inferences from texts and increase their familiarity with a wide range of literary genres.

Composition

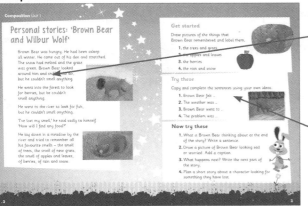

Includes high-quality, annotated text extracts as models for different types of writing.

Children learn how to write effectively and for a purpose.

Vocabulary, Grammar and Punctuation

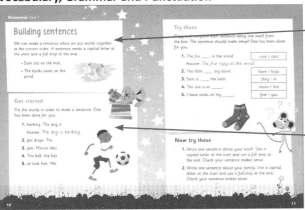

Develops children's knowledge and understanding of grammar and punctuation skills.

A rule is introduced and explained. Children are given lots of opportunities to practise using it.

Spelling

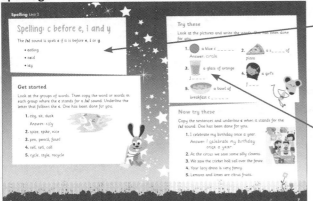

Spelling rules are introduced and explained.

Supports children to remember key spelling rules by investigating how they work.

About Treasure House

Treasure House on Collins Connect

Digital pupil resources for Treasure House are available on Collins Connect, an innovative learning platform designed to support teachers and pupils by providing a wealth of interactive activities.

Treasure House is organised into six core areas on Collins Connect:

- Comprehension
- Composition
- Vocabulary, Grammar and Punctuation
- Spelling
- Reading Attic
- Teacher's Guides and Anthologies.

Features of Treasure House on Collins Connect

The digital resources enhance children's comprehension, composition, vocabulary, grammar, punctuation and spelling skills through providing:

- a bank of varied and engaging interactive activities so children can practise their skills
- audio support to help children access the texts and activities
- auto-mark functionality so children receive instant feedback and have the opportunity to repeat tasks.

Comprehension

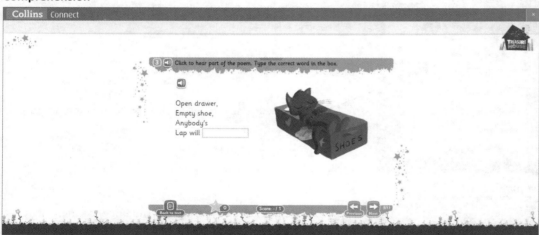

- Includes high-quality, annotated text extracts covering poetry, prose, traditional tales, playscripts and non-fiction.
- Audio function supports children to access the text and the activities.

Composition

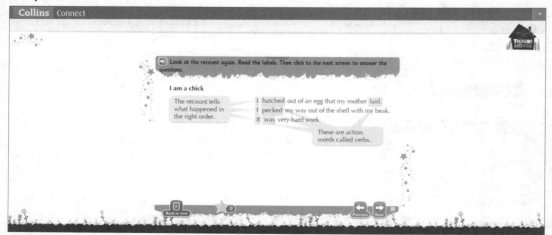

- Activities support children to develop and build more sophisticated sentence structures.
- Every unit ends with a longer piece of writing that can be submitted to the teacher for marking.

About Treasure House

Vocabulary, Grammar and Punctuation

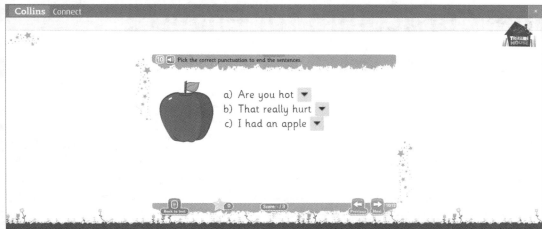

- Fun, practical activities develop children's knowledge and understanding of grammar and punctuation skills.
- Each skill is reinforced with a huge, varied bank of practice questions.

Spelling

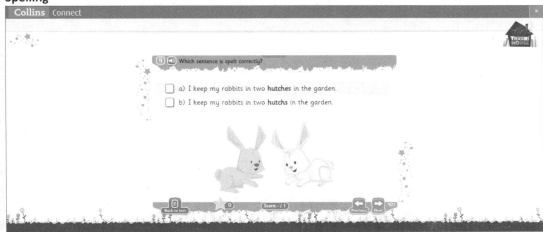

- Fun, practical activities develop children's knowledge and understanding of each spelling rule.
- Each rule is reinforced with a huge, varied bank of practice questions

Reading Attic

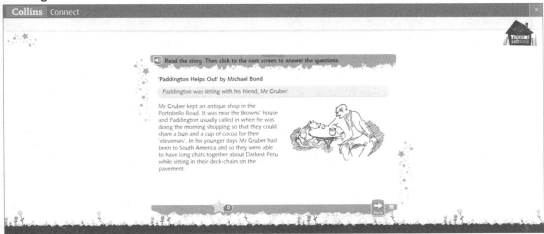

- Children's love of reading is nurtured with texts from the most exciting children's authors.
- Lesson sequences accompany the texts, with drama opportunities and creative strategies for engaging children with key themes, characters and plots.

Treasure House Digital Teacher's Guides and Anthologies

The teaching sequences and anthology texts for each year group are included as a flexible bank of resources on Collins Connect.

The National Curriculum for English: An overview

Purpose and aims

The Treasure House Teacher Guides are designed not only to support teaching of the statutory programmes of study effectively but also as a response to the ethos of the National Curriculum for English. The overarching aim for English in the National Curriculum is to promote high standards of literacy by equipping pupils with a strong command of the written and spoken word, and to develop their love of literature through widespread reading for enjoyment. As the curriculum maintains, reading 'feeds pupils' imagination and opens up a treasure-house of wonder and joy for curious young minds'.

Treasure House encourages children to engage with a wide range of stories, poetry and non-fiction, to apply their literacy skills and develop their vocabulary and knowledge alongside their love of reading. In its study of these varied texts, it incorporates the four core dimensions of the National Curriculum for English:

- Comprehension
- Composition
- Vocabulary, Grammar and Punctuation
- Spelling.

Across these dimensions, it also provides thorough coverage of the underpinning principles and practices of literacy, from oracy and word reading to proofreading.

Spoken language

The National Curriculum states that spoken language is vital to the development of reading, writing and thinking: the quality and variety of language that pupils hear and speak are vital for developing their vocabulary and grammar, and their understanding for reading and writing. We have placed oracy at the heart of every sequence as we (like teachers everywhere) know that spoken language underpins the development of reading and writing. Each sequence, therefore, assists pupils to develop a capacity to explain their understanding of books and other reading, and to prepare their ideas, before they write. This assists them in making their thinking clear to themselves as well as to others.

Reading: Word reading

Alongside comprehension, the curriculum identifies the importance of speedy, accurate word reading. The development of speedy decoding of unfamiliar words and the rapid recognition of known words is utterly vital in every child's progression towards automatic word reading, and every opportunity across the curriculum must be seized to help children towards this goal. Treasure House includes phonics and word recognition in its 'Phonics and spelling' sessions in Phases 1 and 2, and its texts provide ample opportunity to implement the primary strategy for developing this fluency: one-to-one reading. Whole-class, shared reading of the source texts also benefits many children's development in this direction. At these points in the teaching sequences, you can use your knowledge of children's needs to emphasise particular word-reading skills. In the curriculum and in Treasure House, however, the goal of reading is making meaning from texts. Word reading supports comprehension; it is not an end goal independent of application.

Writing: Transcription (spelling and handwriting)

As the curriculum establishes, effective transcription enables composed ideas to flow onto a page in a manner that is legible to any reader.

The National Curriculum requires that children be taught to spell quickly and accurately, requiring phonics, knowledge of conventions and rules, and the learning and application of many words. For transcription, as for word reading, the development of speedy association between spoken and written words is vital. Treasure House includes phonics and word writing in its 'Phonics and

spelling' sessions in Phases 1 and 2, which teach the statutorily required rules and patterns of the National Curriculum (see the core dimension of Spelling, below). Word transcription is furthermore necessary for every composition activity in Treasure House and, at these points in the teaching sequences, you can use your knowledge of children's requirements to emphasise particular word-writing skills as necessary.

Effective writing also requires fluent, legible and eventually speedy handwriting. Handwriting is a filter through which children's ideas must pass and a child with poor handwriting is at risk of achieving poor written outcomes, even if they have the best ideas in the room. Treasure House Teacher's Guides assume discrete teaching and practice of handwriting, as well as high expectations for application in children's own writing. We have not tried to define specific handwriting practices within the sequences, as each school has its own approach and policy designed best to suit the needs of their children. However, during the shared writing session of Phase 3 in each teaching sequence, expected handwriting styles may be modelled. Phase 4, in addition, provides the opportunity for children to edit and redraft their work: a second draft is a chance for a child to concentrate on their very best presentation, as their ideas have already been captured and organised.

The four core dimensions

Comprehension

The National Curriculum states: 'Comprehension skills develop through pupils' experience of high-quality discussion with the teacher, as well as from reading and discussing a range of stories, poems and non-fiction.' The comprehension teaching in Treasure House is built on questions that will stimulate children's ability to think more deeply, and enable dialogue necessary for them to explore meaning in both broader contexts and closer detail. High-quality questioning, as well as space for children to test their ideas about a text through discussion, is key to progressing children's comprehension skills. Phases 1 and 2 of the teaching sequences focus on developing these skills, and also identify appropriate points for drama, storytelling and oracy activities that will further develop children's grasp of the main and underlying ideas within and between texts.

Composition

As the National Curriculum states, composition is the generation, articulation and organisation of ideas in ways that are appropriate to different purposes and audiences. It is also deceptively complex. Some children appear to be natural writers, while others may struggle with ideas, organisation and/or the concept of an intended reader. However, all children have the potential to become effective writers. Imitation, even when unconsciously applied, is at the heart of learning to compose: children who can write stories also know stories. All children may be helped towards better writing if shown how to generate and organise ideas appropriately, for different purposes and audiences, and then how to transfer them successfully from plan to page.

Each Treasure House sequence builds towards children becoming competent writers. Phase 1 provides the inspiration and model for their eventual composition task, Phase 2 supports the generation and organisation of ideas and Phase 3 shows children how to apply vocabulary, grammar and punctuation skills to these ideas while composing collaboratively. In Phase 4, children demonstrate the composition skills they have accrued by planning, writing, redrafting and presenting or performing their own texts. They are encouraged to reflect on the effectiveness of their composition and compare it to the sequence's source texts in order to achieve the desired impact on their readers and learn from their choices for the future.

Vocabulary, Grammar and Punctuation

The Curriculum emphasises the use of Standard English, and growing mastery of grammar and punctuation in context. It also encourages the use of correct terminology for grammar and punctuation, enabling children and teachers to share a common language with which to talk about their reading and writing.

In Treasure House, stress is placed upon the applied use of grammar, rather than discrete grammatical exercises. National Curriculum objectives for vocabulary, grammar and punctuation are introduced in Phases 1 and 3, and woven into composition activities throughout Phase 3. In this way, children are able to implement their new knowledge immediately, and to see and discuss its effects of their writing. The suggested vocabulary, grammar and punctuation activities are not intended to constrain or restrict teachers' creativity: they can be changed or adapted to suit children's needs.

Spelling

Spelling, a priority in the National Curriculum, is a skill that many children find difficult. Ensuring that spelling is taught frequently, to all year groups, is essential. The Treasure House sequences cover all of the National Curriculum objectives, both from its programme of study and its spelling appendix (which are mainly on phonics, spelling patterns, and using prefixes and suffixes). The words on the word lists supplied for each year group in the curriculum, however, are not taught exhaustively. Encouraging the children to use these words in their own writing (perhaps with reference to these lists) will help to embed the vocabulary in their minds.

Treasure House suggests spelling activities in Phases 1 and 2, in discrete teaching sessions. Whilst we have found that grammar and punctuation is most effectively learnt when it is applied in writing in the very same lesson, we regard spelling as having a great deal in common with number bonds and times tables: it requires the frequency of regular 'starter' activities, and does not necessarily have a direct connection to the rest of the lesson. Seeing a particular word or spelling pattern in the model text is helpful, but it is not always possible in texts that have been chosen for their quality and relevance to young readers.

Because the spelling sessions are discrete, they can (like the vocabulary, grammar and punctuation sessions) be changed or adapted to suit children's needs. Each child's progress with spelling will be so variable that your knowledge of children's needs must take precedence, and will allow you to emphasise particular spelling skills as required. Personalised spelling strategies and learning targets, plus practice and application, are vital.

The flexibility inherent to Treasure House will allow you to customise your lessons to fit the needs of your class and your own teaching preferences. The goal of the Treasure House Teacher's Guides is to help you to help children become literate, literary and both confident and competent in English.

Using a Treasure House teaching sequence

This diagram reflects a literacy unit planning process that many schools use, and the process that we apply when supporting teachers with organising their literacy sequences. This is the route that every Treasure House teaching sequence follows.

The structure and content of a Treasure House sequence

Phase 1: Enjoy and immerse

- Firstly, choose a text that will both engage the class and provide the language style and overall structure that you want to see in the children's writing: this is 'the source text'. The source texts are prescribed for each Treasure House sequence, and are available in the anthology.

- Present the children with the 'Big Picture' from the outset: the reasons that they are looking at the source text, and the outcomes it will help them to achieve. The aim is that the children write texts in the style of the source text, but not usually on the same subject matter. Revealing this Big Picture early will help children to notice details that will help them to write their own texts in a similar style.

- Read the source text with the children, bringing it to life in ways that are appropriate to the purpose. The children should be given the chance to enjoy it and fully understand its purpose before they can truly appreciate how it works.

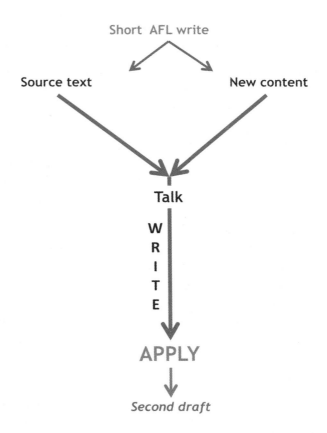

- After reading the text for enjoyment alone, discuss it, generating or researching ideas relating to its content, themes and/or genre. Explore the children's ideas using drama, storytelling and / or oracy activities.

- Help the children to expand their ideas further using incidental writing activities, which could include letters, diary entries, persuasive writing, character profiles or reviews. These are helpful for a range of reasons, including the consolidation of comprehension, the practice of writing in short bursts and the information available for formative assessment.

- Analyse the source text further, focusing on its style and structure and discussing *how* it achieves the effects it does.

Phase 2: Capture and organise

- Remind the children of the Big Picture. This will help to keep them focused on the purpose of their task.

- Discuss ways in which the source text could be rewritten / used as inspiration for a class text. Ask probing questions of the children to assist them to think more deeply.

- Explore the children's ideas using drama, storytelling and / or oracy activities.

- Help the children to expand their ideas further using incidental writing activities.

Phase 3: Collaborate and compose

- Again, remind the children of the Big Picture. This will help to keep them focused on the purpose of their task.

- Teach the children to write, using their newly developed content and the style of the source text, one section at a time. Treasure House teaches vocabulary, grammar and punctuation (VGP) at this point of composition, as this allows for instant application: applied skills are much more likely to be remembered, and also improves the quality of the writing. Lessons in Phase 3 follow the same basic structure:

- Teach a session on an appropriate VGP focus.
- Hold a shared writing session that models writing a section of the class text with reference to the source text, and demonstrates the VGP focus in context.
- Lead the children in an independent writing session, in which they compose their own versions of the modelled section of the class text, applying the VGP focus.
- Hold a plenary that allows children to discuss and assess their own and peers' writing.

- This structure is repeated, in Treasure House, over four lessons (but can, of course, be reduced or extended to suit the complexity of the composition task).
- Encourage the children to rehearse and present or perform their texts to their peers.

Phase 4: Write independently

- Again, remind the children of the Big Picture. This will help to keep them focused on the purpose of their task.

- Having completed the class text, and their own guided texts, the children must then be given the opportunity to apply everything that they have learnt, to plan and write an independent piece of their own, in a similar style. This is a chance for children to combine their literacy skills with their creative thinking. The resulting work may be viewed as an assessment piece: it will tell you what the children have learnt from the unit and the current quality of their writing. However, this aspect should not be emphasised to the children: rather, they should be encouraged to enjoy showing what they can do, and to make their texts their own.

- Give opportunities for editing and redrafting, in order that children work towards the best possible versions or their work they are able to achieve. Then allow the children to assess their own and each other's work using guiding questions.

- Encourage the children to rehearse and present or perform their texts to their peers, and then feedback on one another's work.

The duration of a sequence

To enable you to plan ahead and make decisions about the structure of literacy teaching over the term, a time-frame is suggested at the outset of each sequence. These time-frames are, however, only guidelines: each class will require different amounts of time at each phase, dependent on their particular needs and prior experiences. The only Treasure House phase that specifies a particular number of lessons is the third, as it focuses on the step-by-step teaching of vocabulary, grammar and punctuation applied to different sections of the class text. Even here, we encourage flexibility and adaptation according to need: if a class has experienced and / or composed text in a particular form already, fewer days of teaching may be required before the independence of Phase 4. On the other hand, if a class struggles with a particular concept, skill or style, the reverse may be true.

Differentiation in Treasure House

The Treasure House teaching sequences are structured around the principles of growth mindset, so every effort is made to avoid rigid methods of differentiation.

When differentiated activities are used as the default model of differentiation, it tends to place a ceiling on those identified as 'low ability', ensuring their abilities stay low. Treasure House Teacher's Guides adopt the high-ceiling, low-threshold approach to differentiation, enabling all children to access achievement: everyone can access the learning, but it can also be taken to very high levels. In every dimension of Treasure House, it is important that children master the threshold skills before considering acceleration.

Comprehension

In reading, all children should cross the threshold of reading the Treasure House source texts; however, the depth of their analysis and understanding will vary depending on prior experience, current interests and motivation. Some struggling readers have poor word-reading skills but sound comprehension; if they are always presented with simplified text, their comprehension, and enjoyment, is held back.

Where word reading interferes with comprehension, several tried-and-tested strategies can enable access:

- pre-teaching of concepts or vocabulary
- hearing the text read aloud
- paired reading
- use of visual prompts and dramatisations.

Once a source text has been read, all children can be encouraged to achieve their potential through open questions that pursue the children's own lines of enquiry: much of the teaching in Treasure House is built on questions that stimulate children's ability to think more deeply and enable dialogue. Again, formative assessment is crucial: effective starting-point questions have been provided, but subsequent questions depend entirely upon the children's responses. For example, children are working above age-related expectations may be given the challenge of making increasingly detailed comparisons between the main and extra source texts.

Composition and vocabulary, grammar and punctuation

All teaching of composition and vocabulary, grammar and punctuation should begin with the threshold of composing a simple sentence: all children should be assisted to master this skill and practise it often, to the point of automaticity. Where transcription interferes with composition, allocate extra handwriting practice rather than simplified composition activities: the expectation in Treasure House sequences is that children try to apply their newly acquired composition and vocabulary, grammar and punctuation skills to the best of their ability in their writing.

Levels of ability may then be differentiated through the complexity of changes and/or additions to the sentence, to achieve particular effects. For example, where children are working above age-related expectations, they may be asked to write from a different perspective or to manipulate the vocabulary, grammar and punctuation focus to create a particular effect on readers.

Spelling

Within spelling, all children must cross the threshold of learning new words, rules and patterns. The differentiation within this dimension of the Treasure House sequences should be focused upon application: for example, testing the rule on different root words and ensuring correct application in different writing contexts.

As each child's progress with spelling will be so variable, children should also be prompted to identify recurring personal spelling errors, with support as necessary, and to correct these in their writing during Phases 3 and 4. Where children require additional work on specific skills, Treasure House pupil books can provide additional independent consolidation.

Further ideas

For more ideas on providing access and challenge in Treasure House literacy sessions, please see Accessing achievement strategies.

Accessing achievement strategies

Strategy	Example
Differentiation within the task	• Must – Should – Could: Ensure all children achieve the basic requirement, but then go on to the best of their ability (a simple way of achieving a low-threshold, high-ceiling approach). • Changing targets: Set different success criteria (for example, writing from different viewpoints). • HOT: Prompt children to apply HOT (higher-order thinking) strategies to the main task (for example, extended analysis, comparison, creation of something new, design, investigation, organisation, summarisation or evaluation). • Use and apply: Vary the context of a task (such as describing a game) from familiar to fantastical. • Varied support: Provide varying degrees of support, from full scaffolding to complete independence.
Differentiation through flexible lesson structures	• Cut-aways: Allow the most able children less 'carpet time', starting them working independently but then giving them additional teaching part-way through the lesson. • Timed tasks: Give children varied lengths of time to complete tasks. • Waiting time: Wait a certain amount of time for others to respond before asking more able children for their responses to questions. • Time for review: Have children perform self- and peer evaluation.
Differentiation through choice	• Success selections: Have children self-select their success criteria • Pupil planning: Involve children in the planning process (for example, formatting writing outcomes). • Self-testing: Allow children to devise their own challenges or investigations (such as regarding spelling rules or choosing a research focus).
Differentiation through resourcing	• Vary task prompts to challenge children's responses. • Vary pictures or artefacts to provide more stimulation. • Provide more or fewer supporting resources. • Provide additional texts for comparison. • Provide ICT resources.
Differentiation through method of recording	• Assess learning through spoken responses. • Assess learning through written responses. • Use ICT for assessment (for example, dictation software). • Use graphic organisers to assist children with structural planning. • Use varied levels of formality for reports (oral or written). • Allow children their own choice of recording method.
Access through flexibility in groupings	• Vary the layout of the classroom and the location of resources. • Use guided learning groups or focus groups. • Create different near-ability and mixed-ability pairs, trios and small groups.
Access through pupils as experts	• Form reading, writing and/or response partnerships. • Ask children to think–pair–share ideas. • Allocate roles during group composition (such as spokesperson, scribe and director). • Create peer mentors. • Have children assist others using role-play (such as 'Ask the Expert' or hot seating). • Encourage self- and peer assessment.
Differentiation through questioning and dialogue	• Intervene by questioning, prompting and probing children. • Have sustained dialogues, discussions or debates with children. • Use higher-order questioning. • Have the children ask you questions. • Avoid giving answers that do the work for children.
Differentiated feedback	• Make developmental comments. • Give marks related (only) to children's next steps and targets. • Pose follow-up questions to move children's thinking onwards.

Assessment in Treasure House

Effective teaching is dependent on the assessment cycle delineated by the following questions.

- What can children already do?
- What do they need to learn?
- How is this best taught?
- What can they now do?

This cycle, although it should remain structured and led by the teacher, is most effective when children themselves understand and take an active part in the process. It is always important to keep in mind that, whether or not lesson objectives and intended learning outcomes have been met, children must always tackle their high-frequency errors, no matter how seemingly small. These errors will always hold children back even if, for example, they are mastering fronted adverbials and subordination.

The Treasure House sequences are designed to provide multiple opportunities for this ongoing system of formative assessment by making children's learning visible both to you and to them. By making learning visible, you can respond immediately to misconceptions and breakthroughs, capitalising on every opportunity for formative assessment, phase by phase. This information will help you to plan the course the current sequence should take and to appreciate what may be the most helpful topic for the next sequence.

Visible learning may be achieved through various incidental assessment opportunities (for example, use of mini-whiteboards to display knowledge) and is also attainable through numerous opportunities that are present in every Treasure House sequence.

Diagnostic assessment

Each sequence begins with prior knowledge and diagnostic assessment options that will guide both the starting point of the sequence and the necessary learning focuses as it progresses. You may undertake checks to explore children's current knowledge and understanding about the genre, form and wider context of the source text the text form, as well as the literacy skills to be studied, by engaging the children in discussions, quizzes and short writing activities. You may wish to alter spelling focuses or the sequence's schedule based on this feedback.

Open questions and discussion

In addition, each sequence contains guideline open questions as an integral feature of every phase. In Phase 1, these are comprehension focused; in Phase 2, they support idea generation and organisation; in Phase 3, the focus is on effective application of skills in writing; and in Phase 4 they require reflection and evaluation of independent writing outcomes. In each case, these questions are designed to open up discussion and provoke collaborative thinking; here, children's responses will provide further assessment information useful for tackling any misconceptions and informing the extent to which you adapt the suggested content of the sequence.

Drama, storytelling and performance

Children are encouraged to complete drama, storytelling and/or oracy activities in Phases 1 and 2, engaging with characters in role and with different forms of expression (such as TV news items and puppet shows). Children's responses to these activities will inform your understanding of their deeper appreciation of the content of the source texts and their own compositions, and your plans for when to move on to the next phase. The performance activities suggested at the ends of Phases 3 and 4 will also assist the children's self- and peer-assessment of their work.

Incidental writing

The incidental writing opportunities in Phases 1 and 2 will provide a wealth of information on each child's writing abilities, which can be used to alter the focus of the vocabulary, grammar and punctuation teaching within Phase 3 (the focus suggestions should never take precedent over your knowledge of the children's needs). Additionally, the incidental writing will tell you much about children's broader knowledge and competencies in the relevant text form(s), and this may be used to guide your selection of the next sequence once the current one is completed.

Independent composition

All of the Treasure House sequences, at Phases 3 and 4, result in independent compositions (potentially in more than one draft form). These enable assessment of writing and easy appreciation of the progress a child has made over the course of the Treasure House programme. These compositions may also inform your selection of the next sequence(s), and demonstrate the next steps required to progress children's spelling, grammar and vocabulary.

Preparation for summative assessment

The Treasure House sequences will help children to prepare for summative assessments against all of the National Curriculum English programmes of study by providing structured and contextualised understanding of all of the statutory requirements for learning.

Progression in Treasure House

Progression of source texts

The Treasure House source texts have been very carefully selected in order to stimulate and challenge children in an age-appropriate way, in relation to both their subject matter and their vocabulary choices. All titles have been assigned to year groups based on our pooled experience of what works well for a particular age range and, in some cases, on the age grades already allocated by the excellent Big Cat series from which some titles have been taken. They between those that children should be able to read themselves and more challenging texts that are intended to be explored as a whole class. The National Curriculum requires that children experience both, immersing themselves high-quality literature that is read to them as well as accessing texts independently. How children interact with the source texts is a decision to be informed by your assessment of your class's abilities and requirements.

Progression between year groups

For each year group, each Treasure House Teacher's Guide addresses the programmes of study for all four core dimensions of the National Curriculum for English:

- Comprehension
- Composition
- Vocabulary, Grammar and Punctuation
- Spelling.

In this way, Treasure House is built on the year-by-year progression required by the National Curriculum.

Progression between Key Stages

The English programmes of study are the same for Years 1 and 2. We believe that, rather than dividing the statutory requirements between the year groups, it is more effective to teach the entire range of skills to each year group, revisiting skills in Year 2 to deepen children's understanding by applying them to more challenging texts.

Formative and summative assessments must inform such decisions, though, and you may wish not to revisit certain skills if they have been thoroughly understood by every child. The National Curriculum suggests that teachers should use the programmes of study with some flexibility, as required, so long as all required objectives are achieved by the end of each key stage. This is also our recommendation when using Treasure House: to use formative assessment to repeat of omit practice of skill sets as required.

Progression within year groups

In order to allow for as much flexibility as possible, we have purposely avoided building in a rigid progression between sequences in a given year. This will allow you better to fit the sequences into your school teaching plan, and to make cross-curricular links wherever relevant.

However, we have assigned programmes of study to particular texts so that these are met in context and them applied appropriately. Again, pace and progression within a year must be informed by formative and summative assessments, and you may wish to alter either the order of the sequences or the individual learning objectives within sequences to suit your class's requirements.

Comprehension and composition

Treasure House supports children's progression in reading comprehension within a year group by recommending a wide range of open questions, oracy and drama activities carefully composed to develop their grasp of the age-specific programmes of study. Although sequences can be taught in any order, the children's developing responses to open questions and activities will prompt deeper, more complex and more inferential appreciation and adaptation of the texts, as well as more mature appreciation of linguistic and stylistic choices, as more sequences from one year group are completed.

Vocabulary, grammar and punctuation and spelling

The Treasure House progression in vocabulary, grammar and punctuation, and in spelling, within a year group is similarly adaptable, allowing children to progress in their application of the skills learned and to appreciate their effects on readers to a greater extent.

Sequence overview chart

Sequence number and heading	Anthology texts	Approximate duration
1. Fiction: Story structure	*One Snowy Night* by Nick Butterworth	2 weeks
2. Fairy tales	*Hansel and Gretel* by Malachy Doyle	2 weeks
3. Traditional tales	*The Magic Paintbrush* by Julia Donaldson	2 weeks
4. Rhymes and poems	'Cats' by Eleanor Farjeon 'No Hickory No Dickory No Dock' by John Agard	2 weeks
5. Rhymes and poems	'Busy Day' by John Rice	2 weeks
6. Rhymes and poems	'On Some Other Planet' by Brian Patten 'Fantastic Friends' by Brian Patten	2 weeks
7. Instructions	*How to Make Pop-Up Cards* by Monica Hughes	2 weeks
8. Recounts	*Dougal's Deep-Sea Diary* by Simon Bartram	2 weeks
9. Reports	*Top Dinosaurs* by Maoliosa Kelly, Jon Hughes and Ali Teo	2 weeks
10. Adventure stories	*The Crocodile Under the Bed* by Judith Kerr	2 weeks
11. Magical characters	*The Bog Baby* by Jeanne Willis	2 weeks
12. Imaginary worlds	*Lollipop and Grandpa's Safari* by Penelope Harper	2 weeks
13. Fairy tales	'The Frog Prince' by Margaret Mayo	2 weeks
14. Letters	*Dear Fairy Godmother* by Michael Rosen	2 weeks
15. Information texts	*The Fantastic Flying Squirrel* by Nic Bishop *Spines, Stings and Teeth* by Andy and Angie Belcher	2 weeks

Curriculum map

Reading – comprehension

Reading – comprehension	Sequence 1 Story structure	Sequence 2 Fairy tales	Sequence 3 Traditional tales	Sequence 4 Rhymes and poems	Sequence 5 Rhymes and poems	Sequence 6 Rhymes and poems	Sequence 7 Instructions	Sequence 8 Recounts	Sequence 9 Reports	Sequence 10 Adventure stories	Sequence 11 Magical characters	Sequence 12 Imaginary worlds	Sequence 13 Fairy tales	Sequence 14 Letters	Sequence 15 Information texts
Listen to and discuss a wide range of poems, stories and non-fiction at a level beyond that at which they can read independently.	✓	✓	✓	✓	✓	✓	✓	✓	✓	✓	✓	✓	✓	✓	✓
Be encouraged to link what they read or hear read to their own experiences.	✓	✓	✓	✓	✓	✓	✓	✓	✓	✓	✓	✓	✓	✓	✓
Become very familiar with key stories, fairy stories and traditional tales, retelling them and considering their particular characteristics.	✓	✓	✓					✓		✓	✓	✓	✓	✓	
Recognise and join in with predictable phrases.			✓	✓	✓	✓				✓		✓	✓		
Learn to appreciate rhymes and poems, and to recite some by heart.				✓	✓	✓									
Discuss word meanings, linking new meanings to those already known.	✓	✓	✓	✓	✓	✓	✓	✓	✓	✓	✓	✓	✓	✓	✓
Draw on what they already know or on background information and vocabulary provided by the teacher.	✓	✓	✓	✓	✓		✓	✓	✓	✓	✓	✓	✓	✓	✓
Check that the text makes sense to them as they read and correct inaccurate reading.	✓	✓	✓	✓	✓	✓	✓	✓	✓	✓	✓	✓	✓	✓	✓
Discuss the significance of the title and events.	✓	✓	✓	✓	✓	✓	✓	✓	✓	✓	✓	✓	✓	✓	✓
Make inferences on the basis of what is being said and done.	✓	✓	✓	✓	✓	✓	✓	✓	✓	✓	✓	✓	✓	✓	
Predict what might happen on the basis of what has been read so far.	✓	✓	✓	✓	✓	✓	✓	✓	✓	✓	✓	✓	✓	✓	✓
Participate in discussion about what is read to them, taking turns and listening to what others say.	✓	✓	✓	✓	✓		✓	✓	✓	✓	✓	✓	✓	✓	✓
Explain clearly their understanding of what is read to them.	✓	✓	✓	✓	✓	✓	✓	✓	✓	✓	✓	✓	✓	✓	✓

Curriculum map

Writing – transcription

Skill	Seq 1 Story structure	Seq 2 Fairy tales	Seq 3 Traditional tales	Seq 4 Rhymes and poems	Seq 5 Rhymes and poems	Seq 6 Rhymes and poems	Seq 7 Instructions	Seq 8 Recounts	Seq 9 Reports	Seq 10 Adventure stories	Seq 11 Magical characters	Seq 12 Imaginary worlds	Seq 13 Fairy tales	Seq 14 Letters	Seq 15 Information texts
Spell words containing each of the 40+ phonemes already taught.	✓	✓	✓	✓	✓	✓	✓	✓	✓	✓	✓	✓	✓	✓	✓
Spell common exception words.						✓			✓						
Spell the days of the week.								✓							
Name the letters of the alphabet in order.				✓											
Use letter names to distinguish between alternative spellings of the same sound.														✓	
Use the spelling rule for adding -s or -es as the plural marker for nouns and the third person singular marker for verbs.	✓		✓			✓									
Use the prefix un-.							✓				✓				
Use -ing, -ed, -er and -est where no change is needed in the spelling of root words.	✓	✓	✓	✓	✓	✓	✓	✓	✓	✓	✓	✓	✓		✓
Apply simple spelling rules and guidance, as listed in English Appendix 1.	✓	✓	✓	✓	✓	✓	✓	✓	✓	✓	✓	✓	✓	✓	✓
Write from memory simple sentences dictated by the teacher that include words using the GPCs and common exception words taught so far.	✓	✓	✓	✓	✓	✓	✓	✓	✓	✓	✓	✓	✓	✓	✓

Writing – composition

	Seq 1 Story structure	Seq 2 Fairy tales	Seq 3 Traditional tales	Seq 4 Rhymes and poems	Seq 5 Rhymes and poems	Seq 6 Rhymes and poems	Seq 7 Instructions	Seq 8 Recounts	Seq 9 Reports	Seq 10 Adventure stories	Seq 11 Magical characters	Seq 12 Imaginary worlds	Seq 13 Fairy tales	Seq 14 Letters	Seq 15 Information texts
Say out loud what they are going to write about.	✓	✓	✓	✓	✓	✓	✓	✓	✓	✓	✓	✓	✓	✓	✓
Compose a sentence orally before writing it.	✓	✓	✓	✓	✓	✓	✓	✓	✓	✓	✓	✓	✓	✓	✓
Sequence sentences to form short narratives.	✓	✓	✓	✓	✓	✓		✓		✓	✓	✓	✓	✓	
Re-read what they have written to check that it makes sense.	✓	✓	✓	✓	✓	✓	✓	✓	✓	✓	✓	✓	✓	✓	✓
Discuss what they have written with the teacher or other pupils.	✓	✓	✓	✓	✓	✓	✓	✓	✓	✓	✓	✓	✓	✓	✓
Read aloud their writing clearly enough to be heard by their peers and the teacher.	✓	✓	✓	✓	✓	✓	✓	✓	✓	✓	✓	✓	✓	✓	✓

Writing – vocabulary, grammar and punctuation

	Sequence 1 Story structure	Sequence 2 Fairy tales	Sequence 3 Traditional tales	Sequence 4 Rhymes and poems	Sequence 5 Rhymes and poems	Sequence 6 Rhymes and poems	Sequence 7 Instructions	Sequence 8 Recounts	Sequence 9 Reports	Sequence 10 Adventure stories	Sequence 11 Magical characters	Sequence 12 Imaginary worlds	Sequence 13 Fairy tales	Sequence 14 Letters	Sequence 15 Information texts
Leave spaces between words.	✓			✓	✓										✓
Join words and join clauses using and.		✓	✓					✓	✓	✓	✓		✓	✓	✓
Begin to punctuate sentences using a capital letter and a full stop, question mark or exclamation mark.	✓	✓	✓	✓	✓	✓	✓			✓	✓	✓	✓		
Use a capital letter for names of people, places, the days of the week, and the personal pronoun 'I'.	✓		✓					✓	✓	✓	✓		✓	✓	
Learn the grammar for year 1 in English Appendix 2.	✓	✓	✓	✓	✓	✓	✓	✓	✓	✓	✓	✓	✓	✓	✓
Use the grammatical terminology in English Appendix 2 in discussing their writing.	✓	✓	✓	✓	✓	✓	✓	✓	✓	✓	✓	✓	✓	✓	✓

Curriculum map

English Appendix 1: Spelling

Spelling	Seq 1 Story structure	Seq 2 Fairy tales	Seq 3 Traditional tales	Seq 4 Rhymes and poems	Seq 5 Rhymes and poems	Seq 6 Rhymes and poems	Seq 7 Instructions	Seq 8 Recounts	Seq 9 Reports	Seq 10 Adventure stories	Seq 11 Magical characters	Seq 12 Imaginary worlds	Seq 13 Fairy tales	Seq 14 Letters	Seq 15 Information texts
Spell the /f/, /l/, /s/, /z/ and /k/ sounds ff, ll, ss, zz and ck.				✓									✓		
Spell the /ŋ/ sound n before k.										✓					
Divide words into syllables.		✓													
Spell the /tʃ/ sound tch after a single vowel letter.												✓			
Spell the /v/ sound at the end of words.	✓													✓	
Add s and es to words (plural of nouns and the third person singular of verbs).	✓		✓			✓									
Add the endings -ing, -ed and -er to verbs where no change is needed to the root word.	✓				✓	✓				✓		✓	✓		✓
Add -er and -est to adjectives where no change is needed to the root word.					✓						✓				
Spell words with the digraphs ai, oi.				✓											
Spell words with the digraphs ay, oy.				✓											
Spell words with the split digraph a-e.		✓													
Spell words with the split digraph e-e.															

English Appendix 1: Spelling
[continued]

Spelling objective	Seq 1 Story structure	Seq 2 Fairy tales	Seq 3 Traditional tales	Seq 4 Rhymes and poems	Seq 5 Rhymes and poems	Seq 6 Rhymes and poems	Seq 7 Instructions	Seq 8 Recounts	Seq 9 Reports	Seq 10 Adventure stories	Seq 11 Magical characters	Seq 12 Imaginary worlds	Seq 13 Fairy tales	Seq 14 Letters	Seq 15 Information texts
Spell words with the split digraph i-e.										✓					
Spell words with the split digraph o-e.															
Spell words with the split digraph u-e.															
Spell words with the digraph ar.					✓										
Spell words with the digraph ee.			✓		✓										
Spell words with the digraph ea (/iː/).			✓			✓									
Spell words with the digraph ea (/ɛ/).							✓								
Spell words with the digraph er (/ɜː/).	✓				✓	✓				✓	✓	✓	✓		✓
Spell words with the digraph er (/ə/).	✓				✓	✓				✓	✓	✓	✓		✓
Spell words with the digraph ir.						✓									
Spell words with the digraph ur.						✓									✓
Spell words with the digraph oo (/uː/).					✓										
Spell words with the digraph oo (/ʊ/).					✓										
Spell words with the digraph oa.					✓										
Spell words with the digraph oe.					✓										
Spell words with the digraph ou.															
Spell words with the digraphs ow (/aʊ/), ow (/əʊ/), ue, ew.															

Curriculum map

English Appendix 1: Spelling [continued]

	Sequence 1 Story structure	Sequence 2 Fairy tales	Sequence 3 Traditional tales	Sequence 4 Rhymes and poems	Sequence 5 Rhymes and poems	Sequence 6 Rhymes and poems	Sequence 7 Instructions	Sequence 8 Recounts	Sequence 9 Reports	Sequence 10 Adventure stories	Sequence 11 Magical characters	Sequence 12 Imaginary worlds	Sequence 13 Fairy tales	Sequence 14 Letters	Sequence 15 Information texts
Spell words with the digraph ie (/aɪ/).															
Spell words with the digraph ie (/iː/).															
Spell words with the trigraph igh.					✓										✓
Spell words with the digraph or.					✓										
Spell words with the trigraph ore.					✓										
Spell words with the digraph aw.															
Spell words with the digraph au.					✓				✓						
Spell words with the trigraph air.															
Spell words with the trigraph ear.															
Spell words with the trigraph ear (/ɛə/).					✓										
Spell words with the trigraph are (/ɛə/).					✓										
Spell words ending -y.					✓			✓			✓				
Learn new consonant spellings ph and wh.													✓		
Use k for the /k/ sound.							✓				✓				
Add the prefix -un.												✓			
Spell compound words.															
Spell common exception words.									✓						

30

English Appendix 2:
Vocabulary, grammar and punctuation

Objective	Sequence 1 Story structure	Sequence 2 Fairy tales	Sequence 3 Traditional tales	Sequence 4 Rhymes and poems	Sequence 5 Rhymes and poems	Sequence 6 Rhymes and poems	Sequence 7 Instructions	Sequence 8 Recounts	Sequence 9 Reports	Sequence 10 Adventure stories	Sequence 11 Magical characters	Sequence 12 Imaginary worlds	Sequence 13 Fairy tales	Sequence 14 Letters	Sequence 15 Information texts
Understand regular plural noun suffixes -s or -es, including the effects of these suffixes on the meaning of the noun.	✓		✓			✓									
Use suffixes that can be added to verbs where no change is needed in the spelling of root words.	✓				✓	✓				✓		✓	✓		✓
Understand how the prefix un- changes the meaning of verbs and adjectives.											✓				
Understand how words can combine to make sentences.		✓	✓				✓		✓	✓					
Join words and join clauses using and.	✓	✓	✓	✓	✓	✓		✓	✓	✓	✓	✓	✓	✓	✓
Sequence sentences to form short narratives.	✓	✓	✓	✓	✓	✓	✓	✓		✓	✓	✓	✓	✓	
Separate words with spaces.	✓	✓	✓	✓	✓	✓					✓				
Be introduced to capital letters, full stops, question marks and exclamation marks to demarcate sentences.	✓	✓						✓	✓	✓	✓	✓	✓		✓
Use capital letters for names and for the personal pronoun I.	✓							✓	✓		✓		✓	✓	

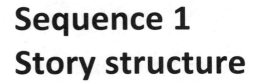

Sequence 1
Story structure

Approximate duration: Two weeks

Big Picture

Through this teaching sequence, children explore the structure of a story in which a park keeper helps animals in need. By the end of the sequence, they will have written their own version for other children to enjoy.

Phase 1: Enjoy and immerse

Children become familiar with the structure of and characters in the model text, *One Snowy Night*.

Phase 2: Capture and organise

Children are supported in developing ideas for a new version of the story.

Phase 3: Collaborate and compose

Children undertake supported writing sessions to develop their own narrative writing.

Phase 4: Write independently

Children write, edit and read aloud their own versions of the model story.

Main source text

Treasure House Anthology Sequence 1 text. *One Snowy Night*, Nick Butterworth, ISBN 978-0-00-714693-2

Background knowledge

The inspiration for the 'Percy the Park Keeper' books came from Nick Butterworth's many walks through his local park. In the books, Percy cares for a wide range of animals found living in the large park, such as foxes, birds, deer, hedgehogs, badgers, rabbits, squirrels, moles and mice. Through the different stories, the children learn how Percy's kind actions help care for the wildlife in his park.

Spoken outcome

To orally recount their own story in a clear sequence

Writing outcome

To rewrite the story, now set during a hot night

Prior knowledge

Check children's knowledge and understanding of:

- wild animals and birds of the UK
- seeing or hearing animals or birds
- animal and bird behaviour when the weather is very cold or very hot
- the role of park keepers.

Diagnostic assessment options

Before starting the unit, you may wish to conduct an initial diagnostic assessment of the children's knowledge and understanding.

Ideas for initial diagnostic assessment options include:

- reviewing children's writing for use of proper nouns, spaces between words and sentence punctuation
- reading aloud a range of sentences for children to identify which are statements, questions and exclamations, showing what they know by drawing the relevant punctuation mark in the air
- speaking and listening activities where children ask each other questions to be answered using statements or exclamations.

Cross-curricular links

KS1 Art and design

- Use drawing, painting and sculpture to develop and share their ideas, experiences and imagination.

KS1 Science – Animals, including humans

- Identify and name a variety of common animals including fish, amphibians, reptiles, birds and mammals.
- Identify and name a variety of common animals that are carnivores, herbivores and omnivores.

KS1 Science – Seasonal changes

- Observe and describe weather associated with the seasons and how day length varies.

Treasure House links

All digital and pupil book units have the same names and numbers, but different questions.

- Treasure House, Year 1, Comprehension Unit 1: Key stories: 'One Snowy Night'
- Treasure House, Year 1, Composition Unit 1: Stories with familiar settings
- Treasure House, Year 1, Punctuation Unit 1: Punctuating sentences
- Treasure House, Year 1, Vocabulary Unit 1: Adding -s and -es
- Treasure House, Year 1, Spelling Unit 7: Adding -s to make a plural
- Treasure House, Year 1, Spelling Unit 8: Adding -es to make a plural
- Treasure House, Year 1, Vocabulary Unit 2: Adding endings to root words (-ing, -ed, -er, -est)
- Treasure House, Year 1, Spelling Unit 9: Adding -ing to a root word
- Treasure House, Year 1, Spelling Unit 10: Adding -er to a root word
- Treasure House, Year 1, Spelling Unit 11: Adding -ed to a root word
- Treasure House, Year 1, Punctuation Unit 2: Capital letter for names and 'I'
- Treasure House, Year 1, Punctuation Unit 3: Capital letter for days of the week and place names

Resources

Props and percussion instruments for drama and storytelling activities (optional); information / images on hot and cold weather and different animals

Source texts – see Anthologies; Percy's story planner; Proofreading sheet / My writing checklist; Proofreading sheet / My writing checklist (blank)

Phase 1: Enjoy and immerse

In Phase 1, the children look at the illustrations and listen to the story, *One Snowy Night* by Nick Butterworth. Over several sessions, the children have opportunities to discuss the story and its characters through comprehension and discussion activities, as well as exploring characters and story structure through drama, storytelling, writing and analysis of the text. Phase 1 also focuses on question marks and includes work on adding -s and -es for plurals.

Programmes of study: Year 1

Comprehension: Become very familiar with key stories, fairy stories and traditional tales, retelling them and considering their particular characteristics.

Comprehension: Recognise and join in with predictable phrases.

Comprehension: Discuss the significance of the title and events.

Comprehension: Participate in **discussion** about what is read to them, taking turns and listening to what others say.

Vocabulary, grammar and punctuation: Begin to punctuate sentences using a capital letter and a full stop, question mark or exclamation mark.

Spelling: Use the spelling rule for adding -s or -es as the plural marker for nouns and the third person singular marker for verbs.

Sparking interest

Show the front cover of *One Snowy Night*. Discuss the weather, and what the animals want. Introduce the sequence by explaining the Big Picture: they will be writing their own story for other children to read.

Reading and discussing

Introduce the text, read it with the class and check their understanding. Use digital screens from Year 1, Comprehension Unit 1 to reinforce discussion.

Discuss the following with the children.

- Why did the animals need help?
- Why do you think the animals came to Percy for help?
- Why couldn't the animals sleep in Percy's bed?
- How was the problem solved?
- Which sleeping place do you think looks the most comfortable?
- Do you think Percy is a good park keeper? Why?

Drama and storytelling

Use a range of activities to reinforce children's understanding of the story's sequence of events and the characters' feelings. Select the activities that suit your class, using mixed-ability groupings.

- **Freeze-framing key moments:** Put the children into different scenes (in the right story order). Use thought-tracking, asking each child in the freeze-frame what they are thinking at that particular moment.
- **Animal mimes:** Have the children pretend to be the animals from the story, using their bodies to show how cold they are. Ask them to imagine getting warm in Percy's hut. Encourage them to consider how their bodies change and how they feel.
- **Animal circles:** Have a child acting as 'Percy' in the middle of a class circle. Allocate each child an animal or bird. Ask 'Percy' to choose an animal; this child has to say why they want to come in from the cold. Repeat multiple times.
- **Dramatic retelling:** Have the children rehearse and perform a key scene from the tale in small groups, with one or two narrators.

Incidental writing

A short writing activity would enhance the children's understanding of the story and help to inform the teaching focuses in the collaborative composition phase. Children could:

- write a thank you card for Percy from all or one of the animals
- write a shape poem in the shape of a snowflake, using words about cold and snow
- draw pictures and write descriptive sentences about each character in the story
- write a diary entry as Percy or one of the animals.

Analysis

Display the text to the children. Discuss the setting of the story and elicit a list of the main characters. Create a sequenced story map using images of the characters and captions or speech bubbles. Have the children contribute orally to help you write the short sentences. Note the story pattern: a noise; a question of who it could be; followed by the answer. Note how Percy's problem regarding where everyone will sleep was sorted at the end of the story. Use the story map for reference.

Grammar: Question marks

Use the text to show how question sentences end with a question mark. Highlight the question mark at the end of the sentence: 'Now who can that be at this time of night?' Discuss the question mark's function, noting that it replaces the full stop. Have children draw question marks in the air. With the children, go through the text to hunt question marks.

Use Year 1, Punctuation Unit 1 for more on question marks.

Phonics and spelling

Display the text and read the sentence 'Standing outside were two shivering rabbits'. Highlight the word 'rabbits'. Write 'rabbit' for the children to see. Explain that when there is more than one rabbit we add '-s' on the end. Add '-s' to 'rabbit' to make it plural. Write and say 'one fox' and 'two foxes'. Emphasise the extra syllable when '-es' is added.

Create a chart with two columns with the headings: '-s' and '-es'. Model a few plural examples of objects and animals to add to the chart, for example: 'moles', 'owls', 'brushes', 'coaches'. Encourage the children to suggest their own plural examples. Let the children hear the extra syllable added by the '-es' ending. Point out the final letters of the root words in the '-es' column: 'x', 'ss', 'ch', 'sh' and so on.

Use Year 1, Vocabulary Unit 1 and Year 1, Spelling Units 7–8 for reinforcement.

Review of the Big Picture

At the end of this phase, discuss with the children what they have learned so far about the story and the characters in *One Snowy Night*. Remind them that this is all working towards writing their own stories.

Year 1, Sequence 1
Story structure

Phase 2: Capture and organise

During Phase 2, children start to develop ideas about new content needed to create a retelling of the story set on a very hot day. Working collaboratively, children decide which animal characters to include, how they are affected by the hot weather and how Percy solves their problems. Phase 2 also includes work on adding -ed and -ing to verbs with no change to the root word.

Programmes of study: Year 1

Comprehension: Draw on what they already know or on background information and vocabulary provided by the teacher.

Comprehension: Be encouraged to link what they read or hear read to their own experiences.

Comprehension: Make inferences on the basis of what is being said and done.

Comprehension: Explain clearly their understanding of what is read to them.

Composition: Say out loud what they are going to write about.

Spelling: Use -ing, -ed, -er and -est where no change is needed in the spelling of root words.

Introduction

Remind the children of the Big Picture. Reread *One Snowy Night*, looking at the story map from Phase 1, and have the children remind each other why the animals asked Percy for help. Have them recap the different animal characters, their needs, the problem regarding sleeping arrangements and how the problem was solved.

Introduce the idea that they are going to work together to create a class story about the animals and Percy called 'One Hot Day'.

Discussing ideas

As a class, discuss the following and make decisions to create their class story.

- What experiences of hot weather can you share with the class?

- What should you do in hot weather to stay cool and stay safe? (for example, drink water, stay in the shade, wear a sun hat, apply sun screen)

- How could the animals in Percy's park be affected by the heat? (for example, no water in the pond, nothing to drink, overheated animals, ground too hard to burrow)

- Which animals could come to Percy to ask for help? (limit this to five)

- In what order will the animals come to ask for Percy's help?

- How will Percy help the overheated animals? (for example, create a makeshift pond from an old bath or paddling pool; put up an umbrella to create shade)

Drama and storytelling

Use a range of activities to allow the children to explore suggestions for their new story plot and the different problems faced by the characters.

- **Feeling hot:** In animal groups, use mime to help the children understand how each animal might feel in hot weather, for example, panting, stretching. Share their movements with the class.

- **Knock Knock!** Put the children into groups: one child to play each animal and one to play Percy. In their groups, each animal takes a turn to knock on an imaginary door. Percy says: 'Who can that be?' The animal says its name and why it needs help. As a class, list the different ideas.

- **Hot-seating Percy:** Put the children into pairs and ask them to imagine they are Percy. Let them think of how Percy could help the animals cool down. Then hot-seat pairs for them to explain their ideas to the class.

- **Freeze-framing key moments:** Once the structure of the story is created, try out the different scenes in the right sequence. Use thought-tracking, asking each child in the freeze-frame what they are thinking at that moment of the story.

Incidental writing

Before you select any incidental writing, make sure the children are able to orally articulate the main events. Select activities that you think appropriate for your class. Children could:

- draw and label a picture of one of Percy's ideas to cool down the animals
- draw a picture, with a caption, of an animal character
- draw and label a picture of Percy's park in hot weather
- write simple animal riddles to share with a partner
- write character diaries and letters.

Organising the new story into a structure

Once the children have thoroughly explored their ideas for their class story, bring them together and use their final suggestions to model how to plot the new story in picture and caption form onto the Percy's story planner. Once recorded, go through the frame and ask the children which aspects of the tale they particularly like and why. Enlarge the frame and display it near the story map from Phase 1 for the children to see and use as reference during the writing phases.

Phonics and spelling

Write the verbs, 'push' and 'roll' on the board and encourage the children to read them out. Explain that these words are verbs and they show actions. Add -ed to the ends of the words and explore the sound change. Explain that we can add -ed onto the ends of most verbs. Focus on the pages in *One Snowy Night* that describe everyone falling out of bed. Let the children help you find words that have -ed, then list them on the board.

Rewrite the root verbs, adding -ing to one of them. Have children come up and add -ing to the rest. Have pairs orally compose sentences using some of the -ed and -ing words.

Use Year 1, Vocabulary Unit 2 and Year 1, Spelling Units 9–11 for reinforcement.

Review of the Big Picture

At the end of this phase, discuss with the children what they have achieved with their planning and ideas for a new story linked to the characters from *One Snowy Night.*

Phase 3: Collaborate and compose

Phase 3 has four writing lessons which support the children in the writing of their new class story, 'One Hot Day'. Each lesson starts with a short vocabulary, grammar and punctuation focus with links to the main text. The children then participate in a shared composition session, applying the VGP focus in context. Independent writing, with plenaries, follows. The VGP focuses are on using capital letters for proper names, identifying and using simple punctuation marks and maintaining gaps between words.

Programmes of study: Year 1

Composition: Say out loud what they are going to write about.

Composition: Compose a sentence orally before writing it.

Composition: Sequence sentences to form short narratives.

Composition: Discuss what they have written with the teacher or other pupils.

Vocabulary, grammar and punctuation: Use a capital letter for names of people, places, the days of the week, and the personal pronoun 'I'.

Vocabulary, grammar and punctuation: Begin to punctuate sentences using a capital letter and a full stop, question mark or exclamation mark.

Vocabulary, grammar and punctuation: Leave spaces between words.

Introduction

Remind the children about the sequence's Big Picture. Explain that over several lessons the children are going to start work on writing their class story about a hot day in Percy's park using their story ideas and the story planner. Use the story map display of *One Snowy Night* to recap on the original story and then look at the writing frame for their new story.

Lesson 1

Capital letters for names and places

Begin the session with a whole class activity on using capital letters for names and places. Write 'Percy' and 'Percy's Park' on the board. Underline the capital letter 'P'. Note that capital letters are used for the first letter of given names. Have children write their names with the correct initial capitals. Write 'fox' on the board and note the absence of a capital (not a proper noun). Name the fox, for example, 'Fred the fox'.

Use Year 1, Punctuation Units 2–3 for more work on capitals.

Shared writing

With the children, using their class Percy's story planner, model writing the opening and the setting of the story. Model the oral composition of sentences before writing

them. Have the children contribute words to show that it is a hot day. Once written, collaboratively check through the work, with attention to accurate use of capital letters for proper nouns and the beginnings of sentences, and checking that the sentences make sense.

Independent writing

The children can now write their own first section, applying the VGP focus on capitals for names and places. Give or show each child Percy's story planner to help with vocabulary and phrasing. Some children may benefit from guided group or peer-paired writing at this stage.

Plenary

Throughout the writing session, ask the children questions to help them focus on their progress and what they have created during that lesson, for example: 'How is your story similar to and different from the original?' 'How does it show that it is a hot day?' 'Where have you used capital letters for names?'

Lesson 2

Capital letters and full stops in sentences

Remind the children about using capital letters for names and places. Explain that capital letters are also used to show the beginnings of sentences. Display the first pages of *One Snowy Night*, highlighting every capital letter at the beginnings of sentences. Ask the children why we use capitals this way (to denote the start of a sentence). Ask the children what symbol we use to show the end of a sentence (full stop). Highlight the full stops in the text.

Slowly read a different part of the story that is not displayed. Have the children listen and physically punctuate at the appropriate moments, for example, putting a hand on their head for capitals and creating a ball with one of their fists for full stops.

Use Year 1, Punctuation Unit 1 for more work on sentence punctuation.

Shared writing

Select the second section of the story (where the animals turn up) from the Percy's story planner, applying the focus: capital letters and full stops. Write one or two sentences incorrectly to prompt children to correct them. Point out repeated or predictable phrases in this section, and link questions to the work on question marks in Phase 1. Once written, collaboratively check that the work makes sense and that the punctuation is correct.

Independent writing

The children can now write their second section, focusing on sentence punctuation. Give or show each child Percy's story planner to help with vocabulary and phrasing. Some children may benefit from guided group or peer-paired writing at this stage.

Plenary

Throughout the writing session, ask the children questions to help them focus on their progress and what they have created during that lesson, for example: 'Where have you used capital letters, full stops and question marks correctly in your writing?' 'How have you followed the story patterns shown in 'One Snowy Night'?'

Lesson 3

Exclamation marks

Write on the board 'I am feeling quite cold.' and 'I am absolutely freezing!' With the children, read the two sentences encouraging intonation for the exclamation sentence. Have the children note the difference between the two sentences. Have them point out the exclamation symbol, name it as an exclamation mark and draw it in the air.

Display the page from *One Snowy Night* which shows the floorboard coming up in Percy's hut. Highlight all the exclamation marks. With the children, read each sentence with and without exclamations and note the difference.

Use Year 1, Punctuation Unit 1 for more work on exclamation marks.

Shared writing

Select the third part of the story (Percy's problem) and model the writing process using Percy's story planner. As you model the writing, add exclamation marks to the end of some sentences. Once written, read the work aloud to check for appropriate use of exclamation marks and that it makes sense.

Independent writing

The children can now write their third section of the story, using exclamation marks. Give or show each child Percy's story planner to help with vocabulary and phrasing. Some children may benefit from guided group or peer-paired writing at this stage.

Plenary

Throughout the writing session, ask the children questions to help them focus on their progress and what they have created during that lesson, for example: 'Where have you used exclamation marks correctly in your writing?' 'How have you made it clear what Percy's problem is with the animals?'

Lesson 4

Separating words with spaces

Write a simple sentence with no gaps between the words and the same sentence with gaps between the words.

Ask the children which sentence is easier to read, and why. Emphasise that gaps between words make reading them much easier.

In pairs, the children read a few sentences taken from different points in the story, noticing the spacing between the words (and the edge of the page). Tell children to open their own writing books and share them with each other to look at how consistent spacing between words is in each others' work.

Shared writing

Use the last part of the story (Percy's solution to the problem), to collaboratively write the final section of the class story using Percy's story planner. Overtly apply the focus on spaces between words. Write one or two sentences with the spaces missing to prompt children to correct them. Once written, read the work aloud together, checking that it makes sense.

Independent writing

The children can now write the final section, focusing on gaps between words. Give or show each child the class story planner to help with vocabulary and phrasing. Some children may benefit from guided group or peer-paired writing at this stage.

Plenary

During the writing session, ask the children questions to help them focus on their progress and what they have created during that lesson, for example: 'How clear are the gaps between your words?' 'How has your story come to a good end?' 'How similar or different is it to the original story ending?'

Rehearsing and performing

Once the children have written their story, encourage them to perform it either as storytellers or by acting it out. Take feedback on what they particularly liked about the stories they have heard.

Review of the Big Picture

Once you have completed all the lessons for this section, remind the children of the sequence's Big Picture. Discuss what they have learned so far.

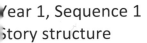

Phase 4: Write independently

This final phase brings all the children's learning and writing skills together so that they can write their own independent story based on the original, but with different animals. Through their writing they will be able to use the different VGP focuses that they have been practising throughout previous phases.

Programmes of study: Year 1

Composition: Say out loud what they are going to write about.

Composition: Compose a sentence orally before writing it.

Composition: Sequence sentences to form short narratives.

Composition: Re-read what they have written to check that it makes sense.

Composition: Discuss what they have written with the teacher or other pupils.

Composition: Read aloud their writing clearly enough to be heard by their peers and the teacher.

Introduction

Introduce the phase by discussing what the children have learned in their story planning and writing sessions, and link it to the Big Picture. Explain that the time has come for the children to bring all their learning together and write their own story about Percy the park keeper. Explain that this time he has to help a set of animals who have escaped from a safari park. Discuss and list different types of animals that they could choose, for example, an elephant, a monkey, a lion, a kangaroo, a snake, a parrot. Ask: 'Where in Percy's hut could the animals sleep?'

Recap the structure of their class story and of the original *One Snowy Night* story. Also revisit their ideas from Phase 2. Highlight that the planning and writing of their own story will take place over several sessions.

Writing

Give each child a blank copy of the 'Percy's Park' story planner. As they plan, draft and write each section of the story, encourage the children to compose their sentences orally before writing them down. Let the children draw a picture to illustrate each section.

All the children should be encouraged to try to write independently to the best of their abilities. Ask open questions such as: 'How will you use your punctuation to show how the animals are feeling?' Make sure that the children have a chance to share their writing with others at appropriate points during each session.

Proofreading and redrafting

Encourage the children to read through their work at the end of each writing session with a partner. Ask them to check whether their writing makes sense. Proofreading and improvement without support means that the writing will happen over a few lessons. Offer the children the Proofreading sheet / My writing checklist, or create your own checklist with the assistance of the blank Proofreading sheet / My writing checklist.

Self- and peer-assessment

Encourage the children to take time to assess their own and others' writing. Make sure that they read out their writing clearly. Ask open questions to encourage self- and peer-assessment such as: 'How similar is this story to the original?' 'What needs do the animals have?' 'How does Percy solve their problems?' Also encourage them to check their VGP focuses on punctuation and sentence sequencing to ensure they have been successfully applied throughout the texts.

Presenting and performing

Have the children make simple illustrated story books to share and read with each other. Encourage the children to use intonation to highlight exclamations and voices of the different characters.

Final review of the Big Picture

Individually or with partners, have children reflect on what they have learned from this sequence and what they will remember to do in future writing.

Sequence 2
Fairy tales

Approximate duration: Two weeks

Big Picture

Through this teaching sequence, children explore the structure, setting and characters of the well-known fairy tale, 'Hansel and Gretel'. By the end of the sequence, they will have written a new version with a new bad character and a new setting.

Phase 1: Enjoy and immerse

Children become familiar with the structure, setting and characters in the model text, 'Hansel and Gretel'.

Phase 2: Capture and organise

Children are supported in developing ideas for a new version of the story with a new bad character and setting.

Phase 3: Collaborate and compose

Children undertake supported writing sessions to develop their own narrative writing.

Phase 4: Write independently

Children write, edit and read aloud their own versions of the model story.

Main source text

Treasure House Anthology Sequence 2 text. *Hansel and Gretel*, Malachy Doyle, ISBN 978-0-00-723602-2

Background knowledge

Hansel and Gretel is an old German fairy tale that was written down by the Brothers Grimm for their collection of tales. Hansel and Gretel are a brother and sister who are captured by a child-eating witch after being abandoned in the woods by their starving parents. The tale may have originated from the Great Famine that ravaged Europe 700 years ago, when children were often left to look after themselves. In this simple version, Hansel and Gretel, abandoned and lost, are captured by an old woman who tries to put them in her cauldron. However, Gretel's quick thinking saves the day and the children escape.

Spoken outcome

To read or perform their class and individual version of *Hansel and Gretel*

Writing outcome

To rewrite the fairy tale, *Hansel and Gretel*, with a new bad character and a new setting

Prior knowledge

Check children's knowledge and understanding of:

- a range of fairy tales
- the story of *Hansel and Gretel*
- how fairy tales were passed down orally from the very distant past.

Diagnostic assessment options

Before starting the unit, you may wish to conduct an initial diagnostic assessment of the children's knowledge and understanding.

Ideas for initial diagnostic assessment options include:

- reviewing children's writing for correct sentence punctuation
- speaking and listening activities where children ask questions and answer using statements or exclamations
- reviewing children's writing to check that their sentences make sense
- reviewing children's writing to check for use of joining simples sentences with 'and'.

Cross-curricular links

KS1 Art and design

- Use drawing, painting and sculpture to develop and share their ideas, experiences and imagination.

Treasure House links

- Treasure House, Year 1, Comprehension Unit 2: Fairy stories: 'Hansel and Gretel'
- Treasure House, Year 1 Composition Unit 2: Fairy Stories
- Treasure House, Year 1, Punctuation Unit 1: Punctuating sentences
- Treasure House, Year 1, Spelling Unit 4: Spelling words with two syllables
- Treasure House, Year 1, Grammar Unit 1: Building sentences
- Treasure House, Year 1, Unit 2: Building sentences using 'and'

Resources

Props and percussion instruments for drama and storytelling activities (optional); paper and writing materials for story maps

Source texts – see Anthologies; Fairy-story planner; Hansel and Gretel sentence cards; Making food sentences; Proofreading sheet / My writing checklist; Proofreading sheet / My writing checklist (blank)

Phase 1: Enjoy and immerse

In Phase 1, the children look at the illustrations and listen to the story, *Hansel and Gretel*. Over several sessions, the children have opportunities to discuss the story and its characters through comprehension and discussion activities as well as exploring characters and story structure through drama, storytelling, writing and analysis of the text. Phase 1 also includes work on recognising and using exclamation marks in sentences.

Programmes of study: Year 1

Comprehension: Become very familiar with key stories, fairy stories and traditional tales, retelling them and considering their particular characteristics.

Comprehension: Discuss the significance of the title and events.

Comprehension: Make inferences on the basis of what is being said and done.

Comprehension: Predict what might happen on the basis of what has been read so far.

Vocabulary, grammar and punctuation: Begin to punctuate sentences using a capital letter and a full stop, question mark or exclamation mark.

Spelling: Divide words into syllables.

Sparking interest

Display page 2 and 3 of the main source text, *Hansel and Gretel*. Read the text from the pages. Ask questions such as: 'Who are Hansel and Gretel?' (They are brother and sister, children of the woodman and his wife) 'How do we know that the family are poor?' 'Why is the woodman not happy about his wife's idea?' 'Who is listening at the door?' 'What do you think he will do next?' Introduce the sequence by explaining the Big Picture: they will be looking at *Hansel and Gretel* stories to help them write their own version.

Reading and discussion

Read the whole story to the class using intonation. Check children's understanding of the content and characters of the story. Use the digital screens from Year 2, Comprehension Unit 2 to reinforce discussion.

Ask questions such as:

- Why do you think Hansel dropped cake bits on the path?
- Look at the picture on page 5. What do you think the woodman asked Hansel and Gretel to do?
- What happened to Hansel's cake trail?
- Why were Hansel and Gretel glad to find the small house?
- How did the sweet granny get Hansel and Gretel into her house?
- What did she really want to do with them?

- Why do you think the birds help them get home?
- Was the woodman glad to see Hansel and Gretel?

Encourage the children to share their thoughts about the granny character and her home. Ask: 'How does the granny and her house change when Hansel and Gretel walk through the gate?'

Drama and storytelling

Use a range of activities to reinforce the children's understanding of the main story and investigate the main characters. Select the activities that would fit in with your lesson timing. Encourage mixed-ability grouping for the chosen activities.

- **Storytelling:** Become a storyteller. The children should accompany your performance, either by using props for sound effects or by taking the roles of the characters.
- **Story map retelling:** Put the children into small groups. Display the story map on pp.14–15 or give each group a copy of the map. In their groups, encourage the children to recount the story in the right sequence order.
- **Freeze-framing key moments:** Put the children into different scenes in the right story order. Use thought-tracking, asking each child in the freeze-frame what they are thinking at that particular moment.

- **Getting lost:** Put the children into pairs or small groups. Ask the children to imagine that they are lost in the forest. Encourage them to consider how they would they find a way to get out and how they would survive.

- **Hot-seating the granny:** This activity can be done in pairs, small groups or as a class situation with the children representing the characters. Questions could include: 'Did you know Hansel and Gretel were coming?' 'Why would you want to eat them?' 'What would you have done, if they had said no to you?'

Incidental writing

A short writing activity would enhance the children's understanding of the story and help to inform the teaching focuses in the collaborative composition phase. Children could:

- write a letter asking for help from Hansel and Gretel
- write character descriptions and recounts
- draw a story map with labels showing the way back home from the granny's house
- design a 'lost children' poster.

Analysis

Display the text to the children. Discuss the setting of the story and, with the children, list the main characters. Encourage the children to decide whether the characters are good or bad and draw a happy or bad-tempered face by each character name. Use the story map on pp.14–15 to explore the plot, focussing on the beginning, the middle and the end parts of the story. Focus on the story sequence from when the children meet the granny: the invitation, being trapped, the escape. Draw three images, write simple captions to show this sequence and display them in order.

Grammar: Using an exclamation mark

Show page 10 from the main source text, *Hansel and Gretel*. Read the text emphasising the intonation for the sentences with an exclamation mark. Point to the exclamation mark at the end of the sentence: 'I will make you fat!' Find out if the children remember what the mark is called and what it tells the reader. Say the sentence without the exclamation mark to show a contrast. Read slowly through the text. When the children hear an exclamation and see an exclamation mark ask them to draw the shape in the air.

Use Year 1, Punctuation Unit 1 for more work on exclamation marks.

Phonics and spelling

This activity can be done in small groups or as a class. Write the two-syllable names 'Hansel' and 'Gretel' on a board. Say each name in turn, clapping the beat for each syllable. Explain how longer words can be split into parts called syllables. Draw a line between the letters in the names to show the two syllable parts (Hans/el, Gret/el).

Write out more two-syllable words from the story such as 'woodman', 'cannot', 'pocket', 'cauldron'. Let the children write each one in turn on their whiteboards, and place a mark to show the break between the two syllables by saying the word and clapping the beats.
Use Year 1, Spelling Unit 4 for more work on spelling words with two syllables.

Review of the Big Picture

At the end of this phase, discuss with the children what they have learned so far about the story and the main characters. Remind the children (or have them remind each other) of the sequence's Big Picture: that this is all working towards writing their own stories.

Year 1, Sequence 2
Fairy tales

Phase 2: Capture and organise

During Phase 2, children start to develop ideas about new content needed to create a retelling of the fairy tale using a new bad character with a different house or building. Working collaboratively, children decide on the new character and setting and the new events and actions that occur from these changes. Phase 2 also includes work on spelling the split digraph, a-e.

Programmes of study: Year 1

Comprehension: Draw on what they already know or on background information and vocabulary provided by the teacher.

Comprehension: Be encouraged to link what they read or hear read to their own experiences.

Comprehension: Participate in discussion about what is read to them, taking turns and listening to what others say.

Comprehension: Explain clearly their understanding of what is read to them.

Composition: Say out loud what they are going to write about.

Spelling: Spell words with the split digraph a-e.

Introduction

Remind the children of the Big Picture. Display and reread the main source text, *Hansel and Gretel* to the children. Highlight how the story has been told in different ways. Display and read the part of the story from when Hansel and Gretel find the gingerbread house. Discuss what is the same and what is different about the house and the 'old woman' in both books. Ask: 'How does the old woman use her house to lure the two hungry children inside?'

Introduce the idea that the children are going to work together to create their own class version of the fairy tale but with a new bad character and a new house.

Discussing ideas

As a class, discuss and make decisions to create their new story character and setting for their class story. Record their ideas for Phase 3 and Phase 4.

Discuss the following with the children.

- What does the bad character use to lure the children into their trap? (for example, food or the smell of food, sweets, toys, cute animals)
- What does the bad character lure the children into? (for example, an attic, a sweet shop, a cage in a pet shop, a magic picnic blanket that folds to trap them)
- Who is the new bad character? How are they linked to the trap that they set? (for example, a shop keeper, a picnicking teddy bear)
- How does the bad character and their trap change once Hansel and Gretel are successfully lured? (for example, bars appear on the windows of the shop)

- How do Hansel and Gretel escape? (for example, they persuade animals to help them, they use toys to trip the bad character, they create a disguise)

Drama and storytelling

Use a range of activities to allow the children to explore suggestions for their new bad character and new setting.

- **Hot- seating bad character:** Put the children into pairs. Ask them to think of questions they would like to ask the bad character. Match the pair with another pair and let them take turns to be the bad character and the interviewers.
- **Freeze-framing key moments:** Once the structure of the story is created, try out the different scenes in the right sequence. Use thought-tracking by asking each child in the freeze-frame what they're thinking at that moment of the story.
- **Escape plans:** Put the children into small groups. Ask them to imagine that they are trapped in the house by their bad character. Ask them to think of ways they can trick them and escape. Be the bad character and let each group in turn, act out their trick and escape ideas. Discuss with the class which ones work well and help them in their final choice.
- **A new story map:** Have the children create a story map to show their new story ideas, for example, how the children encounter the new bad character and their trap. Encourage them to use it, to reinforce their story ideas or to stimulate new ideas.

Incidental writing

Before you select any incidental writing, make sure the children are able to orally articulate the main events. Select activities that you think appropriate for the abilities and interests of your class. Children could:

- draw a simple picture and character description of the new bad character
- draw and label a picture of the new setting/house
- write a diary entry by Hansel or Gretel about what happened
- make a list of food/toys/cute animals/other in the house or building
- write a recipe for Hansel and Gretel's favourite dish, or the bad character's favourite meal.

Organising the new story into a structure

Once the children have thoroughly explored their ideas for their class fairy tale, bring them together and use their final suggestions to model how to plot the new story in picture, diagram or note form onto the Fairy-story planner. Once recorded, go through the frame and ask the children if they are happy with the tale.

Phonics and spelling

Ask the children what Hansel used to leave a trail in the forest (cake crumbs). Write the word, 'cake' on the board and say each segment of the word. Draw a line connecting the 'a' to the 'e'. Highlight that the a-e makes the /ai/ sound. Note that there is no /e/ sound for the 'e' and that the last sound is /k/.

List some a-e words from the story such as: 'cake', 'came', 'gave', 'gate'. Let the children help you list other words with the same a-e spelling patterns, for example: 'take', 'lame', 'save', 'late'.

Review of the Big Picture

At the end of this phase, discuss with the children what they have achieved with their planning and ideas for the new character and new setting.

Year 1, Sequence 2
Fairy tales

Phase 3: Collaborate and compose

Phase 3 has four writing lessons which support the children in the writing of their class version of Hansel and Gretel. Each lesson starts with a short vocabulary, grammar and punctuation focus with links to the main text. The teacher then models writing in a shared composition session, applying the VGP focus in context. Independent writing, with plenaries, follows. The VGP focuses are on combining words to make sentences and joining words and clauses using 'and'.

Programmes of study: Year 1

Composition: Say out loud what they are going to write about.

Composition: Compose a sentence orally before writing it.

Composition: Sequence sentences to form short narratives.

Composition: Discuss what they have written with the teacher or other pupils.

Vocabulary, grammar and punctuation: Understand how words can combine to make sentences.

Vocabulary, grammar and punctuation: Join words and join clauses using 'and'.

Introduction

Remind the children about the sequence's Big Picture. Explain that over several lessons the children are going to start work as a class to draft and write a different version of *Hansel and Gretel* with a new bad character and home/building. Use the class Fairy-story planner from Phase 2 to remind the children of their story plan and final choice of the new character and place.

Lesson 1

Combining words to make sentences

Write 'The woodman was poor.' on the board. Read out the sentence. Note that it starts with a capital letter and ends with a full stop. Write the words for the sentence, 'The birds ate the cake crumbs' individually on cards (including the punctuation). Give a word card each to six children. In no particular order, ask each child to come up and show their card for the class to read out. When all six words are together, ask the children to help you put them in the right order to make a sentence. Point out the punctuation clues. Once completed, ask the children to read the sentence out to check it makes sense. Note that the punctuation alone does not make it a sentence. Remove words but leave the capital letter and full stop, and check the children's understanding that it is not a sentence.

Use Year 1 Grammar Unit 1 for more work on sentences.

Shared writing

With the children, using their Fairy-story planner, model writing the opening of the story (the children become lost). Model the oral composition of sentences before writing. Write one or two sentences with words in the wrong order to encourage the children to use what they have learned about combining words correctly to make sentences. Once written, collaboratively check through the work, with attention to accurate use of sentence punctuation, and that the sentences make sense.

Independent writing

The children can now write their own first section, applying the VGP focus on combining words to make sentences. Give or show each child the class Fairy-story planner to help with vocabulary and structure. Some children may benefit from guided group or peer-paired writing at this stage.

Plenary

Throughout the writing session, ask the children questions to help them focus on their progress and what they have created during that lesson, for example: 'How is your story opening like the original?' 'Where have you used capital letters and full stops properly?' Encourage children to check that the words in the sentences are in the right order and that no words are missing.

Lesson 2

Combining words to make sentences

Remind the children of the last lesson, where they put words together to make a sentence. Discuss the punctuation clues that helped them: a capital letter at the beginning of the sentence and a full stop at the end of a sentence. Reiterate that just putting a capital letter and a full stop doesn't make it a sentence. Tell children they are going to explore more ways words are used in simple sentences.

Write: 'Hansel likes eating gingerbread.' 'Gretel likes eating cake.' Point to the name at the beginning of the sentence; the action words 'likes' and 'eating'; and the object at the end of the sentence. Give the children a copy of the Making food sentences sheet. Let them write out four sentences using the sentence model and then two of their own sentences. Let them share with partners.

Use Year 1, Grammar Unit 1 for more work on sentences.

Shared writing

With the children, using their class Fairy-story planner, model writing the second part of the story (Hansel and Gretel are tricked and trapped by the bad character). Model the oral composition of sentences before writing them. Write one or two sentences with words in the wrong order for the children to correct. Note the main subject, action word and object in the sentence. Once written, collaboratively check through the work, with attention to accurate sentence punctuation, and that the sentences make sense.

Independent writing

The children can now write their second section, focusing on sentence creation and punctuation. Give or show each child the class Fairy-story planner to help with vocabulary and structure. Some children may benefit from guided group or peer-paired writing at this stage.

Plenary

Throughout the writing session, ask the children questions to help them focus on their progress and what they have created during that lesson, for example: 'Where have you used capital letters, full stops and question marks correctly in your writing?' 'How have you followed the story patterns shown in *Hansel and Gretel*?'

Lesson 3

Joining words and clauses using 'and'

Write on the board, 'Gretel brushed the floor.' and 'She washed the dishes.' Encourage the children to read the sentences out. Highlight that they are two sentences by pointing to the capital letters and full stops. Ask the children what small word they could use to join the sentences together to make one sentence. Orally join the sentences together using the word 'and' and then write the sentence out. Underline the 'and' and circle the lowercase 's' for 'she' to show it is not a capital letter. Ask the children for more household jobs that Gretel could have done. Write the suggestions on the board and then with the children join pairs of sentences using 'and'.

Use Year 1, Grammar Unit 2 for more work on building sentences using 'and'.

Shared writing

Select the third part of the story (the children trick the bad character and escape) and model the writing process using the class story planner. As you model the writing, join some of the sentences using 'and'. Once written, read the work aloud to check it makes sense, there is good use of sentence punctuation and some sentences are joined using 'and'.

Independent writing

The children can now write their third section, applying their knowledge on sentences and showing examples of sentences joined with 'and'. Give or show each child the class Fairy-story planner to help with vocabulary and structure. Some children may benefit from guided group or peer-paired writing at this stage.

Plenary

Throughout the writing session, ask the children questions to help them focus on their progress and what they have created during that lesson, for example: 'How have you made it clear how Hansel and Gretel escape from the bad character?' 'Which of your sentences are joined with 'and'?'

Lesson 4

Joining words and clauses using 'and'

Briefly revise last lesson's work on joining sentences using the word 'and'. Write two sentences on the board: 'Hansel ran down the path' 'Hansel jumped over a puddle'. Ask the children to orally join the sentences using 'and'. Note how the sentence sounds clumsy with 'Hansel' twice. Write out the sentence: 'Hansel ran down the path and jumped over a puddle.' Put the children into pairs and give them the Hansel and Gretel sentence cards. Ask them to join two sentences together and then rewrite them as one sentence.

Use Year 1, Grammar Unit 2 for more work on building sentences using 'and'.

Shared writing

Select the final part of the story (the children go home) and model the writing process using the class Fairy-story planner. As you model the writing, join some of the sentences using 'and', noting how some words are taken out. Once written, read the work aloud to check it makes sense, there is good use of sentence punctuation and some sentences are joined using 'and'.

Independent writing

The children can now write their fourth and final section, applying their knowledge of sentences and showing examples of sentences joined with 'and'. Give or show each child their class Fairy-story planner to help with vocabulary and structure. Some children may benefit from guided group or peer-paired writing at this stage.

Plenary

During the writing session, ask the children questions to help them focus on their progress and what they have created during that lesson, for example: 'How has your story come to a good end?' 'How similar or different is it to the original story ending?' 'How can you check the sentences make sense?' 'Which is your best sentence joined with 'and'?' Encourage children to check that they have and/or a partner has used capital letters and full stops correctly.

Presenting and performing

Once the children have written their story, encourage them to retell it either as storytellers or by creating a performance. Take feedback on what they particularly liked about the stories children have heard.

Review of the Big Picture

Once you have completed all the lessons for this section, remind the children of the sequence's Big Picture. Discuss what they have learned so far.

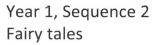

Phase 4: Write independently

This final phase brings all the children's learning and writing skills together so that they can write their own fairy tale independently. Through their writing, they will be able to utilise the different VGP focuses that they have been practising throughout the previous phases.

Programmes of study: Year 1

Composition: Say out loud what they are going to write about.

Composition: Compose a sentence orally before writing it.

Composition: Sequence sentences to form short narratives.

Composition: Re-read what they have written to check that it makes sense.

Composition: Discuss what they have written with the teacher or other pupils.

Composition: Read aloud their writing clearly enough to be heard by their peers and the teacher.

Introduction

Introduce the phase by discussing what the children have learned in their story planning and writing sessions and link it to the Big Picture. Emphasise that the time has come for the children to bring all their learning together and write their own version of the fairy tale with a new bad character and house/building. Review the children's various suggestions for bad characters and settings from Phase 2.

Recap the story structure of their class story and the two versions of the old woman and the house in the *Hansel and Gretel* stories. Explain that the planning and writing of their own story will take place over several sessions.

Writing

Give each child a Fairy-story planner. As they plan, draft and write each section of the story, encourage the children to compose their sentences orally before writing them down. Let the children draw a picture to illustrate each section.

All the children should be encouraged to try to write independently to the best of their abilities. Ask open questions such as: 'How does your story start?' 'How does the bad character lure Hansel and Gretel into the trap?' 'How do Hansel and Gretel get home?' Make sure that the children have a chance to share their writing with others at appropriate points during each session.

Proofreading and redrafting

Encourage the children to read through their work at the end of each writing session with a partner. Ask them to check whether their writing makes sense. Proofreading and improvement without support means that the writing will happen over a few lessons. Offer the children the Proofreading sheet / My writing checklist, or create your own checklist with the assistance of the blank Proofreading sheet / My writing checklist.

Self- and peer-assessment

Encourage the children to take time to assess their own and others' writing. Make sure that they read out their writing clearly. Also encourage them to check their VGP focuses on punctuation and sentence structure to ensure they have been successfully applied throughout the texts.

Presenting and performing

Have the children make simple illustrated story books to share and read with each other or create puppets to perform the story. Encourage the children to use intonation to express exclamations and use different voices for the different characters.

Final review of the Big Picture

Individually or with partners, have children reflect on what they have learned from this sequence and what they will remember to do in future writing.

Sequence 3
Traditional tales

Approximate duration: Two weeks

Big Picture

Through this teaching sequence, children explore the story, structure and characters of the traditional tale, *The Magic Paintbrush*. By the end of the sequence, they will have written a new non-rhyming version of the story with a different setting about a child who uses a magic crayon to help others and to fool a new greedy character.

Phase 1: Enjoy and Immerse

Children become familiar with the story, structure and characters in the model text, *The Magic Paintbrush*.

Phase 2: Capture and organise

Children are supported in developing ideas for a new non-rhyming version of the story with new characters and setting.

Phase 3: Collaborate and compose

Children undertake supported writing sessions to develop their own narrative writing of the class story.

Phase 4: Write independently

Children write, edit and read aloud their own non-rhyming versions of the model story.

Main source text

Treasure House Anthology Sequence 3 text. *The Magic Paintbrush*, Julia Donaldson, ISBN 978-0-33-396443-9

Background knowledge

The Magic Paintbrush is an old Chinese traditional tale. In Julia Donaldson's rhyming version of the tale, a young girl called Shen is given a magic paint brush, with which she must only paint things that become real for poor people. When she refuses to paint riches for the emperor, he throws her into a cell. However she manages to escape and stops the emperor recapturing her by using her paintings to scare him and his army away.

The better-known version of the tale involves a young boy, who uses the magic paintbrush to create fertile fields and streams to help the poor local farmers. He is then kidnapped by the emperor who desires a golden mountain. The boy draws this with a sea before it and with a ship to sail there. Once the emperor and his men are on board, the boy draws a huge wave to drown them all.

Spoken outcome

To read or perform their story, 'The Magic Crayons'

Writing outcome

To rewrite the traditional tale in a different setting about a child with magic crayons

Prior knowledge

Check children's experience, knowledge and understanding of:

- traditional tales from around the world
- traditional Chinese tales (see Digital Comprehension Unit 3 for more work on a Chinese traditional tale)
- how traditional tales were orally passed down from the very distant past
- tales about something that comes to life through magic
- tales about greed and being kind to others.

Diagnostic assessment options

Before starting the unit, you may wish to conduct an initial diagnostic assessment of the children's knowledge and understanding. Ideas for initial diagnostic assessment options include:

- reviewing children's writing for the correct use of sentence punctuation
- speaking and listening activities where children ask questions and answer using statements or questions
- reviewing children's writing to check that their sentences make sense
- reviewing children's writing for simple sentences joined with 'and'.

Cross-curricular links

KS1 Art and design

- Use drawing, painting and sculpture to develop and share their ideas, experiences and imagination.

KS1 Geography – Geographical skills and fieldwork

- Use world maps, atlases and globes to identify the United Kingdom and its countries, as well as the countries, continents and oceans studied at this key stage.

Treasure House links

- Treasure House, Year 1, Comprehension Unit 3: Traditional tales: 'The King of the Forest'
- Treasure House, Year 1, Composition Unit 3: Fantasy Stories
- Treasure House, Year 1, Punctuation Unit 2: Capital letter for names and 'I'
- Treasure House, Year 1, Spelling Unit 7: Adding -s to make a plural
- Treasure House, Year 1, Spelling Unit 8: Adding -es to make a plural
- Treasure House, Year 1, Punctuation Unit 1: Punctuating sentences
- Treasure House, Year 1, Grammar Unit 1: Building sentences
- Treasure House, Year 1, Grammar Unit 2: Building sentences using 'and'

Resources

Props and percussion instruments for drama and storytelling activities (optional); a large paintbrush, a pack of coloured crayons, paper and drawing materials, a globe or world map

Source texts – see Anthologies; Traditional tale map; Mixed-up sentences; Proofreading sheet / My writing checklist; Proofreading sheet / My writing checklist (blank)

Phase 1: Enjoy and immerse

In Phase 1, the children listen to the story, *The Magic Paintbrush*. Over several sessions, the children have opportunities to discuss the story and its characters through comprehension and discussion activities as well as exploring characters and story structure through drama, storytelling, writing and analysis of the text. Phase 1 covers the vocabulary, grammar and punctuation focus on using capital letters for names and includes work on adding -s or -es for third person singular verbs.

Programmes of study: Year 1

Comprehension: Listen to and discuss a wide range of poems, stories and non-fiction at a level beyond that at which they can read independently.

Comprehension: Become very familiar with key stories, fairy stories and traditional tales, retelling them and considering their particular characteristics.

Comprehension: Learn to appreciate rhymes and poems, and to recite some by heart.

Comprehension: Make inferences on the basis of what is being said and done.

Comprehension: Predict what might happen on the basis of what has been read so far.

Vocabulary, grammar and punctuation: Use a capital letter for names of people, places, the days of the week, and the personal pronoun 'I'.

Spelling: Use the spelling rule for adding -s or -es as the plural marker for nouns and the third person singular marker for verbs.

Sparking interest

Show the children a large paintbrush. Ask them to imagine that the brush is magic and that any object or creature they paint will come alive. Have the children each say what they would paint and why. Introduce the tale, *The Magic Paintbrush*. Explain that it is an old Chinese tale that has been retold for many years. Use a globe or world map to show where China is in relation to the UK.

Reading and discussion

Read the story to the class using appropriate intonation. Check children understand any difficult or new words. Stop at different parts of the story to discuss, ask questions, and make predictions and to check children's understanding of the content and characters.

Discuss the following with the children.

- What would Shen rather do than catch food for her family?
- What does Shen paint for the poor villagers? Why did they ask for those things? (discuss each item)
- Why does the emperor not want ordinary, familiar items like the poor people?
- What do you think Shen planned to do when she was in prison?

- What do you think about Shen's ideas to get rid of the emperor? What other ways can you think of?
- How does the story end?
- What do you think happens to Shen and the paintbrush after the end of the story?

Drama and storytelling

Use a range of activities to reinforce children's understanding of the story and characters. Select the activities that would fit in with your lesson timing. Encourage mixed-ability grouping for the chosen activities.

- **Class performance:** Organise a drama performance of the story with children taking on different roles and making props, choosing and playing musical instruments and wearing costumes.
- **Character intonation:** Put the children into groups and give them sections of the story to learn and recite. Highlight the rhythm of the text and the different voices needed for dialogue, for example, bossy, annoyed, happy, scared.

- **Magic paintbrush judging:** Select a small group of children to be magic paintbrush judges. Put the other children in groups of twos or threes. Ask each group to think of what they need from the paintbrush and the reason why. Organise some groups to be poor villagers and others to be rich villagers. The judges are to listen to the villagers and to make a decision based on the villagers' reasons.

Incidental writing

Short writing activities enhance the children's understanding of the story and help to inform the teaching focuses in the collaborative composition phase. Children could:

- paint pictures (with descriptive labels) of objects that Shen painted for the villagers
- write a few sentences about how they would help someone with a magic paintbrush
- write a thank you letter from Shen to the man who gave her the magic paintbrush
- write a review of *The Magic Paintbrush* with details of what they liked/didn't like
- collect words that describe Shen and use them to create a word picture
- create a labelled picture of Shen, describing her appearance and personality.

Analysis

Look at the story in more detail. Note that the story rhymes. Ask: 'How do we know it is set in China?' (Answers could include the Chinese animals, an 'emperor', fields of rice, the name, 'Shen', the Chinese dragon) Remind the children that, in traditional tales or fairy tales, there are usually good characters and bad characters. Discuss who was which in the story and how they know. Note that another common characteristic is the hero fooling another character. Use the Traditional tale map to record the story structure of the tale with the children, highlighting the beginning, middle and end of the story, and any repeated phrases. Discuss Shen's problem (being imprisoned) and how she resolves the problem in the middle part of the story.

Grammar: Capital letters for names

Write, 'Shen' and 'shen' on the board. Explain that one is written incorrectly and one is written correctly. Ask the children to write the correct word. Have them show it at the same time. Confirm that 'Shen' is right and ask the children to explain why (capital letters for names). Have the children write down fictional names for villagers and other characters. Let them share their ideas with each other.

Use Year 1, Punctuation Unit 2 for more on capital letters for names and the personal pronoun 'I'.

Phonics and spelling

Show the main source text and focus on the line 'She paints a pot, then stands and waits …' Underline 'She paints' and remind the children that 'paints' is a verb. (Verbs are doing or being words). Underline 'stands' and 'waits'. Highlight or circle the 's'. Note that we need to add '-s' or '-es' to the ends of regular verbs that describe another person's actions (as opposed to our own actions). Ask the children what other things Shen could do. Write their suggestions on the board, for example: 'she helps', 'she runs', 'she fishes'. Note that the -s and -es endings are spelled the way they sound: if the ending sounds like /s/ or /z/, it is spelled '-s'; if the ending sounds like /es/ and adds a syllable, it is spelled '-es'. In pairs, let the children write a list of five verbs to show Shen's chores in one day before she received the paintbrush, for example: 'she washes', 'she cleans'.

Review of the Big Picture

At the end of this phase, discuss with the children what they have learned so far about the tale and the main characters. Remind them that this is all working towards writing their own stories.

Phase 2: Capture and organise

During Phase 2, children start to develop ideas about new content needed to create a non-rhyming traditional tale based on *The Magic Paintbrush* in a new setting involving magic crayons. Working collaboratively, children decide on the two new main characters, the setting and the new events and actions for their story. The tale can be written in past or present tense. Phase 2 also includes work on alternative spellings with the /ee/ sound.

Programmes of study: Year 1

Comprehension: Draw on what they already know or on background information and vocabulary provided by the teacher.

Comprehension: Be encouraged to link what they read or hear read to their own experiences.

Comprehension: Make inferences on the basis of what is being said and done.

Comprehension: Explain clearly their understanding of what is read to them.
Composition: Say out loud what they are going to write about.
Spelling: Spell words with the digraph ee.
Spelling: Spell words with the digraph ea (/i/).

Introduction

Remind the children of the Big Picture. Reread or with the children recount Julia Donaldson's version of *The Magic Paintbrush*. Highlight that there are many versions of the tale and describe an original version (see Background information). Note how the main message of the story is the same: helping others less fortunate; tricking a mean character. Highlight that many of the versions are still set in China.

Show the children a pack of colourful crayons. Introduce the idea that the children are going to work together to create their own class version of the tale but with a new hero who is given magic crayons instead of a magic paintbrush. Mention that their tale will not rhyme.

Discussing ideas

As a class, discuss and make decisions to create their new story characters, setting and story events for their class story. Suggest that the children keep the traditional tale in the past for the class story. Record the children's ideas for Phase 3 and Phase 4.

Discuss the following with the children.

- Where will the story be set? (for example, in another country, the same Chinese setting or in the UK)
- Who will be our hero? What will they be like? Why is the hero chosen to have magic crayons?
- Who gives the hero magic crayons? What can the crayons do?

- How will the hero use the crayons to help those in need?
- Who will the greedy character be? (for example, a king, an emperor, a rich landowner, a rich family member)
- What will they want the hero to draw and why?
- Where will the hero be imprisoned? How will the hero escape?
- What object will the hero draw to stop the greedy character catching them?
- How will the story end?

Drama and storytelling

Use a range of activities to allow the children to explore suggestions for their new tale.

- **Helping others:** Remind the children how the magic crayons are used to help others. Put the children in groups and give them different characters that need help, for example, poor farmers, sick or hurt people, endangered animals, hungry villagers, lost children. Have them discuss, and then perform short scenes to show the problem and how the crayons are used to solve the problems.

- **Stop and draw!** Have the children imagine that they are running from the greedy character. Call out 'Stop and draw!' Have them mime drawing your suggestion or their own idea to stop the greedy character. Call 'Let it be real!' Have the children act or mime what they have drawn.

- **Exploring the end:** Have a drama session to allow the children to explore how the story will end. Discuss different ending ideas and allocate each one to a group of children. Let them rehearse and then act out their ending to the rest of the class.
- **Freeze-framing key moments:** Once the structure of the story is created, try out the different scenes in the right sequence. Use thought-tracking, asking each child in the freeze-frame what they are thinking at that moment of the story.

Incidental writing

Before you select any incidental writing, make sure the children are able to orally articulate the main events. Select activities that you think appropriate for the abilities and interests of your class. Children could:

- make crayon drawings that could be drawn by the hero in the story, with a caption explaining what the drawing is of and how it helps
- draw a picture of the main character with a simple description of them
- complete the sentence, 'I would draw a _____ to help _____', with various ideas.

Organising the new traditional tale into a structure

Once the children have thoroughly explored their ideas for their class tale, bring them together and use their final suggestions to model how to plot the new story on the traditional tale map in picture and note form. Once recorded, go through the planner and ask the children what they particularly like about the tale and anything they would now change.

Phonics and spelling

On a display board, draw or create two large tree shapes with branches. Write 'ee' above one and 'ea' above the other. Show blank word cards in the shape of round coins. Ask: 'Who wanted Shen to draw a tree with gold coins?' (the emperor) Ask the children to help you spell 'tree' on a coin card. Note the /ee/ sound for 'ee'. Let one of the children stick it onto a branch. Point to 'ea' and discuss how it stands for the same sound as 'ee' but is spelled differently. Let children say the sound. Add a word to the 'ea' tree, for example 'leaf'. Have children suggest 'ee' and 'ea' words to write on the coin cards and add to the trees. Emphasise the /ee/ sound in each word.

Review of the Big Picture

At the end of this phase, discuss with the children what they have achieved with their planning and ideas for their new class tale.

Phase 3: Collaborate and compose

Phase 3 includes three writing lessons, which support the children in writing their class version of *The Magic Paintbrush*. Each lesson starts with a short vocabulary, grammar and punctuation focus with links to the main text. The teacher then models writing in a shared composition session, applying the VGP focus in context. Independent writing, with plenaries, follows. The text should be non-rhyming. The VGP focuses are on the use of question and exclamation marks, how words can combine to make sentences and joining words and clauses using 'and'.

Programmes of study: Year 1

Composition: Say out loud what they are going to write about.

Composition: Compose a sentence orally before writing it.

Composition: Sequence sentences to form short narratives.

Composition: Discuss what they have written with the teacher or other pupils.

Vocabulary, grammar and punctuation: Begin to punctuate sentences using a capital letter and a full stop, question mark or exclamation mark.

Vocabulary, grammar and punctuation: Understand how words can combine to make sentences.

Vocabulary, grammar and punctuation: Join words and join clauses using and.

Introduction

Remind the children about the sequence's Big Picture. Explain that over several lessons the children are going to start work as a class to draft and write a different version of *The Magic Paintbrush* involving new characters and magic crayons. Use the Traditional tale map from Phase 2 to remind the children of their story plan and final choice of the new characters, events and setting.

Lesson 1

Question marks

Display the main source text and read out the first three questions ('Did you catch some shrimps...') with emphasised intonation to show that they are questions. Have the children repeat the questions. Ask: 'What type of sentences are these?' (questions) 'What is used to help us see that they are questions?' (question marks) Say the questions again and have the children draw the question mark in the air at the end of each one. With the children write a few simple questions they would like to ask Shen. Encourage volunteers to come up and add the question mark. Read and write out a few statements so that the children can see and hear the difference between these and question sentences.

Use Year 1 Grammar Unit 1 for more work on sentence punctuation.

Shared writing

With the children, using their Traditional tale map, start model writing the opening of the story. Model the oral composition of sentences before writing them. Include questions, omitting the question marks so that the children can show where they should go. Once written, collaboratively check through the work, with attention to accurate sentence punctuation, correct spellings and to check that the sentences make sense.

Independent writing

The children can now write their own first part of the class tale, focusing on using question marks correctly. Make sure that the class Traditional tale map is available for them to see. Some children may benefit from guided group or peer-paired writing at this stage.

Plenary

Throughout the writing session, ask the children questions t[o] help them focus on their progress and what they have creat[ed] during that lesson, for example: 'How have you introduced [the] characters and setting of the story?' 'How does the hero he[lp] others with the magic crayons?' 'Where have you listed som[e] objects that the hero has drawn?' 'What question sentence[s] have you included?' 'Where have you used question marks[?]' Prompt children to check that their work makes sense, and [is] spelled and punctuated correctly.

Lesson 2

Combining words to make sentences

Write: 'tree. to you a I want paint' Explain that the emperor from *The Magic Paintbrush* has sent a note to Shen but the words have been mixed up. Have the children help you unscramble the words. Point out the clues in the sentence punctuation to help them. Discuss how we can make a sentence when we put words together in the right order. Put the children into small groups and give each of them words from a scrambled sentence using the Mixed-up sentences resource sheet. Once the children have put their sentences in order, ask them to stand up and show the sentence. Have them write sentences and cut them up for other groups to work out.

Use Year 1 Grammar Unit 1 for more work on building sentences.

Shared writing

With the children, using their Traditional tale map, model writing the middle part of the story. Model the oral composition of sentences before writing them. Mix up a few words in a sentence and ask children if the sentence makes sense. Have the children help you put the words and sentence punctuation in the correct order. Once written, collaboratively check through the work, with attention to accurate sentence punctuation, correct spellings and to check that the sentences make sense.

Independent writing

The children can now write their own second part of the class tale, focusing on putting words into the correct order to create a sentence that makes sense. Make sure that the class Traditional tale map is available for them to see. Some children may benefit from guided group or peer-paired writing at this stage.

Plenary

Throughout the writing session, ask the children questions to help them focus on their progress and what they have created during that lesson, for example: 'How have you shown that the greedy character is greedy?' 'How have you described what the greedy character wants?' 'Why won't the hero do what the greedy character wants?' 'How does the hero escape?' 'What type of letter have you used to start your sentences?' 'What have you used to show the end of your sentences?' Prompt children to check that their work makes sense, and is spelled and punctuated correctly.

Lesson 3

Joining sentences using 'and'

Write two sentences: 'The emperor turns his horse.' 'The emperor rides away.' Read the sentences out to the children. Point out that both sentences are about what the emperor does. Explain that you are going to join them into one sentence. Say that you need a little word to glue them together: Ask: 'Which word can I use?' (and). Model joining the sentences using 'and' and removing the second instance of 'The emperor': 'The emperor turns his horse and rides away.' Read it out with the children to check it makes sense. Use the source texts to look for other examples of sentences joined with 'and'.

Shared writing

With the children, using their Traditional tale map, model writing the final part of the story.

Model the oral composition of sentences before writing them. As you model the writing, join some of the sentences using 'and', with children's help. Once written, collaboratively check through the work, with attention to accurate sentence punctuation, correct spellings and to check that the sentences make sense.

Independent writing

The children can now write their own final part of the class tale, focusing on joining sentences using 'and'. Make sure that the class traditional tale map is available for them to see. Some children may benefit from guided group or peer-paired writing at this stage.

Plenary

Throughout the writing session, ask the children questions to help them focus on their progress and what they have created during that lesson, for example: 'How have you described how the hero stops the greedy character?' 'What ending have you used in your tale?' 'Why have you chosen to end your tale like this?' 'What makes this a good ending?' 'Which sentences have you joined together using 'and'?' 'What punctuation marks have you used in your sentences?' Prompt children to check that their work makes sense, and is spelled and punctuated correctly.

Presenting and performing

Once the children have written their tale encourage them to retell it either as storytellers or by creating a performance. Take feedback on what they particularly liked about the tales they have heard.

Review of the Big Picture

Once you have completed all the lessons for this phase, remind the children of the sequence's Big Picture. Discuss what they have learned so far.

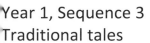

Phase 4: Write independently

This final phase brings all the children's learning and writing skills together so that they can write their own traditional tale about magic crayons independently. Through their writing, they will be able to utilise the different VGP focuses that they have been practising throughout previous phases.

Programmes of study: Year 1

Composition: Say out loud what they are going to write about.

Composition: Compose a sentence orally before writing it.

Composition: Sequence sentences to form short narratives.

Composition: Re-read what they have written to check that it makes sense.

Composition: Discuss what they have written with the teacher or other pupils.

Composition: Read aloud their writing clearly enough to be heard by their peers and the teacher.

Introduction

Introduce the phase by discussing what the children have learned in their story planning and writing sessions and link it to the 'Big picture'. Emphasise the excitement of bringing all their learning together to write their own version of 'The Magic Crayons'. Review the children's different suggestions for the new characters, setting, and events from Phase 2. Clarify that the planning and writing of their own tale will take place over several sessions.

Writing

Give each child a Traditional tale map. As they plan, draft and write each section of the story, encourage the children to compose their sentences orally before writing them down. Have children draw a picture to illustrate each section.

All the children should be encouraged to try to write independently to the best of their abilities. Ask open questions such as 'Where is your story set?' 'How does your story start?' 'Who gives your hero the crayons?' 'How are the crayons used to help others?' 'What does the greedy character want?' 'How does the hero escape?' 'How do they stop the greedy character?' 'How does the story end?' 'What part do you like best?' 'Which part would you change?' Make sure that the children have a chance to share their writing with others at appropriate points during each session.

Proofreading and redrafting

Encourage the children to read through their work at the end of each writing session with a partner. Ask them to check whether their writing makes sense. Proofreading and improvement without support means that the writing will happen over a few lessons. Offer the children the

Proofreading sheet / My writing checklist, or create your own checklist with the assistance of the blank Proofreading sheet / My writing checklist.

Self- and peer-assessment

Encourage the children to assess their own and others' writing. Make sure that they read out their writing clearly. Ask open questions to encourage self- and peer-assessment such as: 'How similar/different is this story to the original?' 'How does the story start?' 'What happens in the middle part of the story?' 'What problem must the hero solve?' 'How does the hero trick the greedy character?' 'Has the story got a good story ending?' 'Which character is good and which is bad?' 'How is the story exciting and fun to read?' Also encourage children to check their VGP focuses on the correct place for a question mark, combining words to create sentences and joining two simple sentences using 'and', to check that they have been successfully applied throughout the texts. Make sure that they read out their writing clearly.

Presenting and performing

Have the children write out their tales from their writing frames with crayon pictures to illustrate their writing. Let them share and read each other's tales or perform their tale to each other. Encourage the children to use intonation to highlight exclamations and voices of the different characters.

Final review of the Big Picture

Individually or with partners, have children reflect on what they have learned from this sequence and what they will remember to do in future writing.

Sequence 4
Rhymes and poems

Approximate duration: Two weeks

Big Picture

Through this teaching sequence, children explore the poem, 'Cats'. By the end of the sequence, they will have written a new version of the poem, based on a different element of a cat's life and behaviour.

Phase 1: Enjoy and immerse

Children become familiar with the content, language and structure of the model text poem, 'Cats'.

Phase 2: Capture and organise

Children are supported in developing ideas for a new poem about cats.

Phase 3: Collaborate and compose

Children undertake supported writing sessions to develop their own writing based on the class poem.

Phase 4: Write independently

Children write, edit and read aloud their own poems about cats.

Main source text

Treasure House Anthology Sequence 4 text. 'Cats', Eleanor Farjeon, *The Puffin Book of Fantastic First Poems*, ISBN 978-01-41-30898-2, p.6

Extra source texts

'No Hickory No Dickory No Dock', John Agard, *The Puffin Book of Fantastic First Poems*, ISBN 978-0-14-130898-2, p.15

Background knowledge

Eleanor Farjeon (1881–1965) was a prolific English author, poet and playwright whose stories, poems and nursery rhymes for children have been universally acclaimed and are still popular today. She grew up in a large, literary, creative family, with a father and two brothers who were also writers and another brother who was a composer. Encouraged to write from an early age, she got her inspirations for her writing from everyday life around her and on her many trips away. Her most well-known work today is her children's hymn, 'Morning has broken' (1931), which is sung to an old Scottish folk tune.

Spoken outcome

To read or perform their poem on cats

Writing outcome

To write a poem about cats

Prior knowledge

Check children's knowledge and understanding of:
- cats and their behaviour
- poems with simple rhymes
- nursery rhymes (including by Eleanor Farjeon)
- poems about animals and cats.

Diagnostic assessment options

Before starting the unit, you may wish to conduct an initial diagnostic assessment of the children's knowledge and understanding.

Ideas for initial diagnostic assessment options include:

- reviewing children's writing for correct sentence punctuation in poems and verses such as capital letters at the beginnings of lines
- speaking and listening activities where children listen to and identify exclamation sentences
- reviewing children's writing for their ability to understand and use compound words
- reviewing children's writing to check for the correct spelling of words with the /k/ sound spelled ck.

Cross-curricular links

KS1 Art and design

- Use drawing, painting and sculpture to develop and share their ideas, experiences and imagination.

KS1 Music

- Use their voices expressively and creatively by singing songs and speaking chants and rhymes.

KS1 Science – Animals, including humans

- Identify and name a variety of common animals including fish, amphibians, reptiles, birds and mammals.
- Identify and name a variety of common animals that are carnivores, herbivores and omnivores.

Treasure House links

- Treasure House, Year 1, Comprehension Unit 4: Rhymes and poems: 'Cats'
- Treasure House, Year 1, Composition Unit 6: Poetry: My Favourite
- Treasure House, Year 1, Punctuation Unit 1: Punctuating sentences
- Treasure House, Year 1, Spelling Unit 2: Spelling ck after a short vowel

Resources

Props and percussion instruments for drama and storytelling activities (optional); information and images of cats and their behaviour

Phase 1: Enjoy and immerse

In Phase 1, the children listen to and perform the poem, 'Cats'. Over several sessions, the children have opportunities to discuss the language and structure of the poem through comprehension and discussion activities as well as exploring the poem's content and structure through drama, performance, writing and analysis of the text. Phase 1 also covers the vocabulary, grammar and punctuation focus on using exclamation marks in sentences and includes work on the digraphs ai and ay.

Programmes of study: Year 1

Comprehension: Listen to and discuss a wide range of poems, stories and non-fiction at a level beyond that at which they can read independently.

Comprehension: Recognise and join in with predictable phrases.

Comprehension: Learn to appreciate rhymes and poems, and to recite some by heart.

Comprehension: Discuss the significance of the title and events.

Vocabulary, grammar and punctuation: Begin to punctuate sentences using a capital letter and a full stop, question mark or exclamation mark.

Spelling: Spell words with the digraphs ai, oi.

Spelling: Spell words with the digraphs ay, oy.

Sparking interest

Show images of cats sleeping in a range of different places. Encourage the children to share their experiences or opinions about how and where cats sleep. Ask: 'If you were a cat, where would you sleep?' Explain that you are going to read a poem that lists places where cats sleep. Highlight that is was written long ago by Eleanor Farjeon who liked to write poems and rhymes about her life, which included her pet cats.

Reading and discussion

Display and then read out the poem using appropriate intonation and putting emphasis on the repeated phrases at the beginning and end of the poem. If possible, repeat the poem with the children joining in. Lead a discussion to check their understanding of the poem.

Use Year 1, Comprehension Unit 4 for more comprehension work on the poem.

Discuss the following with the children.

- What phrase starts and ends the poem?
- What different places do the cats like to sleep in?
- What do you think the word 'any' means? Why is it a good word to use to explain where cats sleep?
- Where on the window-ledge do they sleep?
- What do you think 'frocks' means?

- Do you think the poet minds the cats sleeping in her frock cupboard? Why?
- Do you think cats care where they sleep? Why or why not?

Drama and storytelling

Use a range of activities to reinforce children's understanding of the poem. Select the activities that would fit in with your lesson timing. Encourage mixed-ability grouping for the chosen activities.

- **Class Performance:** Organise a performance of the poem. Give small groups of children one or two lines of the poem to remember and perform. Have them all say the repeated starting and finishing lines. Either have a recitation of the poem or let the children use movement or props for a more dramatic performance.

- **Cat movements:** Have a mime and movement session. Tell the children to use their bodies and facial expressions to be cats. Call 'Time to sleep!' Say where the cats are going to sleep. Encourage them to take their time doing it. Remind them how cats can curl into tight places. Once they are all settled, call 'Wake up cats!' and start the process again.

Cat sleeping circle: Put the children into a circle. Start the circle by asking the question: 'Dear Cat, why are you sleeping in/on/by/under …?' Choose a sleeping place and then roll a ball to one of the children in the circle for their answer, for example: 'I like sleeping on a beanbag because….' Have that child ask another sleeping question before rolling the ball to someone else for the answer. Continue until all the children have had turns.

Incidental writing

Short writing activities enhance the children's understanding of the poem and help to inform the teaching focuses in the collaborative composition phase. Children could:

- draw and label pictures of sleeping cats
- write a vertical list of other places where cats sleep (for example, 'up a tree', 'a cat bed', 'on the sofa', 'under a table', 'under a bed', 'in a bush'
- compose a short lullaby for a cat
- complete sentences such as: 'If I was a cat, I would sleep _____ because _____'
- write two lines to add the model poem.

Analysis

Display the poem, 'Cats', to the children and read through the poem. Note the long layout of the poem and that there is only one to three words on each line. Discuss how the poem is like a long list of places. Cut the poem up into parts. Encourage the children to find and say the repeated phrases used at the start and end of the poem. Highlight the repeated word, 'Any' and discuss how it is used. Read the poem out and help the children discuss the rhythm and speed of the poem, and how the use of exclamation marks makes the poet sound cross by the end. Finally highlight the rhyming words for every other sentence.

Use Year 1, Comprehension Unit 4 as support for analysis of the poem.

Grammar: Punctuating sentences with exclamation marks

Display the poem, 'Cats', to the children and read it with appropriate intonation and emphasis on the two exclamation lines at the end of the poem. Highlight 'Anywhere!' and say it again with exclamation. Hide the exclamation mark, and say the word without exclamation. Ask: 'What is added to 'Anywhere' so that we know to say it with feeling?' Remind the children what the exclamation mark is called. In pairs or individually, let the children think of one or two word exclamations and share them with the class. Write them on a board and let the children add the exclamation marks.

Use Year 1, Punctuation Unit 1 for more work on punctuating sentences.

Phonics and spelling

Draw a cat with a long tail. Ask the children to help you spell 'tail' to use as a label. Underline the 'ai' and say the sound /ai/ with the children. Encourage the children to help you spell other words that use 'ai' with the /ai/ sound. Write them around the cat shape for example, 'rain', 'wait', 'train', 'paid'. Draw a ball of wool and explain how the cat wants to play. Write 'play' next to the wool, underline 'ay' and say the /ai/. Add more 'ay' words around the wool. Discuss how the 'ai' and 'ay' have the same sound but are spelled differently. Note that 'ai' is mostly in the middle of words and 'ay' is mostly at the end of words. You may want to continue this activity by looking at the digraphs, 'oi' and 'oy'.

Review of the Big Picture

At the end of this phase, discuss with the children what they have learned so far about the poem, 'Cats'. Remind them that this is all working towards writing their own poems about cats.

Year 1, Sequence 4
Rhymes and poems

Phase 2: Capture and organise

During Phase 2, children start to develop ideas about the new content needed for their class cat poem that has the same structure as the model text, 'Cats'. Working collaboratively, children decide on what cat behaviour their poem will focus on and the words and phrases they could use. Phase 2 also includes work on alternative spellings with the /ee/ sound.

Programmes of study: Year 1

Comprehension: Be encouraged to link what they read or hear read to their own experiences.

Comprehension: Discuss word meanings, linking new meanings to those already known.

Comprehension: Draw on what they already know or on background information and vocabulary provided by the teacher.

Comprehension: Participate in discussion about what is read to them, taking turns and listening to what others say.

Composition: Say out loud what they are going to write about.

Spelling: Spell the /f/, /l/, /s/, /z/ and /k/ sounds ff, ll, ss, zz and ck.

Introduction

Remind the children of the Big Picture. Reread the model text poem, 'Cats', to the children and encourage them to join in with you on a repeat performance. Discuss the different areas that the children have done to explore the poem.

Introduce the idea that the children are going to work together to create their own class version of the poem but with a focus on a different area of a cat's behaviour.

Discussing ideas

As a class, discuss and make decisions to create their new class poem on cats. Have information and images of cats available as reference during the discussion. Record their ideas for Phase 3 and Phase 4.

Discuss the following with the children.

- Which aspect of a cat's behaviour will our poem focus on? (for example, feeding, movement, noises)
- What words and phrases can we use to describe cats and their behaviour?

Put the children into groups. Give them a behavioural area each and cat images that they can select, stick onto posters and add headings to. Let the children present their picture posters to the class.

Decide on a beginning phrase, for example: 'Cats eat / A lot'; 'Cats move / Everywhere'; 'Cats are / Noisy'.

Drama and performance

Use a range of activities to reinforce children's understanding of the poem. Select the activities that would fit in with your lesson timing. Encourage mixed-ability grouping for the chosen activities.

- **Miming cats:** Use drama, mime and movement to explore the different ways cats behave or move, for example, walking, cleaning, jumping, lapping water.
- **Caterwauling:** Work with the children to create a musical tune using their voices to make different sounds cats make. Write the sounds on the board for the children to learn and follow, for example: 'purr', 'meow', 'hiss', 'howl', 'wail'.
- **Freeze-framing:** Have the children freeze into different examples for a selected area of behaviour. Use thought-tracking, asking each child in the freeze-frame what they are thinking as a cat at that moment.

Incidental writing

Before you select any incidental writing, make sure the children are able to orally articulate the main events. Select activities that you think appropriate for the abilities and interests of your class. Children could:

- compile a long list of actions, objects and places related to the class's selected aspect of cat behaviour
- create a poster to show images and captions or labels showing the selected aspect of cat behaviour
- write a diary entry from the point of view of a cat
- write a list of questions for a cat, for example: 'Why do you wave your tail?' 'How can you jump so high?'.

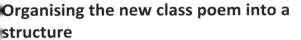

Organising the new class poem into a structure

Once the children have thoroughly explored their ideas for their class poem, bring them together and use their final suggestions to model how to decide its structure and content using the poem, 'Cats' as a model. Record the decisions on the Animal poem planner. Make a final decision on the opening and ending phrase and in what order the cat actions will be listed in the poem. Once recorded, go through the planner and other notes and ask the children if they are happy with the poem.

Phonics and spelling

Display the poem, 'No Hickory No Dickory No Dock'. Read the poem to the children and ask them who they think is speaking. Link it to the nursery rhyme, 'Hickory Dickory Dock'. Highlight the word, 'clock' and say each segment of the word out loud with the children. Underline the 'ck' and ask: 'What sound does 'ck' stand for?' (/k/). Underline and verbally emphasise the 'ck' in the words, 'dock' and 'lock'. Ask: 'What letter is before 'ck'?' (the vowel 'o'). Explain that the /k/ sound is spelled 'ck' if it comes after a vowel letter in short words. Give each child the Sorting 'ck' words resource sheet. Children can use the sheet to practise sorting out 'ck' words into their various vowel groups.

Review of the Big Picture

At the end of this phase, discuss with the children what they have achieved with their planning and ideas for their new class poem.

Phase 3: Collaborate and compose

Phase 3 has two writing lessons which support the children in the writing of their class poem of 'Cats'. Each lesson, starts with a short vocabulary, grammar and punctuation focus with links to the main text. The teacher then models writing in a shared composition session, applying the VGP focus in context. Independent writing, with plenaries, follows. The text should be non-rhyming. The VGP focuses are on separating words with spaces and using capital letters to demarcate sentences.

Programmes of study: Year 1

Composition: Say out loud what they are going to write about.

Composition: Compose a sentence orally before writing it.

Composition: Sequence sentences to form short narratives.

Composition: Discuss what they have written with the teacher or other pupils.

Handwriting: Begin to form lower-case letters in the correct direction, starting and finishing in the right place.

Handwriting: Form capital letters.

Vocabulary, grammar and punctuation: Leave spaces between words.

Vocabulary, grammar and punctuation: Begin to punctuate sentences using a capital letter and a full stop, question mark or exclamation mark.

Introduction

Remind the children about the sequence's Big Picture. Explain that over several lessons the children are going to start work as a class to draft and write their own cat poem. Use the planning and information from Phase 2 to remind the children of their poem ideas and content.

Lesson 1

Separating words with spaces

Write the poem, 'Cats' out on the board without any spaces. Say the poem without pausing between the words. Ask: 'What is wrong with the way I said the poem?' 'What is wrong with how I have written the poem?' (no gaps between the words) Have the children help you rewrite the poem with gaps between the words. Read it with the children again and discuss why it is important to have gaps between the words. Notice how hard it is to read some/all of the words when they merge.

Shared writing

With the children, start to develop the content of their poem, with the help of their Animal poem planner and lists of words and phrases collected in Phrase 2 for the chosen area of cat behaviour. Remind the children of the starting and ending phrase and the order in which things will be listed in the poem. Orally model any rhyming words or patterns that could be used, for example: 'box' and 'fox'; 'train' and 'rain'. Model writing one to three words per line, emphasising the need to leave gaps between the words. Collaboratively, work with the children to decide if the words and phrases are what they want and in the right order. Move the words or phrases around until the children are happy with the rhythm and sound of the poem. Once written, collaboratively check through the work for correct spelling and use of exclamation marks.

Independent writing

The children can now write their own version of the class poem applying the VGP focus on leaving spaces between words. Make sure that the class plans and word lists are available to help with the phrasing and poem structure. Some children may benefit from guided group or peer-paired writing at this stage.

Plenary

Throughout the writing session, ask the children questions to help them focus on their progress and what they have created during that lesson, for example: 'What phrase have you used at the start and end of the poem?' 'How many words do you have in each line?' 'What words and phrases have you used that you particularly like?' 'What words or phrases are you not happy with yet?' 'What rhythm does your poem have?' Prompt children to check that they have put spaces between the words and used exclamation marks correctly.

Lesson 2

Punctuating sentences with a capital letter

Display the extract of the poem, 'Cats', to the children. Ask the children what they notice about the capital letters. Highlight that every line starts with a capital letter even though it is not always the start of a sentence. Explain that in most rhymes and poems each line starts with a capital letter. Briefly look at other poems and rhymes for examples of this. Make a point of how confusing this can be, but emphasise that poetry is a very special type of writing.

Use Year 1, Grammar Unit 1 for more work on building sentences.

Shared writing

Explain to the children that you are going to write out the class poem from Lesson 1. Highlight handwriting skills and focus on the use of capital letters at the start of each line. Once the poem has been written in best, ask the children how it could be presented, for example, with a coloured border, pictures of cats illustrating the actions. Discuss fun ways of performing it to another class. Select a favourite choice and encourage the children to rehearse and perform the poem.

Independent writing

The children write out their poem in best focusing on their handwriting skills and on using capital letters at the beginning of each line. Some children may benefit from writing their poem on the computer.

Let the children share their ideas with others on how they are going to illustrate their poem and present their poem. Have images of cats, colouring resources and border designs available.

Plenary

Throughout the writing session, ask the children questions to help them focus on their progress and what they have created during that lesson, for example: 'What do like about how you have presented your poem?' 'How would you do things differently if you did it again?' Prompt children to check that they have used capital letters at the beginning of each line, have put spaces between words, that their letters are formed correctly and that their poem is neat and easy to read.

Presenting and performing

Once the children have written out their poems, encourage them to read through and recite their poems using appropriate intonation to create a performance for the class. Take feedback on what the children particularly liked about the poems they have heard.

Review of the Big Picture

Once you have completed all the lessons for this section, remind the children of the sequence's Big Picture. Discuss what they have learned so far.

Phase 4: Write independently

This final phase brings all the children's learning and writing skills together so that they can write their own cat poem. Through their writing, they will be able to utilise the different VGP focuses that they have been practising throughout previous phases.

Programmes of study: Year 1

Composition: Say out loud what they are going to write about.

Composition: Compose a sentence orally before writing it.

Composition: Sequence sentences to form short narratives.

Composition: Re-read what they have written to check that it makes sense.

Composition: Discuss what they have written with the teacher or other pupils.

Composition: Read aloud their writing clearly enough to be heard by their peers and the teacher.

Introduction

Introduce the phase by discussing what the children have learned in their poetry planning and writing sessions and link it to the Big Picture. Emphasise the excitement of bringing all their learning together to write their own version of the poem, 'Cats'.

Use the planning and word lists from Phase 2 to review the children's suggestions of different aspects of cat behaviour. Clarify that the planning and writing of their own poem will take place over several sessions. Point out that poems can be rhyming or non-rhyming.

Writing

Give each child an Animal poem planner. As they plan, draft and write their poems, encourage the children to compose their words and phrases orally before writing them down.

All the children should be encouraged to try to write independently to the best of their abilities. Ask open questions such as: 'What cat behaviour is your poem about?' 'What list of words and phrases have you used?' 'Have you used the same phrase at the beginning and at the end of the poem?' 'Have you used any rhyming words?' 'Does your poem have rhythm?' Make sure that the children have a chance to share their writing with others at appropriate points during each session.

Proofreading and redrafting

Encourage the children to read through their work at the end of each writing session with a partner. Ask them to check whether their writing makes sense. Proofreading and improvement without support means that the writing will happen over a few lessons. Offer the children the

Proofreading sheet / My writing checklist, or create your own checklist with the assistance of the blank Proofreading sheet / My writing checklist.

Self- and peer-assessment

Encourage the children to take time to assess their own and others' writing. Make sure that they read out their writing clearly. Ask open questions to encourage self- and peer-assessment such as: 'How does my poem use a list of things a cat does?' 'What phrase have I used at the beginning and end of the poem?' 'What exclamation words and exclamation sentences have I used?' 'What punctuation have I used?' 'What does my partner notice about the rhythm?' 'What rhyming words have I used?' 'How is my poem like the original?' Also encourage children to check their use of exclamation marks and capital letters as well as leaving spaces between words. Make sure that they read out their writing clearly.

Presenting and performing

Once the children have written their poems, display them in class or create a class book for the children to enjoy reading and looking at. Encourage them to use their poems to create a performance to the class using appropriate intonation. Take feedback on what the children particularly liked about the poems they have heard.

Final review of the Big Picture

Individually or with partners, have children reflect on what they have learned from this sequence and what they will remember to do in future writing.

Sequence 5
Rhymes and poems

Approximate duration: Two weeks

Big Picture

Through this teaching sequence, children explore the poem, 'Busy Day'. By the end of the sequence, they will have written a new version of the poem, using a new main repeated word and new busy-day focus.

Phase 1: Enjoy and Immerse

Children become familiar with the content, language and structure of the model text poem, 'Busy Day'.

Phase 2: Capture and organise

Children are supported in developing ideas for a new poem about a busy day.

Phase 3: Collaborate and compose

Children undertake supported writing sessions to develop their own writing based on the class poem.

Phase 4: Write independently

Children write, edit and read aloud their own poems about a busy day.

Main source text

Treasure House Anthology Sequence 5 text. 'Busy Day', Michel Rosen, *The Puffin Book of Fantastic First Poems*, ISBN 978-0-14-130898-2, p.66

Background knowledge

Michael Rosen is an award winning children's author and poet. He was also the British Children's Laureate from 2007 to 2009. He is well-known for his belief in encouraging children to have fun and explore poetry as well as to perform it. The poem 'Busy Day' is a good example of a fun poem that can be performed by young children. It was originally published in a collection of poems called 'You Tell Me' by Roger McGough and Michael Rosen.

Spoken outcome

To perform their poems about a busy day

Writing outcome

To write their own version of the poem, 'Busy Day'

Prior knowledge

Check children's knowledge and understanding of:

- poems by Michael Rosen
- poems with simple rhymes
- poems about shopping or everyday life.

Diagnostic assessment options

Before starting the unit, you may wish to conduct an initial diagnostic assessment of the children's knowledge and understanding.

Ideas for initial diagnostic assessment options include:

- reviewing children's writing for correct sentence punctuation
- speaking and listening activities where children listen to and identify question sentences
- reviewing children's writing for sufficient spaces between the words
- reviewing children's writing and spelling skills to check what phonemes they know and can spell correctly , especially those phonemes represented by various graphemes.

Cross-curricular links

KS1 Art and design

- Use drawing, painting and sculpture to develop and share their ideas, experiences and imagination.

KS1 Geography – Human and physical geography

- Use basic geographical vocabulary to refer to key human features, including: city, town, village, factory, farm, house, office, port, harbour and shop.

KS1 Music

- Use their voices expressively and creatively by singing songs and speaking chants and rhymes.

Treasure House links

- Treasure House, Year 1, Comprehension Unit 5: Rhymes and poems: 'Honey Bear'
- Treasure House, Year 1, Composition Unit 5: Poetry: Patterns
- Treasure House, Year 1, Vocabulary Unit 2: Adding endings to root words (-ing, -ed, -er, -est)
- Treasure House, Year 1, Spelling Unit 10: Adding -er to a root word
- Treasure House, Year 1, Spelling Unit 15: Spelling wh
- Treasure House, Year 1, Punctuation Unit 1: Punctuating sentences

Resources

Props and percussion instruments for drama and storytelling activities (optional); image of a busy street with shops

Source texts – see Anthologies; 'Busy Day' writing frame; Investigating sounds and spellings; Proofreading sheet / My writing checklist; Proofreading sheet / My writing checklist (blank)

Phase 1: Enjoy and immerse

In Phase 1, the children listen to and perform the poem, 'Busy Day'. Over several sessions, the children have opportunities to discuss the language and structure of the poem through comprehension and discussion activities as well as exploring the poem's content through drama, performance, writing and analysis of the text. Phase 1 also covers the vocabulary, grammar and punctuation focus on using questions in sentences and includes work on spelling the /w/ sound 'wh'.

Programmes of study: Year 1

Comprehension: Listen to and discuss a wide range of poems, stories and non-fiction at a level beyond that at which they can read independently.

Comprehension: Recognise and join in with predictable phrases.

Comprehension: Learn to appreciate rhymes and poems, and to recite some by heart.

Comprehension: Explain clearly their understanding of what is read to them.

Reading: Read words with contractions (for example, I'm, I'll, we'll), and understand that the apostrophe represents the omitted letter(s).

Vocabulary, grammar and punctuation: Use suffixes that can be added to verbs where no change is needed in the spelling of root words.

Spelling: Learn new consonant spellings ph and wh.

Sparking interest

Show an image of a busy high street to the children. Encourage them to explore the image, pointing out and describing what different people are doing and observing other elements, such as the traffic, that make it a busy scene. Encourage the children to share their own experiences of being in a place which was very busy. Ask: 'How did you feel?'

Reading and discussion

Display and then read out the poem using appropriate intonation. Emphasise the repeated phrases at the beginning and end of the poem. If possible, repeat the poem with the children joining in. Lead a discussion to check their understanding of the poem.

Discuss the following with the children:

- What is the most used word in the poem?
- Why do you think the poet uses 'pop' a lot? Do you think it is a good word?
- Where does the person go during their busy day? What does the person do?
- How does the poem make the person sound busy?
- Who do you think is asking the questions?
- Do you know someone who is always busy?

- What do you notice about the first part of the poem and the last part of the poem? (it repeats)
- How does the poem make you feel that the person is going round in circles?
- Do you think the person is really busy?

Drama and storytelling

Use a range of activities to reinforce children's understanding of the poem. Select the activities that would fit in with your lesson timing. Encourage mixed-ability grouping for the chosen activities.

- **Class Performance:** Organise a poetry performance of the poem. Give small groups of children one or two lines of the poem to remember and perform. Have them all say the repeated starting and finishing lines.

- **Busy, Busy:** Give each of the children a different line and action phrase from the poem. Discuss the actions intonation and facial expressions, the children could use to go with the lines, including the questions. Start with the class saying the poem in order then let them wander around saying their lines and doing their actions at the same time. Discuss the noise and busyness of the scene.

- **Freeze-framing:** Try out the different scenes from the poem in the right sequence. Use thought-tracking, asking each child in the freeze-frame what they're thinking at that moment of the poem.

- **In and out:** Use a set of opposite pairs of prepositional words to create an imaginary journey, for example: 'go into the hall', 'go out of the door', 'climb up the hill', 'climb down the hill', 'walk over the bridge', 'crawl under the bush'. Let the children mime following your orders. Let them make their own suggestions.

Incidental writing

Short writing activities enhance the children's understanding of the poem and help to inform the teaching focuses in the collaborative composition phase. Children could:

- collect and write simple prepositional words and match them to their opposites, for example: 'over' and 'under'; 'in' and 'out'; 'up' and 'down'
- create a shopping list or to-do list for a shopping trip
- write a recount of their personal experience of a busy day
- draw illustrations or a comic strip of the busy day
- draw a map, with labels, of the route taken on the busy day.

Analysis

Display the poem, 'Busy Day' and read it with them. Indicate how there are three verses describing the busy day with a chorus or refrain (a repeated section) separating each of them. Remind the children again that the first and last verses are the same. Look at the use of repetition in the poem, for example, 'can't stop, got to pop'. Have the children identify the pairs of rhyming words. Note the contraction words and how the apostrophe is in place of missing letters. On a separate piece of paper, list the prepositional words used in the poem, for example: 'in', 'out', 'over', 'down', 'round', 'up'. Discuss how these words tell us the direction in which the action is taking place.

Grammar: Adding the suffix -er to root verbs

Write the word 'walk' on the board for the children to see. Have the children stand up and walk on the spot. Remind them that the word is an action word or 'verb'. Point to them and say: 'You are walkers.' Write the word sum: 'walk + er = walker'. Underline the 'er' and explain how we can add -er onto the end of doing words. Write 'talk' and, with the children, write another sum to add -er. Discuss the change in meaning from talking to being a talker.

Write a list of root verbs on the board or give them to children on a sheet. Ask them to choose three of the verbs and write -er word sums. Let them share their sums with others and discuss how adding -er changes the meaning of the root verb (it becomes a noun).

Use Year 1, Vocabulary Unit 2 and Year 1, Spelling Unit 10 for more work on adding -er to root words.

Phonics and spelling

Display the poem, 'Busy Day'. Highlight the question phrases, 'pop where?', 'pop what?' and point out 'where' and 'what'. With the children, say each segment of each word out loud and underline the 'wh'. Ask: 'What sound does the 'wh' make? (/w/) Tell children that five question words, 'when', 'where', 'who', 'which', and 'what', all start with 'wh' which stands for the /w/ sound. Have the children help you say each word, spell them and list them on the board. Put the children into pairs. Ask them to choose and write a question word starting with 'wh' and then use it to think of an answer to ask the busy person in the poem. Let them share their questions with the class.

Use Year 1, Spelling Unit 15 for more work on words spelled with 'wh'.

Review of the Big Picture

At the end of this phase, discuss with the children what they have learned so far about the poem, 'Busy Day'. Remind them that this is all working towards writing their own poems about a busy day.

Phase 2: Capture and organise

During Phase 2, children start to develop ideas about the new content needed for their class poem about a busy day that has the same structure as the model text, 'Busy Day'. Working collaboratively, children decide on the words and phrases they could use to create a different version of the poem. Phase 2 also includes work on distinguishing between alternative spellings of the same sound.

Programmes of study: Year 1

Comprehension: Be encouraged to link what they read or hear read to their own experiences.

Comprehension: Discuss word meanings, linking new meanings to those already known.

Comprehension: Draw on what they already know or on background information and vocabulary provided by the teacher.

Comprehension: Participate in discussion about what is read to them, taking turns and listening to what others say.

Composition: Say out loud what they are going to write about.

Spelling: Use letter names to distinguish between alternative spellings of the same sound.

Introduction

Remind the children of the Big Picture. Reread the model text poem, 'Busy Day', to the children and encourage them to join in with you on a repeat performance. Discuss the different areas that the children have done to explore the poem.

Introduce the idea that the children are going to work together to create their own class version of the poem.

Discussing ideas

As a class, discuss and make decisions to create their new class poem about a busy day. Record their ideas for Phase 3 and Phase 4.

Discuss the following with the children:

- Who could the busy person be?
- What word could we use to replace 'pop'? (for example, 'whizz', 'skip', 'hop', 'run', 'jump', 'jog', 'dash', 'nip')
- What different places could the busy person go to? (for example, school, a swimming pool, shops, a library)
- What tasks and activities could the busy person do on their busy day? (for example, gardening, swimming, playing, working, eating, drinking)

Drama and storytelling

Use a range of activities to allow the children to explore suggestions for their new tale.

- **Pop, whoosh, hop:** This activity need a big space. Using the list of possible replacements for the word 'pop', ask the children to carry out an activity for one of words. For example, children whizz around the room for the word 'whizz'. Call out the various words so that they change the activity.
- **What a busy day!** Put the children into pairs and encourage them to have a pretend telephone conversation about their busy day. Have one ask the questions and the other talk about the day and then change roles.
- **Busy circles:** Let each child choose two phrases they could use in the class poem with a selected replacement 'pop' word. Start with the children in a circle and then call 'Busy!' Let them work around saying their phrases at the same time. Discuss what phrases they used.

Incidental writing

Before you select any incidental writing, make sure the children are able to orally articulate the main events. Select activities that you think appropriate for the abilities and interests of your class. Children could:

- make a fun and brightly coloured collection of word cards using the list of words that could be used to replace 'pop'
- recount a character's busy day, for example, a farmer, a teacher, a singer, a pupil, a builder
- draw a story map, with labels, to show the places and events that the children have decided on for the class poem.

Organising the new poem into a structure

Once the children have thoroughly explored their ideas for their class poem, bring them together and use their final suggestions to model how to decide its structure and content using the poem, 'Busy Day', as a model. Use the planning and lists of rhyming words to help you. Record the information on a flip chart. Make a final decision on which word will replace, 'pop', what events and places will be included, and rhyming pairs for each verse. Once recorded, go through the plans and ask the children if they are happy with the poem.

Phonics and spelling

Display the poem 'Busy Day' and read out the poem. Highlight how in each verse there are rhyming words. Read the first and then the second verses slowly and ask the children to put their hands up when they hear any rhyming words. Highlight the words, 'walk', 'talk', 'shop', 'stop', 'pop', 'round', 'town', 'see', 'tea'. Note that some words that have the same sound and the same spelling pattern while others do not, for example, 'round' and 'town'. Put the children in pairs and give them each an Investigating sounds and spellings resource sheet. Ask them to think of another rhyming word to go with the given word that could be used in the class poem, for example, 'shed', 'bed', 'mouse', 'house', 'tree', 'pea'. Let them write the rhyming word by the given word and share it with the class. Have the words on display for reference.

Review of the Big Picture

At the end of this phase, discuss with the children what they have achieved with their planning and ideas for their new class poem.

Phase 3: Collaborate and compose

Phase 3 has two writing lessons which support the children in writing their class poem, 'Busy Day'. Each lesson starts with a short vocabulary, grammar and punctuation focus with links to the main text. The teacher then models writing in a shared composition session, applying the VGP focus in context. Independent writing, with plenaries, follows. The text could be rhyming or non-rhyming. The VGP focuses are on punctuating sentences using question marks and full stops, and leaving spaces between words.

Programmes of study: Year 1

Composition: Say out loud what they are going to write about.

Composition: Compose a sentence orally before writing it.

Composition: Sequence sentences to form short narratives.

Composition: Discuss what they have written with the teacher or other pupils.

Handwriting: Begin to form lower-case letters in the correct direction, starting and finishing in the right place.

Handwriting: Form capital letters.

Vocabulary, grammar and punctuation: Begin to punctuate sentences using a capital letter and a full stop, question mark or exclamation mark.

Vocabulary, grammar and punctuation: Separate words with spaces.

Introduction

Remind the children about the sequence's Big Picture. Explain that over several lessons the children are going to start work as a class to draft and write their own 'Busy Day' poem. Use the recorded planning and information from Phase 2 to remind the children of their poem ideas and content.

Lesson 1

Punctuating sentences with question marks and full stops

Show the children the 'wh' question word cards from the Grammar lesson in Phase 1. Select one of them and use it to model writing a simple question sentence, omitting the question mark, for example: 'Where is my pencil'. Write an answering statement without the full stop, for example: 'Your pencil is on the table by the window'. Draw a question mark and a full stop. Ask: 'What are these two punctuation marks called?' Ask the children to match the marks to the right sentences and explain why. Put the children in pairs and give them each a piece of paper with either a full stop or question mark on it. Ask them to think of a question or a statement sentence. In turn let each pair say their sentence to the class. Ask the children to point to the punctuation mark that needs to be used.

Shared writing

With the children, model writing the 'Busy Day' class poem with the help of their planning and list of words and phrases collected in Phase 2. Say each line and then write the poem within the 'Busy Day' poem writing frame. Remind them of the starting word and the order of actions and events that fit into the poem frame. Ask the children what two question words with the 'wh' spelling could be used. Ask: 'What should we add after a question?' Collaboratively, work with the children to decide if the words and phrases are what they want and in the right order. Move the words or phrases around until the children are happy with the rhythm and sound of the poem. Once written, collaboratively check through the work.

Independent writing

The children can now write their own version of the class poem applying the VGP focus of adding question marks in the right places. Make sure that the class plans and word lists are available for them to see. Give each child a 'Busy Day' writing frame to help with the phrasing and poem structure. Some children may benefit from guided group or peer-paired writing at this stage.

Plenary

Throughout the writing session, ask the children questions to help them focus on their progress and what they have created during that lesson, for example: 'What direction words have you used?' 'How have you described your characters actions?' 'What places have you described and how have you described them?' 'What questions or phrases have you repeated?' 'How have you punctuated the questions?' 'What rhyming words have you used?' 'How have you made the poem sound busy and fast, when you read it out?'

Lesson 2

Leaving spaces between words

With the children, recite a well-known nursery rhyme or poem such as 'Little Miss Muffet'. Write the rhyme out on the board without any spaces. Say the rhyme again without pausing between words. Ask: 'What is wrong with the way I said the rhyme?' 'What is wrong with how I have written the rhyme?' (there are no gaps between the words) Have the children help you rewrite the rhyme with gaps between the words. Read it with the children again and discuss why it is important to have gaps between words.

Use Year 1, Punctuation Unit 1 for more on punctuating sentences.

Shared writing

Explain to the children that you are going to write out the class poem that you wrote in the writing frame in Lesson 1. Emphasise handwriting skills and focus on leaving spaces between words. Note how the first verse is repeated again at the end. Discuss fun ways of performing it to another class. Select a favourite choice and encourage the children to rehearse and perform the poem.

Independent writing

The children write out their poem in best, with focus on handwriting skills and the VGP focus on using spaces between words. Some children may benefit from writing their poem on the computer.

Let the children share their ideas with others on how they are going to illustrate their poem and present their poem. Have a selection of images and border designs available for inspiration.

Plenary

Throughout the writing session, ask the children questions to help them focus on their progress and what they have created during that lesson, for example: 'How have you illustrated your work?' 'What do like about how you have presented your poem?' 'How would you do things differently if you did it again?' Prompt children to check that they have used capital letters at the beginning of each line, have put spaces between words, that their letters are formed correctly and that their poem is neat and easy to read.

Presenting and performing

Once the children have written out their poems, encourage them to read through and recite their poems using appropriate intonation to create a performance to the class. Encourage the class to participate by taking part in the repeated phrases. Take feedback on what the children particularly liked about the poems they have heard.

Review of the Big Picture

Once you have completed all the lessons for this section, remind the children of the sequence's Big Picture. Discuss what they have learned so far.

Phase 4: Write independently

This final phase brings all the children's learning and writing skills together so that they can write their own 'Busy Day' poem. Through their writing, they will be able to utilise the different VGP focuses that they have been practising throughout previous phases.

Programmes of study: Year 1

Composition: Say out loud what they are going to write about.

Composition: Compose a sentence orally before writing it.

Composition: Sequence sentences to form short narratives.

Composition: Re-read what they have written to check that it makes sense.

Composition: Discuss what they have written with the teacher or other pupils.

Composition: Read aloud their writing clearly enough to be heard by their peers and the teacher.

Introduction

Introduce the phase by discussing what the children have learned in their poetry planning and writing sessions and link it to the Big Picture. Emphasise the excitement of bringing all their learning together to write their own 'Busy Day' poem.

Use the planning and word lists from Phase 2 to review the children's suggestions, busy words and events. Clarify that the planning and writing of their own poem will take place over several sessions. Highlight that they can choose to use another word for 'Pop' or use the word, 'Pop', if they would rather.

Writing

Give each child a 'Busy Day' writing frame. As they plan, draft and write their poems, encourage the children to compose their words and phrases orally before writing them down.

All the children should be encouraged to try to write independently to the best of their abilities. Ask open questions such as: 'What word have you chosen as your main repeated word for the poem?' 'Why have you chosen it?' 'What places does the person go to in the poem?' 'What direction words have you used?' 'Have you used repeated questions and phrases?' 'Have you added in question marks in the right places?' 'Are you using any rhyming pairs of words in your poem? If so, what are they?' 'Does the poem sound busy and fast?' 'Does it look like a list of things to do?'

Make sure that the children have a chance to share their writing with others at appropriate points during each session.

Proofreading and redrafting

Encourage the children to read through their work at the end of each writing session with a partner. Ask them to check whether their writing makes sense. Proofreading and improvement without support means that the writing will happen over a few lessons. Offer the children the Proofreading sheet / My writing checklist, or create your own checklist with the assistance of the blank Proofreading sheet / My writing checklist.

Self- and peer-assessment

Encourage the children to take time to assess their own and others' writing. Make sure that they read out their writing clearly. Ask open questions to encourage self- and peer-assessment such as: 'Have I used the same layout as 'Busy Day'?' 'Is the poem long, and like a list?' 'Does my main repeating word, work well in the poem?' 'Does it make the person in the poem, sound busy?' 'Is it clear where they are going?' 'Does the person visit a range of places or do a mix of things?' 'Does my poem sound busy and fast, when I read it out?' 'Is my poem, neatly written?' 'Are there spaces between my words?'

Also encourage them to check their VGP focuses on the use of question marks in the correct place as well as leaving spaces between words. Make sure that they read out their writing clearly.

Presenting and performing

Once the children have written their poems, arrange them in a display with pictures drawn by the children. Link the verses so that they become a very long busy day. Encourage the children to use their individual poems to create a performance to the class or have groups working together to perform a long back to back 'Busy Day' poetry performance. Take feedback on what the children particularly liked about the poems they have heard.

Final review of the Big Picture

Individually or with partners, have children reflect on what they have learned from this sequence and what they will remember to do in future writing.

Sequence 6
Rhymes and poems

Approximate duration: Two weeks

Big Picture

Through this teaching sequence, children explore the poem, 'On Some Other Planet'. By the end of the sequence, each child will have composed one or two new verses for a new version of the poem.

Phase 1: Enjoy and immerse

Children will become familiar with the content, language and structure of the model text poem.

Phase 2: Capture and organise

Children are supported in developing ideas for two new verses for the model poem.

Phase 3: Collaborate and compose

Children undertake supported writing sessions to develop their own writing based on the class poem verses.

Phase 4: Write independently

Children write, edit and read aloud their own new verses for their class version of, 'On Some Other Planet'.

Main source text

Treasure House Anthology Sequence 6 text. 'On Some Other Planet', John Rice, *First Poems*, SBN 978-1-84-121550-1, p.9

Extra source text

'Fantastic Friends', Brian Patten, *First Poems*, SBN 978-1-84-121550-1, p.8

Background knowledge

John Rice is a Scottish poet, story-teller and author. Most of his work is written for children although he has also written for adults. Many of his stories and poems have been written with the emphasis on performance whether it is poetry or telling stories.

John Rice is particularly keen to encourage children to develop a love of and ability to enjoy and perform poetry. The poem 'On Some Other Planet' is a good example of one of John Rice's performance poems with repeated phrases and fun images.

Spoken outcome

To perform their new 'On Some Other Planet' verse or verses

Writing outcome

To write and contribute one or two new verses to a class version of the poem, 'On Some Other Planet'

Prior knowledge

Check children's knowledge and understanding of:

- poems and rhymes by John Rice
- science fiction themed poems about, for example, space, aliens, superheroes
- planets and space.

Diagnostic assessment options

Before starting the unit, you may wish to conduct an initial diagnostic assessment of the children's knowledge and understanding.

Ideas for initial diagnostic assessment options include:

- reviewing children's writing for the correct use of sentence punctuation.
- speaking and listening activities where children identify the changes to words when -ing, -s and -es are added.
- reviewing children's blending and segmenting skills
- speaking and listening spelling activities to test children's recognition of the /ar/ sound spelled 'ar'.

Year 1, Sequence 6
Rhymes and poems

Cross-curricular links

KS1 Art and design

- Use drawing, painting and sculpture to develop and share their ideas, experiences and imagination.

KS1 Music

- Use their voices expressively and creatively by singing songs and speaking chants and rhymes.

Treasure House links

- Treasure House, Year 1, Comprehension Unit 6: Rhymes and poems: 'A Chubby Little Snowman'
- Treasure House, Year 1, Composition Unit 4: Poetry: The Senses
- Treasure House, Year 1, Vocabulary Unit 2: Adding endings to root words (-ing, -ed, -er, -est)
- Treasure House, Year 1, Spelling Unit 9: Adding -ing to a root word
- Treasure House, Year 1, Vocabulary Unit 1: Adding -s and -es
- Treasure House, Year 1, Punctuation Unit 1: Punctuating sentences

Resources

Props and percussion instruments for drama and storytelling activities (optional); images of planets and planet Earth; root verb cards for Phase 1 (for example, 'jump', 'fall', 'climb', 'swing', 'walk', 'eat', 'fly', 'curl', 'read', 'paint', 'stand', 'zoom', 'pack'); a space themed wall display with a large planet shape in the middle; star shapes for writing on in Phase 2

Source texts – see Anthologies; 'On some other planet' verse planner / writing frame; Proofreading sheet / My writing checklist; Proofreading sheet / My writing checklist (blank)

Phase 1: Enjoy and immerse

In Phase 1, the children listen to and perform the poem, 'On Some other Planet'. Over several sessions, the children discuss the language and structure of the poem through comprehension and discussion activities as well as exploring the poem's content through drama, performance, writing and analysis of the text. Phase 1 also covers the vocabulary, grammar and punctuation focus on adding -ing to the ends of verbs. The children also work on spellings with 'ir' and 'ur' that stand for the same /ur/ sound.

Programmes of study: Year 1

Comprehension: Listen to and discuss a wide range of poems, stories and non-fiction at a level beyond that at which they can read independently.

Comprehension: Recognise and join in with predictable phrases.

Comprehension: Learn to appreciate rhymes and poems, and to recite some by heart.

Comprehension: Explain clearly their understanding of what is read to them.

Vocabulary, grammar and punctuation: Use suffixes that can be added to verbs where no change is needed in the spelling of root words.

Spelling: Spell words with the digraph ir.

Spelling: Spell words with the digraph ur.

Sparking interest

Show an image of Earth to the children and ask them what it is (our planet). Ask children if they know the names of any other planets and what they know about them. Introduce the poem, about aliens living on planets. Check that the children understand what 'alien' means.

Reading and discussing

Display and read the poem using expression. If possible, repeat the poem with the children joining in with the line, 'On some other planet'. Check that children understand vocabulary such as: 'estate car', 'trillion', 'time zone', 'intelligent', 'duplicate'.

Discuss the following with the children.

- How many planets are there in the poem?
- How are the aliens and their actions like those on Planet Earth?
- Why do you think the aliens are similar?
- Why do you think the intelligent beginnings are alone?
- How would you feel if there was a planet with an identical person like you there? What would you say or ask them?
- Which planet would you like to go to and why?
- Do you think that there are planets with aliens on them? Why?

Drama and storytelling

Use a range of activities to reinforce children's understanding of the poem. Select the activities that would fit in with your lesson timing. Encourage mixed-ability grouping for the chosen activities.

- **Class Performance:** Organise a performance of the poem. Give groups of children sections of the poem to perform. Use props and musical instruments for the performance and use mime to act out the actions of the aliens.
- **Planet groups:** Put the children into groups and allocate each a planet from the poem. Children create scenes of life as an alien on their planet. For example, the first planet could be all music-loving aliens. Have them perform their scenes to the class.
- **Meeting me:** Read out the last verse of the poem. Discuss how the poet meets an identical person to themselves. In a space, put the children into pairs and explain that they are looking at the exact copy of themselves. Let each child take turns to copy the physical actions of the other child.
- **Alien movement:** Have a mime and movement session where the children imagine they are an alien. Ask them to use their bodies and facial expressions to show what the alien looks like and how it moves.

Incidental writing

Short writing activities enhance the children's understanding of the poem and help to inform the teaching focuses in the collaborative composition phase. Children could:

- write a simple log recording a visit to a planet
- compose a song or rhyme sung by the music-loving alien
- draw a picture of an alien with labels to describe it
- draw and label pictures of each planet scene
- think of names for the planets (punctuating each name with a capital letter).

Analysis

Display and read the poem, 'On Some Other Planet'. Look at the structure of the poem. In one colour, highlight the first line for each verse. Using another colour, highlight that the second line of each verse says where the planet may be. Go through each verse, noting words such as 'near', 'on', 'in'. Using another colour, highlight the last two lines of the poem about the alien and what they may be doing. Go through each verse at a time asking children to put up hands when they hear a rhyme. List the pairs of words, for example: 'star' and 'car'; 'away' and 'play'.

Grammar: Adding -ing to root verb words

Create a space wall display with a large planet shape in the middle and write the title: 'Planet 'ing''. With the children, read out 'ing'. Explain how we can add -ing onto the end of some words. With links to each alien in the poem, write the verb root words on the planet: 'sing', 'sleep', 'play', 'think', 'talk'. Say the words and then, with the children's support, add 'ing' to the ends. Give out root-verb cards to the children (see resources) and ask them to add -ing to the ends. Collect the cards and add them to the planet shape. Let the children choose two -ing words and orally compose a sentence for each one.

Use Year 1, Vocabulary Unit 2 and Year 1, Spelling Unit 9 for more work on the suffix -ing.

Phonics and spelling

Read 'Fantastic Friends'. Draw two large superhero style t-shirt shapes on the board with 'ir' in the middle of one and 'ur' in the middle of the other. With the children, say both the digraphs and discuss how they have the same /ur/ sound. Add 'ir' words and 'ur' words into the correct t-shirt, for example, 'girl', 'bird', 'shirt', 'first', 'turn', 'hurt', 'burst', 'Thursday'. Have the children draw their own superhero t-shirts and then select an 'ir' and 'ur' word to go on it. Encourage them to say each segment of the words out loud as they spell them.

Review of the Big Picture

At the end of this phase, discuss with the children what they have learned so far about the poem, 'On Some Other Planet'. Remind them that this is all working towards writing new verses for the poem.

Phase 2: Capture and organise

During Phase 2, children start to develop ideas about the new content needed to create new verses for the model poem. Working collaboratively, children decide on the words and phrases they could use in the new verses. Phase 2 also includes spelling the digraph 'ar'.

Programmes of study: Year 1

Comprehension: Be encouraged to link what they read or hear read to their own experiences.

Comprehension: Discuss word meanings, linking new meanings to those already known.

Comprehension: Draw on what they already know or on background information and vocabulary provided by the teacher.

Comprehension: Participate in discussion about what is read to them, taking turns and listening to what others say.

Composition: Say out loud what they are going to write about.

Spelling: Spell words with the digraph 'ar'.

Introduction

Remind the children of the Big Picture. Reread the model text to the children and encourage them to join in with you on a repeat performance. Introduce the idea that the children are going to work together to create two new verses of the poem.

Discussing ideas

As a class, discuss and make decisions to create their new verses for the planet poem. Record their ideas for Phase 3 and Phase 4. Use the poem 'Fantastic Friends' to help with ideas.

Discuss the following with the children.

- What aliens could we invent? How can we describe them?
- Where could the planets be? How can we describe them?
- What will the aliens be doing?
- What rhyming words can we use?
- What direction words can we use to describe where the planets are?

Drama and storytelling

Use a range of activities to reinforce children's understanding of the poem. Select the activities that would fit in with your lesson timing. Encourage mixed-ability grouping for the chosen activities.

- **Space travel:** Have a drama session, where the children prepare for and then set off for a journey in a space rocket. Suggest events during the journey such as avoiding comets. Once they have landed, children enact exploring a planet.
- **Hot-seating:** Have half the children role-play aliens and half role-play humans. Encourage a question and answer session about life on both planets.

Incidental writing

Before you select any incidental writing, make sure the children are able to orally articulate the main events. Select activities that you think appropriate for the abilities and interests of your class. Children could:

- write a postcard from an alien
- draw pictures with captions describing a planet
- draw and label a picture of an alien
- compile a kit list for a space traveller
- describe a day in the life of an alien.

Organising the new class verses into a structure

Once the children have thoroughly explored their ideas for their class verses, bring them together and make final decisions on the content. Record the information on two copies of the 'On Some Other Planet' writing frame. Note that each sheet shows the verse plans first to help with writing the verses later. Go through the plans, asking the children if they are happy with the poem.

Phonics and spelling

Have children make lots of paper stars. Show the children one of the star shapes and ask them what it is. With the children, say each segment of the word as you write it onto the star shape. Underline 'ar' and ask children what sound the 'ar' spells (/ar/). Ask children to suggest more words where the /ar/ sound is spelled 'ar'. Say each segment of each word as you write them on a board, for example: 'arm', 'car', 'card', 'garden', 'far'. Give out the star shapes and let the children write the words on the stars. Add them to the planet picture display from Phase 1.

Review of the Big Picture

At the end of this phase, discuss with the children what they have achieved with their planning and ideas for their new class verses for the poem.

Phase 3: Collaborate and compose

Phase 3 has two writing lessons which support the children in writing two new verses for the poem, 'On Some Other Planet'. Each lesson starts with a short vocabulary, grammar and punctuation focus with links to the main text. Children then have the opportunity to participate in a shared composition session, applying the VGP focus in context. Independent writing, with plenaries, follows. The VGP focuses are on regular plural noun suffixes -s or -es and using full stops at the ends of sentences.

Programmes of study: Year 1

Composition: Say out loud what they are going to write about.

Composition: Compose a sentence orally before writing it.

Composition: Sequence sentences to form short narratives.

Composition: Discuss what they have written with the teacher or other pupils.

Vocabulary, grammar and punctuation: Understand regular plural noun suffixes -s or -es, including the effects of these suffixes on the meaning of the noun.

Vocabulary, grammar and punctuation: Begin to punctuate sentences using a capital letter and a full stop, question mark or exclamation mark.

Introduction

Remind the children about the sequence's Big Picture. Explain that the children are going to work as a class to draft and write two new verses for the poem, 'On Some Other Planet'. Use the planning from Phase 2 to remind the children of their verses' ideas and content.

Lesson 1

Regular plural noun suffixes -s or -es

Remind the children that the young aliens in the poem liked to play in parks. Write the word, 'park'. Explain that when there is more than one park we add -s to the end of the word. Write 'beach'. Note that the aliens liked to play on more than one beach. Add -es to the end to show this. Note that we add -es to words that end in 'ch', 'sh', 's', 'x' or 'z' and have an extra syllable. Give out a set of word cards that could end in -s and -es to small groups of children. Ask them to sort out the nouns into -s and -es endings and then write them out.

Use Year 1, Vocabulary Unit 1 and Year 1, Spelling Unit 7–8 for more work on plural nouns.

Shared writing

With the children, model writing the first new verse using the first copy of the 'On some other planet' verse planner / writing frame. Model the oral composition of the simple sentences before writing. Encourage children to help you write the correct plural noun endings. Once written, collaboratively check through the work for correct spelling and sentence punctuation.

Independent writing

The children can now write their own version of the class verse applying the VGP focus on plural noun suffixes. Make sure that the class plans and word lists are available to them. Give each child the first copy of their 'On some other planet' verse planner / writing frame to help with the phrasing and poem structure. Some children may benefit from guided group or peer-paired writing at this stage.

Plenary

Throughout the writing session, ask the children questions to help them focus on their progress and what they have created during that lesson, for example: 'How does the first line of your verse begin?' 'How have you said where the planet is in the second line?' 'How have you described the planet in the third and fourth line?' 'Which words ending in -ing have you used?' 'Which -es and -s plural nouns have you used?' 'What rhyming words have you used?'

Lesson 2

Using full stops at ends of sentences

Read out a verse of 'On Some Other Planet' without showing it to the children. Ask them to put their hands up when they think a full stop should be used. Discuss their reasoning and repeat with the other verses. Have children work in groups to look at examples of texts and discuss the use of the full stop and why it is needed. Let them read out sentences to each other to hear where a sentence naturally ends.

Use Year 1, Punctuation Unit 1 for more on punctuating sentences.

Shared writing

With the children, model writing a second new verse using a second copy of the 'On some other planet' verse planner / writing frame. Model the oral composition of sentences before writing. Note the full stop at the end of the verse. Once written, collaboratively check through the work for correct spelling and sentence punctuation.

Independent writing

The children can now write their second verse applying the VGP focus on full stops. Make sure that the class plans and word lists are available to them. Give each child the second copy of the 'On some other planet' verse planner / writing frame to help with the phrasing and poem structure. Some children may benefit from guided group or peer-paired writing at this stage.

Plenary

Throughout the writing session, ask the children questions to help them focus on their progress and what they have created during that lesson, for example: 'How does the first line of your verse begin?' 'How have you said where the planet is in the second line?' 'How have you described the planet in the third and fourth line?' 'What rhyming words have you used?' 'What does your partner say about the rhythm of your poem?' 'Where have you added a full stop?'

Presenting and performing

Once children have written their verses, model writing out the verses in best. Read out the original poem and add the two class-written verses onto the end. Encourage the children to offer feedback on what they particularly liked about the verses they have heard.

Review of the Big Picture

Once you have completed all the lessons for this section, remind the children of the sequence's Big Picture. Discuss what they have learned so far.

Phase 4: Write independently

This final phase brings all the children's learning and writing skills together so that they can write their own verses for 'On Some Other Planet' independently. Through their writing, they will be able to utilise the different VGP focuses that they have been practising.

Programmes of study: Year 1

Composition: Say out loud what they are going to write about.

Composition: Compose a sentence orally before writing it.

Composition: Re-read what they have written to check that it makes sense.

Composition: Discuss what they have written with the teacher or other pupils.

Composition: Read aloud their writing clearly enough to be heard by their peers and the teacher.

Handwriting: Begin to form lower-case letters in the correct direction, starting and finishing in the right place.

Introduction

Introduce the phase by discussing what the children have learned in their planning and writing sessions and link it to the Big Picture. Emphasise the excitement of bringing all their learning together to write their own verses for 'On Some Other Planet'. Explain that the verses will be put together to create poems of five or six verses. Review the children's suggestions for planets and aliens from Phase 2. Clarify that the planning and writing of their verses will take place over several sessions. Depending on the child's ability, some may be able to write one verse, others may be able to write two.

Writing

Give each child one or two copies of the 'On some other Planet' verse planner / writing frame. As they plan, draft and write their verses, encourage the children to compose their words and phrases orally before writing them down.

All the children should be encouraged to try to write independently to the best of their abilities. Ask open questions such as: 'Where is your planet?' 'What position word have you used to say where it is?' 'What is on your planet?' 'How have you described the inhabitants?' 'Have you using any rhyming words?' 'If so, what rhyming words have you used?' 'Does your poem have rhythm?' Make sure that the children have a chance to share their writing with others at appropriate points during each session.

Proofreading and redrafting

Encourage children to read through their work at the end of each writing session with a partner. Ask them to check whether their writing makes sense. Proofreading and

improvement without support means that the writing will happen over a few lessons. Offer the children the Proofreading sheet / My writing checklist, or create your own checklist with the assistance of the blank Proofreading sheet / My writing checklist.

Self- and peer-assessment

Encourage the children to take time to assess their own and others' writing. Make sure that they read out their writing clearly. Offer them a set of self-assessment questions, such as: 'How does the first line start?' 'Where I have I said where the planet is?' 'What position words have I used to say where the planet is?' 'Where have I described what is on the planet?' 'What am I particularly happy with?' 'What would I like to change?' 'Do the verses work with the model poem?' Encourage children to check their plural nouns, adding the -ing to verbs, and full stops at the ends of sentences.

Presenting and performing

Once the children have written their verses, encourage them to write them out in best. Compile the verses into poems of five or six verses. Have each child perform their own verse or verses as part of their group poem performance to the rest of the class. Take feedback on what the children particularly liked about the poems they have heard. Put up the poems in a Space themed wall display with pictures and images of the aliens drawn by the children.

Final review of the Big Picture

Individually or with partners, have children reflect on what they have learned from this sequence and what they will remember to do in future writing.

Sequence 7
Instructions

Approximate duration: Two weeks

Big Picture

Through this teaching sequence, children look at instructions. By the end of the sequence, each child will have written a simple instruction for a favourite game or activity.

Phase 1: Enjoy and immerse

Children become familiar with the content, language and structure of the model instruction text, *How to Make Pop-Up Cards*.

Phase 2: Capture and organise

Children are supported in developing ideas for an instruction text for a favourite class game or activity.

Phase 3: Collaborate and compose

Children undertake supported writing sessions to develop their own writing based on the class instruction text.

Phase 4: Write independently

Children write, edit and read aloud their own instructions for a game or activity.

Main source text

Treasure House Anthology Sequence 7 text. *How to Make Pop-Up Cards*, Monica Hughes, ISBN 978-0-00-718601-3, pp.2–7

Background knowledge

Instruction texts for Year 1 should be simple with a clear chronological order. During Year 1, children begin to develop a knowledge and understanding of the basic features of instructions including a clear title, use of command sentences, number connectives, simple labelled diagrams or pictures and easy to follow language. The main source text focuses on making pop-up cards. The sequence offers children the opportunity to create their own class instruction book with easy to follow games and activities.

Spoken outcome

To read out their instructions for others to follow

Writing outcome

To write instructions for a game or activity for other children to use

Prior knowledge

Check children's knowledge and understanding of:

- playground games and activities
- popular games and activities played at school or at home
- following and orally giving simple instructions.

Diagnostic assessment options

Before starting the unit, you may wish to conduct an initial diagnostic assessment of the children's knowledge and understanding.

Ideas for initial diagnostic assessment options:

- reviewing children's writing for correct sentence punctuation for information captions
- speaking and listening activities to check that children can give or follow instructions
- reviewing children's writing to check that they are able to sequence simple instructions.

Cross-curricular links

KS1 Art and design

- Use drawing, painting and sculpture to develop and share their ideas, experiences and imagination.

KS1 Physical Education

- Master basic movements including running, jumping, throwing and catching, as well as developing balance, agility and co-ordination, and begin to apply these in a range of activities.
- Participate in team games, developing simple tactics for attacking and defending.
- Perform dances using simple movement patterns.

Treasure House links

- Treasure House, Year 1 Comprehension Unit 7: Reading instructions: Test your taste buds
- Treasure House, Year 1, Composition Unit 7: Writing instructions
- Treasure House, Year 1, Punctuation Unit 1: Punctuating sentences
- Treasure House, Year 1, Spelling Unit 17: Adding the prefix un-
- Treasure House, Year 1, Grammar Unit 1: Building sentences

Resources

Paper and pencils for paper spinner; materials to make pop-up cards (optional)

Source texts – see Anthologies; Instructions writing frame; Proofreading sheet / My writing checklist; Proofreading sheet / My writing checklist (blank)

Year 1, Sequence 7
Instructions

Phase 1: Enjoy and immerse

In Phase 1, children listen to and read the instruction text, *How to Make Pop-Up Cards*. Over several sessions, the children discuss the language and structure of the instruction text through comprehension and discussion activities and explore the instruction text's content through activities, writing and analysis of the text. Phase 1 also covers the vocabulary, grammar and punctuation focus on using capitals and full stops for sentences and includes work on spelling -er at the ends of words.

Programmes of study: Year 1

Comprehension: Listen to and discuss a wide range of poems, stories and non-fiction at a level beyond that at which they can read independently.

Comprehension: Discuss word meanings, linking new meanings to those already known.

Comprehension: Check that the text makes sense to them as they read and correct inaccurate reading.

Comprehension: Explain clearly their understanding of what is read to them.

Vocabulary, grammar and punctuation: Begin to punctuate sentences using a capital letter and a full stop, question mark or exclamation mark.

Spelling: Spell words with the digraph 'er' [representing the unstressed schwa sound] (/ə/).

Sparking interest

Explain to the children that you are going to show them how to make something (for example, the paper spinner from the extract). Give the children clear instructions for each part of the process. Once done, ask the children how they knew what to do. Introduce the term, 'instructions' and discuss how they tell us how to do something.

Reading and discussion

Explain that the children are going to listen to and read instructions for another craft. Let them read out the title of the book, *How to Make Pop-Up Cards*. Check that the children understand the vocabulary. Encourage them to read along with you or repeat after you.

Discuss the following with the children.

- How does the front page help you find different parts of the instructions?
- What page lists what we need to make the cards?
- What are 'Tips'? Why have they been put in a separate place to the instructions?
- Why do you think the instructions are numbered?
- Why is it important that the sentences short and easy to understand?
- How is the flowchart helpful?

Drama and storytelling

Use a range of activities to reinforce children's understanding of instructions. Select the activities that would fit in with your lesson timing. Encourage mixed-ability grouping for the chosen activities.

- **Human flowchart**: In groups, have the children create a human flowchart with each child saying one part of the instructions.
- **Show and tell:** In pairs or small groups, children make things, explaining how to make them as they go. Offer learning support to those children who are not yet skilled in using the scissors.
- **Verbal instructions**: Give verbal instructions for the children to follow, for example, making something, creating human statues, a game or dance.
- **Follow the book**: Let the children use *How to Make Pop-Up Cards* to make their own cards.

Incidental writing

Short writing activities enhance the children's understanding of the instruction text and help to inform the teaching focuses in the collaborative composition phase. Children could:

- compile new greeting words for cards
- draw a flowchart of instructions for creating other type of cards or booklets
- write a shopping list of what is needed to make cards.

Analysis

Look at the structure and language of the instructions in *How to Make Pop-Up Cards*. Start by discussing the use of the contents page and why it is important to show what items are needed. Point out that the book uses a labelled photograph but a list of items would also work. Go through the book to discuss the use of headings, simple captions, key words, labels, numbered and/or bulleted points, a flowchart and an ending sentence.

Use Year 1, Comprehension Unit 7 for more instruction text examples.

Grammar: Capital letters and full stops

Copy out the sentences from the 'Making the frame' section without the capital letters or full stops. Encourage the children to read out the sentences. Ask: 'What is wrong with each sentence?' (no capitals and no full stops). Encourage the children to correct the sentences, adding the capital letters and full stops to the correct places in the sentences.

Use Year 1, Punctuation Unit 1 for more on punctuating sentences.

Review of the Big Picture

At the end of this phase, discuss with the children what they have learned so far about instruction texts. Remind them that this is all working towards writing their own instruction texts.

Phonics and spelling

Write the title: 'Soft 'er' words'. List the words, 'ruler', 'border' and 'paper' under the title. Underline the 'er' for each word. Highlight that the 'er sound at the end of the words makes a soft sound like an 'uh'. Have the children copy the sound with you and then with each word. Compare it with the stressed -er sound in 'person' which has a hard /er/ sound. Encourage the children to help you add more unstressed -er words to the list, for example 'stapler', 'finger', 'sister', 'summer', 'winter', 'under'. Underline the 'er' and encourage the children to make the /uh/ sound for the end of each word.

Phase 2: Capture and organise

During Phase 2, children start to develop ideas about the new content needed for a new class instruction text. Working collaboratively, children decide on the words and layout they will use. Phase 2 also includes work on the prefix un-.

Programmes of study: Year 1

Comprehension: Be encouraged to link what they read or hear read to their own experiences.

Comprehension: Draw on what they already know or on background information and vocabulary provided by the teacher.

Comprehension: Participate in discussion about what is read to them, taking turns and listening to what others say.

Comprehension: Explain clearly their understanding of what is read to them.

Composition: Say out loud what they are going to write about.

Spelling: Use the prefix un-.

Introduction

Remind the children of the Big Picture. Re-read and discuss the model instruction text, *How to Make a Pop-up Book*. Introduce the idea that the children are going to work together to create a new instruction text about a favourite class game or activity that other children can follow.

Discussing ideas

As a class, discuss and make decisions to create their new instruction text. Record their ideas for Phase 3 and Phase 4.

Discuss the following with the children.

- What games and activities do you enjoy at school or at home? Can you describe the game/activity? Why is this game/activity fun?
- What games or activities could we have instructions for?
- What items or equipment would be needed.
- In what order must we do things in?
- What other helpful sections could we add to the text? (for example, photographs, tip or fact boxes, flowcharts, labels)

Drama and storytelling

Use a range of activities to reinforce children's understanding of their instruction text ideas. Select the activities that would fit in with your lesson timing. Encourage mixed-ability grouping for the chosen activities.

- **Instruction show and tell:** To help with the process of choosing the final game or activity, have the children try them out and then feed back to the rest of the class.
- **Human flowchart:** Organise a human flowchart for instructions for various games or activities. Let the children say what they are doing for each section.
- **Wrong order:** Put the children into groups and have them decide on the instructions for a given game or activity. Each child says one section of the instructions. Ask them to present their instructions to the others but in the wrong sequence order. Have the rest of the children work out the correct order.

Incidental writing

Before you select any incidental writing, make sure the children are able to orally articulate the main parts to the instruction text. Select activities that you think appropriate for the abilities and interests of your class. Children could:

- list items needed for the game or activity
- compile helpful tips for the instructions
- plan the design and layout of a contents page
- make a list of diagrams and images needed for the instruction text.

Organising the new instruction text into a structure

Once the children have thoroughly explored their ideas for their class instruction text, bring them together and make a final decision on the content. List items that are needed for the game or activity and make a final decision on other features such as images (pictures or photographs) and tip boxes. Once recorded, go through all the information and ask the children if they are happy with their instruction text plan.

Phonics and spelling

Write a list of words on the board: 'tie', 'lock', 'wrap', 'do', 'knot', 'dress', 'stick', 'pack', 'hook', 'load'. Highlight that they are all action words. Discuss each word with an example of how each word is used, for example, 'wrap presents', 'lock the door'. Write 'un' and ask the children to say the sound. Explain that we can add 'un' to the beginnings of words without having to change how the root word is spelled. Add 'un' to each word and discuss their now opposite meanings, giving examples of how each word is used. Put the children into pairs or small groups and give them a root word card and a blank card. Ask them to write the word with 'un' on the blank card and then mime actions for both words for the other children to guess.

Use Year 1, Spelling Unit 17 and Year 1, Vocabulary Unit 3 for more work on the prefix un-.

Review of the Big Picture

At the end of this phase, discuss with the children what they have achieved with their planning and ideas for their new class instruction text.

Phase 3: Collaborate and compose

Phase 3 has two writing lessons which support the children in the writing of their class instruction text. Each lesson starts with a vocabulary, grammar and punctuation focus with links to the main text. The children then have the opportunity to participate in a shared composition session, applying the VGP focus in context. Independent writing, with plenaries, follows. The VGP focuses are on combining words to make sentences: using verbs at the start of instruction sentences.

Programmes of study: Year 1

Composition: Say out loud what they are going to write about.

Composition: Compose a sentence orally before writing it.

Composition: Re-read what they have written to check that it makes sense.

Composition: Discuss what they have written with the teacher or other pupils.

Composition: Read aloud their writing clearly enough to be heard by their peers and the teacher.

Vocabulary, grammar and punctuation: Understand how words can combine to make sentences.

Vocabulary, grammar and punctuation: Begin to punctuate sentences using a capital letter and a full stop, question mark or exclamation mark.

Introduction

Remind the children about the sequence's Big Picture. Explain that over several lessons the children are going to start work as a class to draft and write their instruction texts. Use the planning and other information from Phase 2 to remind the children of their ideas and content.

Lesson 1

Combining words to make sentences

Display *How to Make Pop-Up Cards*. Focusing on the starts of the instruction sentences, highlight the starting verbs at the beginnings of the sentences. Ask the children what kind of words they are (doing words or verbs). Discuss why it is a good idea to have a doing word at the start of instruction sentences (to say what to do). Have the children think of verbs that they could use at the starts of the sentences in their instruction text. Record their suggestions on a flip chart.

Use Year 1, Grammar Unit 1 for more work on sentences.

Shared writing

With the children, model writing the instruction text using the Instructions writing frame. With the children's input, model writing the heading, list of items and the bulleted sequence of instruction sentences. Model the oral composition of content before writing. As the sentences are written, encourage the children to suggest a verb to start

each sentence. Once written, collaboratively check through the work for accurate sentence punctuation and correct spellings.

Independent writing

The children can now write their own version of the class instruction text applying the VGP focus on using verbs as the first starting words of the sentences. Make sure that the class plans and word lists are available to them. Give each child a copy of the Instructions writing frame to help with the structure. Some children may benefit from guided group or peer-paired writing at this stage.

Plenary

Throughout the writing session, ask the children questions to help them focus on their progress and what they have created during that lesson, for example: 'What items or equipment have you listed?' 'How easy to understand are your sentences?' 'What verbs have you used to start your sentences?'

Lesson 2

Punctuating sentences

Use Year 1, Punctuation Unit 1 on punctuating sentences.

Shared writing

With the children, read through the instruction text, written in the last lesson. Remind the children of the flowchart at the back of the model text, *How to Make Pop-Up Cards*. Model creating a pictorial flowchart with simple captions underneath. Say the sequences for the flowchart before writing them down. Write a few out of sequence and check to see if children can advise in which order they go. Once written, collaboratively check through the work for accurate sentence punctuation, correct sequencing and correct spelling.

Independent writing

The children can now create their pictorial flowchart with accompanying captions, making sure they sequence the instructions in the correct order. Make sure that the class plans and word lists are available to them. Some children may benefit from guided group or peer-paired writing at this stage.

Plenary

Throughout the writing session, ask the children questions to help them focus on their progress and what they have created during that lesson, for example: 'How has the flowchart helped to organise your instructions?' 'How have you shown the order your instructions should be completed in?' 'How easy to understand are your sentences?' 'What pictures have you included?' 'How easy are your pictures to follow?'

Presenting and performing

Once the children have written their instructions and flowcharts, encourage them to work in groups to follow the instructions to see if the instructions are clear. Allow them to show them to other children in different classes for feedback.

Review of the Big Picture

Once you have completed all the lessons for this section, remind the children of the sequence's Big Picture. Discuss what they have learned so far.

Phase 4: Write independently

This final phase brings all the children's learning and writing skills together so that they can write their own instruction text for a favourite game or activity. Through their writing, they will be able to utilise the different VGP focuses that they have been practising throughout previous phases.

Programmes of study: Year 1

Composition: Say out loud what they are going to write about.

Composition: Compose a sentence orally before writing it.

Composition: Re-read what they have written to check that it makes sense.

Composition: Discuss what they have written with the teacher or other pupils.

Composition: Read aloud their writing clearly enough to be heard by their peers and the teacher.

Introduction

Introduce the phase by discussing what the children have learned in their planning and writing sessions and link it to the Big Picture. Emphasise the excitement of bringing all their learning together to write their own instruction texts for another game or activity that they know.

Use the planning from Phase 2 to review the children's different game and activity suggestions. Spend some time discussing the sequencing of some of the ideas. Clarify that the planning and writing of their instructions will take place over several sessions.

Writing

Give each child the Instructions writing frame. As they plan, draft and write their instructions, encourage the children to compose their words and sentences orally before writing them down.

All the children should be encouraged to try to write independently to the best of their abilities. Ask open questions such as: 'What game or activity are you using?' 'What are you calling your instructions?' 'What is needed for the game/activity?' 'Have you decided on the order of the instructions?' 'What verbs will you use at the start of your sentences?' Make sure that the children have a chance to share their writing with others at appropriate points during each session.

Proofreading and redrafting

Encourage the children to read through their work at the end of each writing session with a partner. Ask them to check whether their writing makes sense. Proofreading and improvement without support means that the writing will happen over a few lessons. Offer the children the Proofreading sheet / My writing checklist, or create your own checklist with the assistance of the blank Proofreading sheet / My writing checklist.

Self- and peer-assessment

Encourage the children to take time to assess their own and others' writing. Make sure that they read out their writing clearly. Offer them a set of self-assessment questions, such as: 'What is the title of the instruction text?' 'Does it include a list of what is needed?' 'What order should the instructions be in?' 'Have I numbered or bulleted each instruction?' 'What verbs have I started my sentences with?' 'How have I used a flowchart to make things clearer?' 'Are my sentences easy to read and follow?' Encourage them to check the capital letters and full stops in sentences, the use of verbs at the beginning of instruction sentences and the correct sequencing of sentences.

Presenting and performing

Once the children have written their instructions and flowcharts, have them share their work with another partner or with a group. Encourage feedback on how clear the instructions are. Have time for the children to carry out the instructions and share them with other children.

If needed or suggested, have photographs taken for each part of the instructions. Encourage the children to use them alongside their work.

Final review of the Big Picture

Individually or with partners, have children reflect on what they have learned from this sequence and what they will remember to do in future writing.

Sequence 8
Recounts

Approximate duration: Two weeks

Big Picture

Through this teaching sequence, children explore the language and structure of writing a diary recount using the model text, *Dougal's Deep-Sea Diary*. By the end of the sequence, the children will have written their own diary recount about an imaginary adventure.

Phase 1: Enjoy and immerse

Children become familiar with the content, language and structure of the model text, *Dougal's Deep- Sea Diary*.

Phase 2: Capture and organise

Children are supported in developing ideas for a diary recount by Dougal about another amazing adventure.

Phase 3: Collaborate and compose

Children undertake supported writing sessions to develop their own writing based on the class diary recount.

Phase 4: Write independently

Children write, edit and read aloud their own diary recount about an amazing imaginary adventure they experienced.

Main source text

Treasure House Anthology Sequence 8 text. *Dougal's Deep-Sea Diary*, Simon Bartram, ISBN 978-1-84-011509-3

Background knowledge

A recount retells events in chronological order to inform or entertain and can be imaginative, personal or factual. In Year 1, children should be able to orally compose and write simple sentences or sentences joined by 'and' for an ordered sequence of events over a day or over a week.

In the main source text, *Dougal's Deep-Sea Diary*, the children are able to explore a first person recount using the personal pronoun, 'I', and diary recount entries for each day of the week.

Spoken outcome

To read out their diary adventure recounts for others to enjoy

Writing outcome

To write their own diary recount about a week's adventure (real or imaginary)

Prior knowledge

Check children's knowledge and understanding of:

- the story series by Simon Bartram
- underwater environments
- being underwater
- sea myths
- deep-sea diving
- diaries.

Diagnostic assessment options

Before starting the unit, you may wish to conduct an initial diagnostic assessment of the children's knowledge and understanding.

Ideas for initial diagnostic assessment options include:

- reviewing children's writing for correct capitalisation of days of the week and place names
- speaking and listening activities where children recognise and spell the days of the week
- reviewing children's writing to check that they use 'and' to build sentences
- reviewing children's writing to check that recounts are written in the right time order

Cross-curricular links

KS1 Art and design

- Use drawing, painting and sculpture to develop and share their ideas, experiences and imagination.

KS1 Geography - Human and physical geography

- Refer to key physical features, including: beach, cliff, coast, forest, hill, mountain, sea, ocean, river, soil, valley, vegetation, season and weather.

KS1 Science - Animals, including humans

- Identify and name a variety of common animals including fish, amphibians, reptiles, birds and mammals.
- Describe and compare the structure of a variety of common animals (fish, amphibians, reptiles, birds and mammals, including pets).

Treasure House links

- Treasure House, Year 1, Comprehension Unit 8: Reading recounts: 'Man on the Moon'
- Treasure House, Year 1, Composition Unit 9: Writing Simple Recounts
- Treasure House, Year 1, Punctuation Unit 2: Capital letter for names and 'I'
- Treasure House, Year 1, Spelling Unit 19: Spelling the days of the week
- Treasure House, Year 1, Spelling Unit 14: Spelling ph
- Treasure House, Year 1, Punctuation Unit 3: Capital letter for days of the week and place names
- Treasure House, Year 1, Grammar Unit 2: Building sentences using 'and'

Resources

Props and percussion instruments for drama and storytelling activities (optional); a simple diary showing one week; photograph of a dolphin or dolphins.

Source texts – see Anthologies; Diary storyboard; Diary adventure writing frame; Match the 'ph' labels; Proofreading sheet / My writing checklist; Proofreading sheet / My writing checklist (blank)

Phase 1: Enjoy and immerse

In Phase 1, the children listen to the story, *Dougal's Deep-Sea Diary*. Over several sessions, the children have opportunities to discuss the language and structure of the recount diary text through comprehension and discussion activities as well as exploring the poem's content through drama, performance, writing and analysis of the text. Phase 1 also covers the vocabulary, grammar and punctuation focus on capitalising the personal pronoun, 'I', and includes work on spelling the days of the week.

Programmes of study: Year 1

Comprehension: Listen to and discuss a wide range of poems, stories and non-fiction at a level beyond that at which they can read independently.

Comprehension: Discuss the significance of the title and events.

Comprehension: Predict what might happen on the basis of what has been read so far.

Comprehension: Explain clearly their understanding of what is read to them.

Vocabulary, grammar and punctuation: Use a capital letter for names of people, places, the days of the week and the personal pronoun 'I'.

Spelling: Spell the days of the week.

Sparking interest

Show and read out the title of the main text story, *Dougal's Deep-Sea Diary* to the children. Ask the children what they think a diary is. Show the children a simple week diary. Note that the diary shows the days of the week and the dates. Highlight that the character in the story is writing a diary for every day of his week's holiday. Ask: 'Why would he want to do that?' (To record what happened, to record his feelings, to remember.) Encourage the children to share their own experiences of writing down or telling others what they did for a trip away.

Reading and discussion

Read and show the story, *Dougal's Deep-Sea Diary* using appropriate intonation. Check that the children understand the meaning of new or difficult words. Lead a discussion to check their understanding of the story. Stop just before the end of the story, to allow the children to decide what Dougal was going to do next.

Discuss the following with the children.

- Why did Dougal wish that tomorrow would come soon?
- What did Dougal hope he would find while he was deep-sea diving?
- Who did Dougal perform with on Monday?
- What did Dougal find in the ancient treasure chest? What did he find the most interesting?
- Why did the king and queen give Dougal a submarine?
- How did Dougal find Atlantis?

- What was Atlantis like? Who lived there?
- Do you think Dougal would go back to his job?
- What do you think Dougal did instead?
- What would you do if you found Atlantis and had a submarine?
- Which day of his holiday do you think was the best?
- Who was Dougal writing the diary for? (himself)

Drama and storytelling

Use a range of activities to reinforce children's understanding of the recount text. Select the activities that would fit in with your lesson timing. Encourage mixed-ability grouping for the chosen activities.

- **Dougal's week:** Split the children into seven groups and give them a day each from Dougal's diary. Let them perform or mime the scenes while you take on Dougal's voice. Create a class performance.

- **Mime and movement:** Ask the children to imagine that they are going on a deep-sea dive to visit an underwater city like Atlantis. Have them mime getting into their diving suits, jumping into the sea, swimming and doing activities underwater.

- **A new submarine:** In groups, children design a submarine. They could use props or pictures to present their ideas to the rest of the class.

Back to work discussion: In a circle, discuss whether Dougal should have gone back to work or dive for pearls. Use open questioning to encourage the discussion.

Incidental writing

Short writing activities enhance the children's understanding of the recount and help to inform the teaching focuses in the collaborative composition phase. Provide information about deep-sea diving if needed. Children could:

- research and write information about deep-sea diving
- draw and label pictures of the underwater city of Atlantis
- design and write a postcard from Dougal to his cousin, Bob, about Atlantis
- design an Atlantis t-shirt or mug
- draw one of the old maps that show where Atlantis was
- write a one day diary recount of a special day trip.

Analysis

Reread the title of the story to the children and ask: 'How do we know that it is a diary?' Look at the days of the week for each entry. Discuss how Dougal has written down what he did and how he felt about the different events on his holiday. Use the Diary story board to help record the events of the week to show the time sequencing and the story plan. Highlight that the recount is written by Dougal so he uses 'I' a lot. Note that when he asks questions, he is asking himself in the diary as if he is a friend.

Grammar: Capital letter for the personal pronoun, 'I'

Remind the children that, in Dougal's diary, Dougal writes about himself and so uses the word 'I'. Highlight 'I' on page 1. Note that when we write the word 'I' it is a capital letter. Reinforce this by holding up a card with 'I' on it. Say a few sentences and hold up 'I' when it is said, for example: 'I went to the zoo today. I saw a monkey who took my hat. I was cross.'

Give the children a piece of paper each and ask them to write 'I' on it. In pairs let them take turns to talk about something they have done. Have them hold up the 'I' whenever they say it.

Use Year 1, Punctuation Unit 2 for more work on the personal pronoun, 'I'.

Phonics and spelling

Remind the children that in Dougal's diary, the days of the week have been written down. Encourage the children to say the days of the week with you. Explain that they are going to work on spelling the days to help them with their diary writing. Write and display the days of the week on word cards. Using the information frame from Pupil Book 1, Spelling Unit 19, work on the spelling for each day. Reinforce the spellings throughout the subsequent planning and writing lessons in Phases 2, 3, and 4.

Review of the Big Picture

At the end of this phase, discuss with the children what they have learned so far about the diary recount, *Dougal's Deep-Sea Diary*. Remind them that this is all working towards writing a new diary adventure.

Phase 2: Capture and organise

During Phase 2, children work collaboratively to develop ideas for the new content needed for a diary recount of another Dougal adventure. Phase 2 also includes work on spelling the /f/ sound 'ph'.

Programmes of study: Year 1

Comprehension: Be encouraged to link what they read or hear read to their own experiences.

Comprehension: Discuss word meanings, linking new meanings to those already known.

Comprehension: Draw on what they already know or on background information and vocabulary provided by the teacher.

Comprehension: Participate in discussion about what is read to them, taking turns and listening to what others say.

Composition: Say out loud what they are going to write about.

Spelling: Learn new consonant spellings 'ph' and 'wh'.

Introduction

Remind the children of the Big Picture. Reread the model text, *Dougal's Deep-Sea Diary* to the children and if possible show the illustrations. Discuss the work children have done to explore the diary recount.

Introduce the idea that the children are going to work together to create another adventure for Dougal to write in his diary.

Discussing ideas

As a class, discuss and make decisions to create Dougal's adventure. Record their ideas for Phase 3 and Phase 4. Use the extra source text, *Man on the Moon* as another adventure idea.

Discuss the following with the children.

- What does Dougal want to do? (for example, find a sea monster, find a long-lost wreck, go to an underwater sporting event)
- On what day of the week does he start his trip?
- What does he do or see on each day of the week?
- What exciting thing happens during the week?
- Who does he meet?
- Does he enjoy the trip?
- What happens on the last day of the week?

Drama and storytelling

Use a range of activities to reinforce children's ideas and thoughts about the new diary. Select the activities that would fit in with your lesson timing. Encourage mixed-ability grouping for the chosen activities.

- **A Dougal adventure:** Once the children have listed their ideas for a new Dougal adventure, have a drama session to explore the different adventure events. Put them into groups and give them an adventure each to discuss and perform back to the class.
- **Freeze-frame events:** Once Dougal's adventure has been chosen, have the children freeze-frame the different events that happen for each day of the week. Use thought-tracking, asking each child in the freeze-frame what they're thinking at that moment of the story.
- **Look what I have found!** Put the children into small groups and give them a prop such as a shell, a costume ring or an old map. Ask each group to discuss how the prop would fit into Dougal's adventure.

Incidental writing

Before you select any incidental writing, make sure the children are able to orally articulate the main events. Select activities that you think appropriate for the abilities and interests of your class. Children could:

- write a postcard from Dougal to a friend about one of the events in the trip
- list equipment needed for the trip
- draw a storyboard of the adventure with days of the week above each picture
- design a new adventure t-shirt for Dougal.

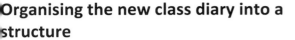

Organising the new class diary into a structure

Once the children have thoroughly explored their ideas for Dougal's new adventure diary, bring them together and make a final decision on the content. Use the diary story board to help plan and record the events under each day's heading. Use words and pictures if needed. Once recorded, go through the plans and ask the children if they are happy with their new adventure.

Phonics and spelling

Remind the children that in Dougal's diary, some of Dougal's sea friends were dolphins. Show a photograph of a dolphin and write a label for it. Ask: 'What sound do the letters 'ph' stand for?' (/f/) Note that the dolphin is in a photograph. Write out the word and ask: 'Which two letters spell the /f/ sound?' Underline 'ph' at the beginning and end of the word.

Give pairs of children a set of 'ph' word labels and some images from the 'Match the 'ph' labels' resource sheet. Ask the children to match the labels to the images. Once done, encourage them to say each word out loud with emphasis on the 'ph'.

Use Year 1, Spelling Unit 14 for more work on spellings with 'ph'.

Review of the Big Picture

At the end of this phase, discuss with the children what they have achieved with their planning and ideas for their new diary adventure.

Phase 3: Collaborate and compose

Phase 3 has three writing lessons which support the children in the writing of a class diary recount for a new Dougal adventure. Each lesson starts with a vocabulary, grammar and punctuation focus with links to the main text. The children then have the opportunity to participate in a shared composition session, applying the VGP focus in context. Independent writing, with plenaries, follows. The VGP focuses are on joining words and joining clauses using 'and' and sequencing sentences to form short narratives.

Programmes of study: Year 1

Composition: Say out loud what they are going to write about.

Composition: Compose a sentence orally before writing it.

Composition: Re-read what they have written to check that it makes sense.

Composition: Discuss what they have written with the teacher or other pupils.

Composition: Read aloud their writing clearly enough to be heard by their peers and the teacher.

Vocabulary, grammar and punctuation: Use a capital letter for names of people, places, the days of the week, and the personal pronoun 'I'.

Vocabulary, grammar and punctuation: Join words and join clauses using and.

Vocabulary, grammar and punctuation: Sequence sentences to form short narratives.

Introduction

Remind the children about the sequence's Big Picture. Explain that the children are going to work as a class to draft and write another adventure for Dougal's diary. Remind the children that they need to write as if they are Dougal. Use the planning from Phase 2 to remind the children of their ideas.

Lesson 1

Capital letters for days of the week and place names

With the children, revise the spellings for the days of the week. Highlight that each day of the week starts with a capital letter. Encourage the children to help you spell and write out the days onto cards with a different colour for the capital letters. Remind the children that place names also start with a capital letter. Let the children decide on place names to match each day of the week for an amazing trip. Write the names on cards with a colour for the capital letters. Use the cards to inspire a class adventure.

Use Year 1, Punctuation Unit 3 and Year 1, Spelling Unit 19 for more work on days of the week.

Shared writing

With the children, model writing the first two days of the diary within the Diary story board. Model the oral composition of sentences before writing. Encourage the children to help you spell the specific days of the week and check that they remember that they start with a capital letter. Ask whether a place name needs a capital letter or not. Once written, collaboratively check through the work for accurate sentence punctuation, capitalisation of the personal pronoun, 'I', and correct spelling.

Independent writing

The children can now write their version of the first two days of Dougal's diary applying the VGP focus on capital letters for days of the week, place names, and for the personal pronoun, 'I'. Make sure that the class plans and story boards are available to them. Give each child a copy of the Diary storyboard to help with the language and structure. Some children may benefit from guided group or peer-paired writing at this stage.

Plenary

Throughout the writing session, ask the children questions to help them focus on their progress and what they have created during that lesson, for example: 'What day of the week did the adventure start on?' 'How has Dougal's adventure started?' 'Where has Dougal gone?' 'What has Dougal been doing?' 'How have you set up the adventure to be exciting?' Encourage children to check that they have included the days of the week and that these are spelled correctly and have capital letters; that events are described in the correct order; that the writing is in the first person with the personal pronoun, 'I', capitalised; and that any place names are correctly capitalised.

Lesson 2

Joining clauses with 'and'

On a board, write out two sentences: 'I saw a shark.' 'I saw a dolphin.' Read out the two sentences with the children. Underline 'I saw a...' and ask: 'What do you notice about these words? (they are the same). Note how saying the same words twice sounds odd, like a robot. Write 'and' and say that it can join sentences to make them sound better. Show how you cut out the repetition of 'I saw a...' and add 'and': 'I saw a shark and a dolphin.' Put the children into pairs and ask them to each say one short sentence of what they might have seen when exploring. Once they have shared their sentences, let them work together to orally join the sentences with 'and' then write it out.

Use Year 1, Grammar Unit 2 for more work on building sentences using 'and'.

Shared writing

Model writing more days of the diary using the Diary storyboard. Model the oral composition of sentences before writing. Encourage the children to help you join simple sentences and clauses using, 'and'. Once written, collaboratively check that the sentences make sense and spelling and sentence punctuation is correct.

Independent writing

The children can now write their class version of the next few days of Dougal's diary applying the VGP focus on joining clauses using 'and'. Make sure that the class plans and story boards are available to them. Give each child a copy of the Diary adventure writing frame to help with the language and structure. Some children may benefit from guided group or peer-paired writing at this stage.

Plenary

Throughout the writing session, ask the children questions to help them focus on their progress and what they have created during that lesson, for example: 'What days of the week have you written about?' 'How has Dougal's adventure continued?' 'Where has Dougal gone?' 'What has Dougal been doing?' 'How have you made the adventure exciting?' Encourage children to check that they have included the days of the week and that these are spelled correctly and have capital letters; that events are described in the correct order; that the writing is in the first person with the personal pronoun, 'I', capitalised; and that any place names are correctly capitalised. Ask children to check their work for sentences that could be joined using 'and'.

Lesson 3

Sequencing sentences to form short narratives

Write the following sentences on cards. 'I put on my diving suit.' 'I jumped into the sea.' 'I saw a treasure chest.' 'I opened it up.' 'I found lots of gold coins.' Display the cards in the wrong order. Explain that Dougal has written some of his sentences in the wrong order and needs the children's help to sort them out. Read through the sentences and then encourage the children to put the sentences in the correct order.

Shared writing

Model writing the last part of the diary using the Diary storyboard. Model the oral composition of the sentences before writing. Remind the children of the VGP focus on sequencing sentences to create a narrative. Check that the sentences are in the correct sequence order so that they make sense. Once written, collaboratively check that sentences make sense and that spelling and sentence punctuation is correct.

Independent writing

The children can now write their class version of the last days of Dougal's diary applying the VGP focus on sequencing sentences to create a narrative. Make sure that the class plans and story boards are available to them. Give each child a copy of the Diary story board to help with the language and structure. Some children may benefit from guided group or peer-paired writing at this stage.

Plenary

Throughout the writing session, ask the children questions to help them focus on their progress and what they have created during that lesson, for example: 'What days of the week have you written about?' 'How has Dougal's adventure ended?' 'How does Dougal feel about his adventure?' 'How have you made the ending exciting?' Encourage children to check that they have included the days of the week and that these are spelled correctly and have capital letters; that events are described in the correct order; that the writing is in the first person with the personal pronoun, 'I', capitalised; and that any place names are correctly capitalised.

Presenting and performing

Once the children have written their diary entries for each day, encourage them to share their work, taking turns to read it to each other. Encourage the children to offer feedback on what they particularly liked.

Review of the Big Picture

Once you have completed all the lessons for this section, remind the children of the sequence's Big Picture. Discuss what they have learned so far.

Phase 4: Write independently

This final phase brings all the children's learning and writing skills together so that they can write their own week's diary about their own amazing imaginary adventure. Through their writing, they will be able to utilise the different VGP focuses that they have been practising throughout previous phases.

Programmes of study: Year 1

Composition: Say out loud what they are going to write about.

Composition: Compose a sentence orally before writing it.

Composition: Sequence sentences to form short narratives.

Composition: Re-read what they have written to check that it makes sense.

Composition: Discuss what they have written with the teacher or other pupils.

Composition: Read aloud their writing clearly enough to be heard by their peers and the teacher.

Introduction

Introduce the phase by discussing what the children have learned in their planning and writing sessions and link it to the Big Picture. Emphasise the excitement of bringing all their learning together to write their own diary of an imaginary holiday or adventure.

Review the children's ideas from Phase 2. Have a discussion session to help the children think of new ideas and events for their diaries. Clarify that the planning and writing of their diaries will take place over several sessions.

Writing

Give each child a copy of the Diary storyboard and the Diary adventure writing frame. As they plan, draft and write their diary entries for their week's adventure, encourage the children to say their sentences before writing them down.

All the children should be encouraged to try to write independently to the best of their abilities. Ask open questions such as 'What adventure are you describing in your diary?' 'What happens on the first day of your adventure?' 'Have you described what happens on that day clearly?' 'What events happen during the week?' 'What happens on the most exciting day of the week?' 'What happens on the last day of the adventure?' 'What will you say about it in your diary?'

Make sure that the children have a chance to share their writing with others at appropriate points during each session.

Proofreading and redrafting

Encourage the children to read through their work at the end of each writing session with a partner. Ask them to check that their writing makes sense. Proofreading and improvement without support means that the writing will happen over a few lessons. Offer the children the Proofreading sheet / My writing checklist, or create your own checklist with the assistance of the blank Proofreading sheet / My writing checklist.

Self- and peer-assessment

Encourage the children to take time to assess their own and others' writing. Make sure that they read out their writing clearly. Offer them a set of self-assessment questions, such as: 'Are the events described in the right order?' 'Does the first entry describe how the adventure starts?' 'Have I written two or more sentences for each day of my diary?' 'Have I written the right day of the week by each day section?' 'How have I made the adventure interesting and fun to read?' 'Have I got a good ending to my week?' 'Does my writing make sense?' 'Would I add anything else to it?' 'Would others be interested in reading it?'

Also encourage them to check their VGP focuses on using capital letters for days of the week, place names and the personal pronoun, 'I'; building sentences using 'and'; and sequencing sentences into a narrative.

Presenting and performing

Once the children have written their adventure diaries, encourage them to either cut out their writing from the writing frame and stick it onto separate sheets of paper or rewrite the sentences on a new sheet of paper with room for them to illustrate each day. Once completed, compile the work into books for the children to read. Have the children share their diaries within groups and encourage them to feed back on each other's work.

Final review of the Big Picture

Individually or with partners, have children reflect on what they have learned from this sequence and what they will remember to do in future writing.

Sequence 9
Reports

Approximate duration: Two weeks

Big Picture

Through this teaching sequence, children look at the structure, content and language of a report text, *Top Dinosaurs*. By the end of the sequence, each child will have created an information report poster about three different dinosaurs.

Phase 1: Enjoy and immerse

Children become familiar with the content, language and structure of the model report text, *Top Dinosaurs*.

Phase 2: Capture and organise

Children are supported in developing ideas to create a poster about three different dinosaurs.

Phase 3: Collaborate and compose

Children undertake supported writing sessions to develop their own writing based on the class dinosaur poster.

Phase 4: Write independently

Children write, edit and read aloud their own report poster about three more dinosaurs.

Main source text

Treasure House Anthology Sequence 9 text. *Top Dinosaurs*, Maoliosa Kelly, Jon Hughes and Ali Teo, ISBN 978-0-00-718571-9

Background knowledge

A report is a text that describes and provides information on something in the third person. During Year 1, the children begin to develop their knowledge and understanding of, and ability to read and write simple report texts on a variety of topics.

In this sequence, the children will have the opportunity to study and write a report on dinosaurs using typical report characteristics: a title, subheadings, descriptive information sentences, use of topic-specific vocabulary, and labels and captions.

Spoken outcome

To show and tell their report posters describing three dinosaurs

Writing outcome

To write a report poster describing three dinosaurs

Prior knowledge

Check children's knowledge and understanding of:

- report texts covering a wide range of subjects
- the characteristics of simple report texts
- what dinosaurs were and when they lived
- definitions of 'carnivores', 'herbivores' and 'omnivores'.

Diagnostic assessment options

Before starting the unit, you may wish to conduct an initial diagnostic assessment of the children's abilities and knowledge and understanding.

Ideas for initial diagnostic assessment options include:

- reviewing children's writing for use of capital letters for proper names
- reviewing children's writing to check that they are beginning to join words and clauses using 'and'
- listening activities where children identify the correct order of words in sentences
- spelling and listening activities where children recognise common exception words within sentences.

Year 1, Sequence 9
Reports

Cross-curricular links

KS1 Art and design

- Use drawing, painting and sculpture to develop and share their ideas, experiences and imagination.

KS1 Science - Animals, including humans

- Identify and name a variety of common animals including fish, amphibians, reptiles, birds and mammals.
- Identify and name a variety of common animals that are carnivores, herbivores and omnivores.
- Describe and compare the structure of a variety of common animals (fish, amphibians, reptiles, birds and mammals including pets).

Treasure House links

- Treasure House, Year 1, Comprehension Unit 9: Reading reports: 'Your Nose'
- Treasure House, Year 1, Composition Unit 8: Writing Simple Reports
- Treasure House, Year 1, Punctuation Unit 2: Capital letter for names and 'I'
- Treasure House, Year 1, Grammar Unit 1: Building sentences
- Treasure House, Year 1, Grammar Unit 2: Building sentences using 'and'

Resources

Images and a range of information about dinosaurs; a range of simple information books

Source texts – see Anthologies; Dinosaur report writing frame; Dinosaur information sheet; Making 'au' pairs; Proofreading sheet / My writing checklist; Proofreading sheet / My writing checklist (blank)

Phase 1: Enjoy and immerse

In Phase 1, the children listen to and read the report text, 'Top Dinosaurs'. Over several sessions, the children have opportunities to discuss the language and structure of the report through comprehension and discussion activities as well as exploring the information's content through activities, writing and analysis of the text. Phase 1 also covers the vocabulary, grammar and punctuation focus, using capital letters for names, and includes work on spelling the /or/ sound 'au'.

Programmes of study: Year 1

Comprehension: Listen to and discuss a wide range of poems, stories and non-fiction at a level beyond that at which they can read independently.

Comprehension: Recognise and join in with predictable phrases.

Comprehension: Discuss word meanings, linking new meanings to those already known.

Comprehension: Check that the text makes sense to them as they read and correct inaccurate reading.

Vocabulary, grammar and punctuation: Use a capital letter for names of people, places, the days of the week, and the personal pronoun 'I'.

Spelling: Spell words with the digraph 'au'.

Sparking interest

Show the children a picture of Tyrannosaurus Rex and ask them what it is (a dinosaur). Tell children that dinosaurs lived millions of years before humans. Encourage the children to share their knowledge of dinosaurs including those they may have seen in museums, films and books. Introduce *Top Dinosaurs* to the children. Tell children that they are going to be writing their own reports on dinosaurs.

Reading and discussion

Read *Top Dinosaurs* with the children. Check children understand the language and help them read and say each dinosaur name. Discuss or ask questions to check children's understanding of the content.

Discuss the following with the children.

- What type of book is this?
- What information does the book contain? What sorts of things does the book tell us about dinosaurs?
- How does the 'Contents' page help the reader?
- What tells you which dinosaur each section is about? (subheadings)
- How did the Stegosaurus' plates and spikes protect it?
- Why has the weight of the Brachiosaurus been compared to the weight of elephants?
- How does the fact list at the back of the book help the reader?

Drama and storytelling

Use a range of activities to reinforce children's understanding of the report text. Select the activities that would fit in with your lesson timing. Encourage mixed-ability grouping for the chosen activities.

- **Be a dinosaur:** Use the descriptive information in *Top Dinosaurs* for children to explore each dinosaur's movements. Once they have explored each dinosaur, call out 'Dinosaur Park!' and have the children be any dinosaur.
- **Guess which dinosaur:** Have a dinosaur guessing game using the phrase: 'It is as _____ as a _____.' Taking turns in pairs, let the children describe one of the dinosaurs using the phrase while others guess or use the book to find out the answer.
- **Dinosaur documentaries:** In groups, children choose a dinosaur to enact a wildlife documentary about. Have one or two of them act as the documentary presenter or presenters. The others in the group enact the dinosaur or dinosaurs that the documentary is about.
- **Dinosaur musical words:** Have a rhythmic music session to help the children pronounce the dinosaur words using percussion.

Incidental writing

Short writing activities enhance the children's understanding of the information text and help to inform the teaching focuses in the collaborative composition phase. Children could:

- draw and label pictures of dinosaurs
- create a dinosaur display with models, pictures, captions and labels
- compile a word bank of the words used to describe the dinosaurs in the book.

Analysis

Look at how the information in *Top Dinosaurs* has been organised. Note the title of the book and the contents page. Discuss how the two simple sentences and the layout of pages 2 and 3 introduce what the report is about. Note that each dinosaur section starts with the name of the dinosaur. Focus on the descriptive sentences for each section including the comparison sentences and their uses. Discuss why there are simple to read dinosaur descriptions at the back of the book. Ask: 'How do they help the reader?' Finally look at the captions and labels used in the report.

Use the extract text, *Your Nose*, for another example of a simple report text.

Grammar: Capital letters for names

Show the children pages 2 and 3 from *Top Dinosaurs* and point to the names of the dinosaurs. Ask: 'What do you notice about the first letter for each name?' (Each starts with a capital letter.) Remind the children that proper names always start with a capital letter and that these words are the proper names for each dinosaur. Have the children invent their own dinosaur and name it. Encourage them to draw the dinosaur and write out its name with a capital letter. Have them write out the capital letter in a different colour or underline it. Display their work.

Use Year 1, Punctuation Unit 2 for more on capital letters for names.

Phonics and spelling

Write the word, 'dinosaur' on the board. Ask the children to read it out loud. Underline the 'au' and ask what sound it spells /or/. Highlight how a few words with the letters 'au' have the /or/ sound. Give out the resource sheet Making 'au' pairs. Children add the missing 'au' letters to the pairs of words and then cut out the words to play a pairs game in pairs. Encourage them to say the words as they pair them with emphasis on the /or/ sound for 'au'.

Review of the Big Picture

At the end of this phase, discuss with the children what they have learned so far about the report text, *Top Dinosaurs*. Remind them that this is all working towards writing their own reports about other dinosaurs.

Phase 2: Capture and organise

During Phase 2, children start to develop ideas about the new content needed for their class report poster about dinosaurs. Working collaboratively, children decide on the words and layout they could use for the report poster. Phase 2 also includes work on spelling some common exception words.

Programmes of study: Year 1

Comprehension: Be encouraged to link what they read or hear read to their own experiences.

Comprehension: Draw on what they already know or on background information and vocabulary provided by the teacher.

Comprehension: Participate in discussion about what is read to them, taking turns and listening to what others say.

Comprehension: Explain clearly their understanding of what is read to them.

Composition: Say out loud what they are going to write about.

Spelling: Spell common exception words.

Introduction

Remind the children of the Big Picture. Reread or discuss the report text, *Top Dinosaurs*. Discuss the work that the children have done so far. Remind the children that reports provide information on things such as how dinosaurs move or look.

Introduce the idea that the children are going to work together to create a report poster on how three different dinosaurs look, move and what they eat. Have the Dinosaur information sheet and other information about six new dinosaurs available for the children to see and read.

Discussing ideas

As a class, discuss and make decisions to create their new class report poster about three new dinosaurs. Use the Dinosaur information sheet and other information to help them choose three dinosaurs for their poster. Record their ideas for Phase 3 and Phase 4.

Discuss the following with the children.

- What shall we call our report poster?
- What sentence could we use to introduce our information?
- How do we say the dinosaur's name?
- What words could we use to describe how the dinosaurs look and move?
- What could we compare the dinosaur to?
- What food does it eat? How does it eat it?
- What pictures shall we add to the poster?
- What labels or captions could we use?

Drama and storytelling

Use a range of activities to reinforce children's ideas. Select the activities that would fit in with your lesson timing. Encourage mixed-ability grouping for the chosen activities.

- **Dinosaur moves:** Have a movement session for the children to explore the movements of each of the three dinosaurs including their speeds.
- **Herbivore, carnivore and omnivore sorting:** Hold up cards with the terms 'herbivore', 'carnivore' and 'omnivore'. Explain their meaning. Put the children into groups and allocate each group a dinosaur. Groups enact and describe what and how their dinosaur eats. Let the class discuss and decide what category each dinosaur belongs to.
- **Amazing dinosaur facts:** Let the children work in pairs to find two amazing facts about dinosaurs including the ones that are being focused on for the poster. Children then present their facts to the class.

Incidental writing

Before you select any incidental writing, make sure the children are able to orally articulate the main parts to the information text. Select activities that you think appropriate for the abilities and interests of your class. Children could:

- compile a list of words that describe how the dinosaurs move, look and eat
- create a chart to show which dinosaurs are carnivore, herbivore and omnivore
- write comparison sentences such as 'An elephant is as tall as a bus.' 'My Nan is as strong as an ox.' 'I am as hungry as a giant.'

Organising the new report into a structure

Once the children have thoroughly explored their ideas for their class report poster, bring them together to make a final decision on the content and layout. On a blank poster record where each section of information should go including the title, introductory sentence, headings, three descriptive sentences and labelled dinosaur pictures. Go through all the other information including the descriptive word lists before asking the children if they are happy with their report poster plan.

Phonics and spelling

Remind the children how some words have tricky letters in them that make them hard to spell. Write a list of common exception words that are used in *Top Dinosaurs*, for example: 'they', 'were', 'one', 'of', 'go', 'there', 'here', 'are', 'some'. Go through each word, saying each segment and focusing on the tricky part of the word. Have the children practise spelling by looking, saying, covering, writing, and then checking their spelling of each word.

Review of the Big Picture

At the end of this phase, discuss with the children what they have achieved with their planning and ideas for their class report poster.

Phase 3: Collaborate and compose

Phase 3 has two writing lessons which support the children in writing their class report poster. Each lesson starts with a vocabulary, grammar and punctuation focus with links to the main text. The children then participate in a shared composition session, applying the VGP focus in context. Independent writing, with plenaries, follows. The VGP focuses are on how words combine to make sentences, and joining words and joining clauses using 'and'.

Programmes of study: Year 1

Composition: Say out loud what they are going to write about.

Composition: Compose a sentence orally before writing it.

Composition: Re-read what they have written to check that it makes sense.

Composition: Discuss what they have written with the teacher or other pupils.

Composition: Read aloud their writing clearly enough to be heard by their peers and the teacher.

Vocabulary, grammar and punctuation: Understand how words can combine to make sentences.

Vocabulary, grammar and punctuation: Join words and join clauses using 'and'.

Introduction

Remind the children about the sequence's Big Picture. Explain that over several lessons the children are going to work as a class to draft and write their report texts for their class poster. Use the planning and recorded information from Phase 2 to remind the children of their ideas.

Lesson 1

Combining words to make sentences

This activity can be done as a class or in groups. Remind the children that words in sentences need to be in the right order to make sense. Write 'claws. They big, sharp had'. Have the children read it out to hear if it makes sense. Ask: 'What do we always start a sentence with?' (a capital letter) 'What do we usually end a sentence with? (a full stop) Write: 'They _____ _____ _____ claws.' With the children, work out the rest of the sentence focusing on the position of the verb and the descriptive words. Provide a few more mixed up sentence examples for the children to unscramble.

Use Year 1, Grammar Unit 1 for more on combining words to make sentences.

Shared writing

Display the Dinosaur report writing frame. With the children's input, use the writing frame's sentence structures to model writing the introduction, the heading with its explanation of pronunciation and three descriptive information sentences for one of the dinosaurs. Encourage the children to compose the sentences orally before writing them. Suggest a few mixed-up sentences for children to correct. Demonstrate adding the descriptive words into the sentences. Once written, collaboratively check that the sentences make sense, the information is clear and the punctuation and spelling is correct.

Independent writing

The children can now write their own version of the introduction and information for one of the dinosaurs ensuring they combine words correctly to make sentences. Make sure that descriptive word lists are available to them. Give each child a copy of the Dinosaur report writing frame to help with the language and structure. Some children may benefit from guided group or peer-paired writing at this stage.

Plenary

Throughout the writing session, ask the children questions to help them focus on their progress and what they have created during that lesson, for example: 'What title have you written?' 'What have you written to introduce the dinosaur?' 'What words have you used to describe the dinosaur?' 'What have you compared it to and why?' 'How have you checked to see if your sentences make sense?'

Lesson 2

Joining words and clauses using 'and'

Show page 13 of *Top Dinosaurs*. Read the sentence: 'They had plates on their backs and spikes on their tails.' Underline the word 'and'. Remind children of previous work where they joined sentences using 'and'. Let the children work in pairs or small groups to write a sentence with 'and' in that describes parts of a dinosaur's body, for example: 'They had a long neck and four legs.'

Use Year 1, Grammar Unit 2 for more work on words and phrases joined with 'and'.

Shared writing

Display the Dinosaur report writing frame. Use the writing frame's sentence structures to model writing the heading and three descriptive sentences for the last two dinosaurs. Encourage the children to compose the sentences orally before writing them. Suggest short sentences that could be combined using 'and'. Demonstrate adding the descriptive words into the sentences. Once written, collaboratively check that the sentences make sense, the information is clear and sentence punctuation and spelling is correct.

Independent writing

The children can now write their own reports for the last two dinosaurs, joining words and clauses using 'and.' Make sure that descriptive word lists are available for them to see. Give each child a copy of the Dinosaur report writing frame to help with the language and structure. Some children may benefit from guided group or peer-paired writing at this stage.

Plenary

Throughout the writing session, ask the children questions to help them focus on their progress and what they have created during that lesson, for example: 'What key words have you used to describe the dinosaurs?' 'What have you compared them to and why?' 'Which sentences have you joined using 'and'?' 'How have you checked to see if your sentences make sense?'

Presenting and performing

Once the class report text has been written on the writing frame, model cutting the information out and sticking it onto the poster. Model writing out the headings for each dinosaur with their pronunciations and the title with the introductory sentences stuck underneath. Add pictures and label them, emphasising the capital letters for names. Let the children do the same by either cutting out and sticking their text onto the poster or writing it directly onto the poster. They can draw their own dinosaur pictures or cut out images. Let the children share their posters with each other and encourage feedback on whether the report describes the dinosaurs well.

Review of the Big Picture

Once you have completed all the lessons for this section, remind the children of the sequence's Big Picture. Discuss what they have learned so far.

Phase 4: Write independently

This final phase brings all the children's learning and writing skills together so that they can write their own report texts for a poster on three more dinosaurs that have been looked at in Phase 2. Through their writing, they will be able to utilise the different VGP focuses that they have been practising throughout previous phases.

Programmes of study: Year 1

Composition: Say out loud what they are going to write about.

Composition: Compose a sentence orally before writing it.

Composition: Re-read what they have written to check that it makes sense.

Composition: Discuss what they have written with the teacher or other pupils.

Composition: Read aloud their writing clearly enough to be heard by their peers and the teacher.

Introduction

Introduce the phase by discussing what the children have learned in their planning and writing sessions and link it to the Big Picture. Emphasise the excitement of bringing all their learning together to write their own report posters about three more dinosaurs. Clarify that the planning and writing of their report poster will take place over several sessions.

Writing

Give each child the Dinosaur report writing frame, relevant dinosaur information, the descriptive word list and blank poster paper. As they plan, draft and write their dinosaur report poster, encourage children to compose their words and phrases orally before writing them.

All the children should be encouraged to try to write independently to the best of their abilities. Ask open questions such as: 'What title will you use for your report poster and why?' 'What descriptive words will you use to describe your dinosaurs?' 'What will you compare each dinosaur to?' 'What pictures will you use for your poster?' 'How are you going to label the pictures?' 'Where will you put the information on the poster?' Make sure children have a chance to share their writing with others at appropriate points during each session.

Proofreading and redrafting

Encourage the children to read through their work at the end of each writing session with a partner. Ask them to check that their writing makes sense. Proofreading and improvement without support means that the writing will happen over a few lessons. Offer the children the Proofreading sheet / My writing checklist, or create your own

checklist with the assistance of the blank Proofreading sheet / My writing checklist.

Self- and peer-assessment

Encourage the children to take time to assess their own and others' writing. Make sure that they read out their writing clearly. Ask open questions to encourage self/peer-assessment such as: 'What title have you given your information booklet?' 'How does you first sentence or sentences introduce us to the dinosaurs?' 'What key words have you used to describe the dinosaur?' 'What things have you used to compare the dinosaurs with?' 'How do we know which dinosaur you are writing about?' 'Which sentences have you joined with 'and' and why?' 'How does your report tell readers what a dinosaur is like?'

Also encourage children to check their VGP focuses on using capital letters for proper names, combining words to make sentences and joining words and clauses using 'and'.

Presenting and performing

Once the children have written their text on their writing frames, have an extra session set aside for them to spend time creating their posters. Encourage the use of labelled pictures and correct punctuation for headings and names. Have a class 'show and tell' session for the children to share their posters with each other. Display their posters for all the children to see.

Final review of the Big Picture

Individually or with partners, have children reflect on what they have learned from this sequence and what they will remember to do in future writing.

Sequence 10
Adventure stories

Approximate duration: Two weeks

Big Picture

Through this teaching sequence, children explore the content and characters of the story, *The Crocodile Under the Bed*. By the end of the sequence, they will have written a new flying adventure story for the main child character from *The Crocodile Under the Bed*.

Phase 1: Enjoy and immerse

Children become familiar with the content, language and structure of the model text, *The Crocodile Under the Bed*.

Phase 2: Capture and organise

Children are supported in developing ideas for a new flying adventure story for the main child character from *The Crocodile Under the Bed*.

Phase 3: Collaborate and compose

Children undertake supported writing sessions to develop their own writing.

Phase 4: Write independently

Children write, edit and read aloud their own new flying adventure story.

Main source text

Treasure House Anthology Sequence 10 text. *The Crocodile Under the Bed*, Judith Kerr, ISBN 978-0-00-758675-2

Background knowledge

Judith Kerr, the award winning author of *The Crocodile Under the Bed*, is also well-known for her 'Mog' series and *The Tiger Who Came to Tea*.

In *The Crocodile Under the Bed*, a boy called Matty is upset because he is not well enough to go a party for the Queen's jubilee. However, while everyone is out, a crocodile from under his bed flies him to the King of the Jungle's party. Matty enjoys the party, goes on fun rides created by the animals before being flown home again by the crocodile that lives under his bed.

Spoken outcome

To read and perform their short story to others

Writing outcome

To write a short story about a child's flight on an imaginary creature to visit someone or something

Prior knowledge

Check children's knowledge and understanding of:

- crocodiles and their habitat
- street parties for Queen Elizabeth II's jubilees
- jungle and African animals
- staying at home when not well.

Diagnostic assessment options

Before starting the unit, you may wish to conduct an initial diagnostic assessment of the children's knowledge and understanding.

Ideas for initial diagnostic assessment options include:

- reviewing children's writing for the correct use of question marks at the end of sentences
- reviewing children's writing for words or clauses joined with 'and'
- reviewing children's writing to assess their ability to combine words correctly to make simple sentences
- spelling and sorting activities using words with the split vowel digraph, i-e, and words ending in 'nk'.

Cross-curricular links

S1 Art and design

- Use drawing, painting and sculpture to develop and share their ideas, experiences and imagination.

S1 Science - Animals, including humans

- Identify and name a variety of common animals including fish, amphibians, reptiles, birds and mammals.

Treasure House links

- Treasure House, Year 1, Vocabulary Unit 2: Adding endings to root words (-ing, -ed, -er, -est)
- Treasure House, Year 1, Spelling Unit 10: Adding -er to a root word
- Treasure House, Year 1, Spelling Unit 3: Spelling nk
- Treasure House, Year 1, Punctuation Unit 1: Punctuating sentences
- Treasure House, Year 1, Grammar Unit 1: Building sentences
- Treasure House, Year 1, Grammar Unit 2: Building sentences using 'and'

Resources

Props and percussion instruments for drama and storytelling activities (optional)

Source texts – see Anthologies; Matty's storyboard; Split vowel digraph, i-e'; Proofreading sheet / My writing checklist; Proofreading sheet / My writing checklist (blank)

Phase 1: Enjoy and immerse

In Phase 1, the children listen to the story, *The Crocodile Under the Bed*. Over several sessions, the children have opportunities to discuss the language and structure of the story through comprehension and discussion activities as well as exploring the story's content through drama, performance, writing and analysis of the text. Phase 1 also covers the vocabulary, grammar and punctuation focus on using exclamation marks for exclamation sentences and includes work on spelling words with the split vowel digraph, i-e.

Programmes of study: Year 1

Comprehension: Listen to and discuss a wide range of poems, stories and non-fiction at a level beyond that at which they can read independently.

Comprehension: Be encouraged to link what they read or hear read to their own experiences.

Comprehension: Make inferences on the basis of what is being said and done.

Comprehension: Recognise and join in with predictable phrases.

Vocabulary, grammar and punctuation: Use -ing, -ed, -er and -est where no change is needed in the spelling of root words.

Spelling: Spell words with the split digraph i-e.

Sparking interest

Explain to the children that you are going to read a story about a boy who was too sick to go a party that he really wanted to go to. Encourage the children to share their own experiences of when they had to miss out on something because they were sick. Ask: 'What did you do to pass the time when you were not well?'

Reading and discussion

Read and show the illustrations in *The Crocodile Under the Bed*. Lead a discussion to check their understanding of the story.

Discuss the following with the children.

- Why did Matty want to go to the party?
- Who was going to look after Matty? Do you think he was going to be any good?
- How did Matty help the crocodile fly?
- What was the crocodile like? (for example scary, friendly, kind)
- Who was the king?
- What things did Matty do at the king's birthday?
- Which ride did he seem to enjoy the most?
- Which ride would you have liked to go on? Why?
- How do you think Matty felt at the end of the story?

Drama and storytelling

Use a range of activities to reinforce children's understanding of the story and the characters. Select the activities that would fit in with your lesson timing. Encourage mixed-ability grouping for the chosen activities.

- **Freeze-framing events:** Have the children freeze-frame the different events of the story in sequence. Use thought-tracking, asking each child in the freeze-frame what they're thinking at that moment of the story.

- **A flying experience:** Have the children imagine that they are able to fly for the first time. Play music to inspire them. Use words to encourage different movements such as swooping and gliding.

- **Shared ride:** Put the children in pairs. Let them take turns to be the crocodile and Matty, with Matty following every flying movement behind the crocodile. Provide a narrative of a flying journey for the children to follow or let them create their own journey to the king's party.

Incidental writing

Short writing activities enhance the children's understanding of the story and help to inform the teaching focuses in the collaborative composition phase. Children could:

- devise and draw a diagram of an animal party ride
- design party invitations for the queen's or king's birthday
- design a birthday cake or party food for the king's party
- write a thank-you letter from Matty to the crocodile
- write instructions for making a party blower
- draw a story map.

Analysis

Display the Matty's storyboard. Use it to discuss and explore the structure and language of the story. With the children, record the start, middle and end of the story. Note how the middle part of the story showed Matty enjoying four things: the cake, and the three rides. Note and record the repeated phrases in the story, such as 'I want to go to a party!' 'Grandpa will see to it' and 'It was a very good … ride'. Encourage the children to say the repeated phrases for reinforcement.

Grammar: Adding -er to verbs

Show the children a party blower or show the illustration from *The Crocodile Under the Bed*. Ask: 'Why is it called a blower?' Demonstrate blowing it or describe how it can be blown to make a noise. Write the word 'blow' on the board and explain that it is a verb (a doing or being word). Write the word sum: 'blow + er = blower'. Underline the 'er'. Note how by adding -er the verb turns into a noun (a naming word). Provide one more word sum with the children's help, for example: 'fly + er = flyer'. Write a list of verbs that can have -er on the end. Ask the children to write word sums to make new nouns.

Use Year 1, Vocabulary Unit 2 and Year 1, Spelling Unit 10 for more work on adding -er to verbs.

Phonics and spelling

Remind the children that Matty went on a ride in the air with the crocodile. Write 'ride' on the board and say each segment of the word. Underline the 'i' and the 'e' and link them with a line. Explain how words with i-e have the long vowel /igh/ sound. Circle the 'd' and explain that 'i' and 'e' are split by a consonant letter which is the last sound of the word, in this case, /d/. Provide another example: 'slide'. Give out the resource sheet Split vowel digraph, i-e for children to add the missing split digraph to words and complete a sentence.

Review of the Big Picture

At the end of this phase, discuss with the children what they have learned so far about the story, *The Crocodile Under the Bed*. Remind them that this is all working towards writing their own new flying adventure story for Matty.

Phase 2: Capture and organise

During Phase 2, children start to develop ideas about the new content needed for their class story about another imaginary flight to another place. Working collaboratively, children decide on the words and phrases they could use for their stories. Phase 2 also includes work on spelling the /ŋ/ sound 'n' before 'k'.

Programmes of study: Year 1

Comprehension: Listen to and discuss a wide range of poems, stories and non-fiction at a level beyond that at which they can read independently.

Comprehension: Recognise and join in with predictable phrases.

Comprehension: Draw on what they already know or on background information and vocabulary provided by the teacher.

Comprehension: Participate in discussion about what is read to them, taking turns and listening to what others say.

Composition: Say out loud what they are going to write about.

Spelling: Spell the /ŋ/ sound 'n' before 'k'.

Introduction

Remind the children of the Big Picture. Reread *The Crocodile Under the Bed* and encourage children to join in on a repeat performance. Discuss the work that children have done to explore the story. Tell children they are going to work together to create a new flying adventure story.

Discussing ideas

As a class discuss and make decisions to create their new story. Record their ideas for Phase 3 and Phase 4.

Discuss the following with the children.

- What does Matty want to do or see? (for example, be in the school play, visit the seaside, go on a carnival float, visit the zoo, go to a wedding, go camping, go sledging)
- Why can't he go?
- What animal is going to take Matty flying?
- How will Matty help the animal fly?
- Where are they going?
- What three things does Matty do there?
- What happens when he gets home?

Drama and storytelling

Use a range of activities to reinforce children's understanding of the story. Select the activities that would fit with your lesson timing. Encourage mixed-ability grouping for the chosen activities.

- **Flying dreams:** Play gentle music for flying. Have the children close their eyes and imagine flying somewhere with their favourite animal to do their favourite thing or something they have always wanted to do. Let the children share their imaginings with the class.
- **Enacting the story:** Once the children have decided on the animal and destination, have them perform in groups or freeze-frame the sequence of the story from the start to the end. Encourage the use of repeated phrases, as used in the model story.

Incidental writing

Before you select any incidental writing, make sure the children are able to articulate orally the main events. Select activities that you think appropriate for the abilities and interests of your class. Children could:

- compile a word bank of verbs for flying such as 'swoop' and 'dive'
- write a rhyme or poem about flying
- write a diary entry by Matty about his new adventure
- draw a story map of the new adventure.

Organising the new story into a structure

Once the children have thoroughly explored their ideas for their class story, bring them together and make a final decision on the content. Record the information on Matty's adventure storyboard. Once recorded, go through the plans and ask the children if they are happy with their ideas.

Phonics and spelling

Remind the children that Matty was worried about who would give him a drink while his family were away. Write the word, 'drink' on the board. Underline 'nk' and note how the n before k stands for the /ŋ/ sound. Suggest exploring more words that end in 'nk'. Create a table with the column headings '-ank', '-ink', '-onk', '-unk' and encourage the children to help you add words to it, for example: 'bank', 'think', 'honk', 'sunk'. Once the table is completed, emphasise the spelling rule: the /ŋ/ sound is spelled 'n' after 'k'.

Use Year 1, Spelling Unit 3 for more on words with 'nk'.

Review of the Big Picture

At the end of this phase, discuss with the children what they have achieved with their planning and ideas for their new class story.

Phase 3: Collaborate and compose

Phase 3 has three writing lessons which support the children in the writing of their new class story. Each lesson starts with a vocabulary, grammar and punctuation focus with links to the main text. Children then participate in a composition session, applying the VGP focus in context. Independent writing, with plenaries, follows. Over the two lessons, the VGP focuses are on question marks in sentences, how words combine to make sentences and joining words and clauses using 'and'.

Programmes of study: Year 1

Composition: Say out loud what they are going to write about.

Composition: Compose a sentence orally before writing it.

Composition: Sequence sentences to form short narratives.

Composition: Discuss what they have written with the teacher or other pupils.

Vocabulary, grammar and punctuation: Begin to punctuate sentences using a capital letter and a full stop, question mark or exclamation mark.

Vocabulary, grammar and punctuation: Understand how words can combine to make sentences.

Vocabulary, grammar and punctuation: Join words and join clauses using 'and'.

Introduction

Remind the children about the sequence's Big Picture. Explain that over several lessons the children are going to work as a class to draft and write a new flying adventure for Matty. Use the planning, the story board and other recorded information from Phase 2 to remind the children of their letter ideas and content.

Lesson 1

Using question marks at the ends of sentences

Read *The Crocodile Under the Bed* from page 4, starting: 'I don't want to have a little party…'. Encouraging the children to join in with the repeated text, 'Grandpa will see to it.' Emphasize the questions as you say them. Discuss the difference in intonation for questions compared to other sentences. Ask: 'What do we put at the ends of sentences to show that they are questions?' In pairs, have the children come up with more 'What if...' questions Matty could ask. Write the questions out and get the children to add the question marks.

Use Year 1, Punctuation Unit 1 for more sentence punctuation work.

Shared writing

Model writing first part of the class story using the story board from Phase 2 as a guide. Model the oral composition of the sentences before writing. Use the repeated questions and answers used in the model text with emphasis on the question marks. Once written, collaboratively check it makes sense and that the sentence punctuation and spelling is correct.

Independent writing

The children can now write their own version of the start of the class story focusing on using question marks correctly. Make sure that the class plans are available for them to see. Some children may benefit from guided group or peer-paired writing at this stage.

Plenary

Throughout the writing session, ask the children questions to help them focus on their progress and what they have created during that lesson, for example: 'Have you said why Matty can't go out?' 'What questions have you included and have you punctuated them correctly?' 'Have you included how Matty helps the animal fly?' 'Which sentences could you improve?' Encourage them to check that their sentences make sense.

Lesson 2

Combining words to make sentences

Write the sentence, 'It was a very good birthday cake.' onto cards and display them in the wrong order. Ask the children to help you reorder the words so that they make sense. If needed, point out the clues in the punctuation to help them. Move the words around until the sentence makes sense. Emphasise the need to read out their sentences to check that they make sense too. Try a few more mixed up sentences for reinforcement either in groups or as a class.

Use Year 1, Grammar Unit 1 for more work on combining words to make sentences.

Shared writing

Model writing the middle part of the class story using the story board from Phase 2 as a guide. Model the oral composition of the sentences before writing. Encourage the children to help you write descriptive sentences and sentences that repeat. Once written, collaboratively check that it makes sense and that sentence punctuation and spelling is correct.

Independent writing

The children can now write their own version of the middle of the class story paying attention to how words combine to make sentences. Make sure that the class plans are available for them to see. Some children may benefit from guided group or peer-paired writing at this stage.

Plenary

Throughout the writing session, ask the children questions to help them focus on their progress and what they have created during that lesson, for example: 'What three things does Matty do?' 'What sentences have you repeated?' 'How have you used them?' 'What names have you given your characters?' Encourage children to check that their sentences make sense, are correctly punctuated and are in an order that makes sense.

Lesson 3

Joining words and joining clauses using 'and'

Write on the board: 'Matty's mummy came home. Matty's daddy came home.' Read out the two sentences. Remind children of previous work they have done joining sentences using 'and'. Ask: 'What would these two sentences sound like as one sentence?' ('Matty's mummy and daddy came

home.') Guide the children as they make suggestions for the sentence. Discuss why the correct answer works well.

Write two more sentences on the board, for example: 'I went on the slide. I went on the swing.' Have the children work in pairs, to join the two sentences using 'and' and write the sentence on their whiteboards or on paper. Let them share their sentences with others.

Use Year 1, Grammar Unit 2 for more on joining words and clauses using 'and'.

Shared writing

Model writing the final part of the class story using the story board from Phase 2 as a guide. Model the oral composition of the sentences before writing. Encourage the children to help you join simple sentences and words using 'and'. Once written, collaboratively check that it makes sense and that the sentence punctuation spelling is correct.

Independent writing

The children can now write their own version of the final part of the class story focusing on joining sentences and words with 'and'. Make sure that the class plans are available for them to see. Some children may benefit from guided group or peer-paired writing at this stage.

Plenary

Throughout the writing session, ask the children questions to help them focus on their progress and what they have created during that lesson, for example: 'Have you described how Matty got home?' 'How does your story end?' 'How have you given your story a good ending?' 'Where have you used 'and' to join sentences?' Encourage children to check that their sentences make sense.

Presenting and performing

Once the children have written their stories let them read out and share them within a group or as a pair. Encourage the children to offer feedback on what they particularly liked about the verses they have heard. Have children perform their class story using props and music.

Review of the Big Picture

Once you have completed all the lessons for this section, remind the children of the sequence's Big Picture. Discuss what they have learned so far.

Phase 4: Write independently

This final phase brings all the children's learning and writing skills together so that they can write their own version of the story. Through their writing, they will be able to utilise the different VGP focuses that they have been practising throughout previous phases.

Programmes of study: Year 1

Composition: Say out loud what they are going to write about.

Composition: Compose a sentence orally before writing it.

Composition: Sequence sentences to form short narratives.

Composition: Re-read what they have written to check that it makes sense.

Composition: Discuss what they have written with the teacher or other pupils.

Composition: Read aloud their writing clearly enough to be heard by their peers and the teacher.

Introduction

Introduce the phase by discussing what the children have learned in their planning and writing sessions and link it to the Big Picture. Emphasise the excitement of bringing all their learning together to write their own new flying adventure story,

Use the planning from Phase 2 to review the children's suggestions for the problems Matty could have at the start of the story, the new flying animal and their destination. Clarify that the planning and writing of their stories will take place over several sessions.

Writing

Give each child a copy of the Matty's adventure storyboard. As they plan, draft and write their stories encourage the children to compose their words and phrases orally before writing them down.

All the children should be encouraged to try to write independently to the best of their abilities. Ask open questions such as: 'Why is Matty sad?' 'Which animal will take him flying?' 'Where are they going?' 'What three things will Matty do there?' 'How will he feel about them?' 'What happens when he gets home?' 'Is he sad or happy at the end of the story?' 'Do the sentences make sense?' Make sure that the children have a chance to share their writing with others at appropriate points during each session.

Proofreading and redrafting

Encourage the children to read through their work at the end of each writing session with a partner. Ask them to check that their writing makes sense. Proofreading and improvement without support means that the writing will

happen over a few lessons. Offer the children the Proofreading sheet / My writing checklist, or create your own checklist with the assistance of the blank Proofreading sheet / My writing checklist.

Self- and peer-assessment

Encourage the children to take time to assess their own and others' writing. Make sure that they read out their writing clearly. Ask open questions to encourage self- and peer-assessment such as: 'How have I written a good start to my story?' 'How have I made it clear why Matty is sad?' 'What repeating sentences have I used from the book?' 'How have I shown what Matty does with the flying animal?' 'How have I ended the story?' 'What makes my story fun to read?' 'How similar is my story to the story from the book?'

Also encourage children to check their work to see if they can improve it by joining words and joining clauses using 'and', and check that they punctuate questions with question marks.

Presenting and performing

Once the children have written their stories, encourage them to illustrate their work. Encourage them to read their stories with the class or in small groups. Support those children who may want to perform their story using props and music.

Final review of the Big Picture

Individually or with partners, have children reflect on what they have learned from this sequence and what they will remember to do in future writing.

Sequence 11
Magical characters

Approximate duration: Two weeks

Big Picture

Through this teaching sequence, children explore the story and characters of, *The Bog Baby*. By the end of the sequence, they will have written a description of a new magical creature.

Phase 1: Enjoy and Immerse

Children become familiar with the story and characters in *The Bog Baby*.

Phase 2: Capture and organise

Children are supported in developing ideas to create a description booklet on a new magical creature.

Phase 3: Collaborate and compose

Children undertake supported writing sessions to develop their own description booklets on the chosen magical creature.

Phase 4: Write independently

Children write, edit and read aloud their own descriptions of a new magical creature.

Main source text

Treasure House Anthology Sequence 11 text. *The Bog Baby*, Jeanne Willis, ISBN 978-0-14-150030-0

Background knowledge

In the story, *The Bog Baby*, the narrator recalls the time when she and her sister were young and they found a magical creature in a magic pond. They take it away from its natural habitat and look after it as a much loved secret pet. At first the bog baby is happy but after a while it becomes sad and ill. The girls' mother helps them to realise that to really love him, they have to let the bog baby return back to his magical pond where he would be happy.

The story provides examples of good character description: how the bog baby looks, moves and what it likes to eat. The story also has a prominent environmental message about preserving nature and caring for and respecting wildlife in its natural habitats.

Spoken outcome

To show and tell their descriptions of their magical creature.

Writing outcome

To write simple descriptions about a magical creature and put them into a booklet

Prior knowledge

Check children's knowledge and understanding of:

- magical or fantasy stories set in everyday situations
- magical or fantasy characters in everyday situations
- caring for and respecting other living things
- the needs of other living things.

Year 1, Sequence 11
Magical characters

Diagnostic assessment options

Before starting the unit, you may wish to conduct an initial diagnostic assessment of the children's knowledge and understanding.

Ideas for initial diagnostic assessment options include:

- reviewing children's writing for correct sentence punctuation, especially full stops
- speaking and listening activities where children identify changes to adjectives when 'un-', '-er' and '-est' are added to them
- reviewing children's writing to see if they are beginning to join some words or clauses with 'and'
- spelling and speaking activities to test children's recognition of words that end in '-y' and have the /ee/ sound.

Cross-curricular links

KS1 Art and design

- Use drawing, painting and sculpture to develop and share their ideas, experiences and imagination.

KS1 Science - Living things and their habitats

- Identify that most living things live in habitats to which they are suited and describe how different habitats provide for the basic needs of different kinds of animals and plants, and how they depend on each other.

Treasure House links

- Treasure House, Year 1, Vocabulary Unit 3: Adding the prefix un-
- Treasure House, Year 1, Spelling Unit 17: Adding the prefix un-
- Treasure House, Year 1, Spelling Unit 13: Spelling words ending in y
- Treasure House, Year 1, Spelling Unit 12: Adding -er and -est to adjectives
- Treasure House, Year 1, Vocabulary Unit 2: Adding endings to root words (-ing, -ed, -er, -est)
- Treasure House, Year 1, Grammar Unit 2: Building sentences using 'and'
- Treasure House, Year 1, Punctuation Unit 1: Punctuating sentences

Resources

Props and percussion instruments for drama and storytelling activities (optional); images of bogs; information and images of different habitats; booklets made from two folded A4 pieces of paper

Source texts – see Anthologies; Adjective word cards; Magical creature sentence starters; Proofreading sheet / My writing checklist; Proofreading sheet / My writing checklist (blank)

Phase 1: Enjoy and immerse

In Phase 1, the children listen to the story, *The Bog Baby*. Over several sessions, the children have opportunities to discuss the story and its characters through comprehension and discussion activities as well as exploring characters and the story's meaning through drama, storytelling, writing and analysis of the text. Phase 1 also covers the vocabulary, grammar and punctuation focus on how the prefix un- changes the meaning of adjectives and includes work on spelling words ending in the /ee/ sound spelled -y.

Programmes of study: Year 1

Comprehension: Listen to and discuss a wide range of poems, stories and non-fiction at a level beyond that at which they can read independently.

Comprehension: Be encouraged to link what they read or hear read to their own experiences.

Comprehension: Make inferences on the basis of what is being said and done.

Comprehension: Predict what might happen on the basis of what has been read so far.

Comprehension: Explain clearly their understanding of what is read to them.

Vocabulary, grammar and punctuation: Understand how the prefix un- changes the meaning of verbs and adjectives.

Spelling: Spell words ending -y.

Sparking interest

Show the children the front page of *The Bog Baby*. Read out the title and ask the children if they think the bog baby is a real or a magical creature. Discuss their reasoning. Ask children if they know what a 'bog' is (permanently wet, muddy ground). Let the children share their experiences of seeing a bog or walking on one and discuss where bogs are generally found.

Read and discuss

Read *The Bog Baby* to the class using appropriate intonation. Check children's understanding of any difficult or new words. Stop at different parts of the story to discuss or ask questions to check children's understanding of the content and characters.

Discuss the following with the children.

- Why did the two girls go into Bluebell Wood?
- Why did the girls blow on the bog baby's wings? Did the girls want to keep the bog baby a secret?
- Why did the bog baby become sick? (Discuss the diet, the wrong bits chosen for his home, a non-magical habitat, making him walk, the stress of others looking at or trying to attack him.)
- Why do you think the girls loved the bog baby so much? Do you think he loved them too?
- Why was returning the bog baby back to the pond a sign that the girls loved him?
- How do you think the bog baby felt when he was taken back to his home?
- Why is it important to care for and respect other living things and the places where they live?

Drama and storytelling

Use a range of activities to reinforce children's understanding of the main story and investigate the main characters. Select the activities that fit with your lesson timing. Encourage mixed-ability grouping for the chosen activities.

- **Storytelling:** Become a storyteller. The children should accompany your performance, either by using props for sound effects or by taking the roles of the characters.
- **Freeze-framing key moments:** Put the children into different scenes in the right story order. Use thought-tracking, ask each child in the freeze-frame what they are thinking at that particular moment.
- **Bog baby movements:** Use movement and drama to explore how the bog baby moves, talks and eats when he is in the pond. Do a similar exercise to show how he changes when he is captured and compare the two.
- **Bog baby thoughts:** Have the children work in groups of four. Ask them to imagine that they are the bog baby. One pair explains why they like living in the pond and why they wanted to go back. The other pair explain why they like living with the girls.

Incidental writing

Short writing activities enhance the children's understanding of the story and help to inform the teaching focuses in the collaborative composition phase. Children could:

- write thought bubbles of what the bog baby is thinking at different parts of the story
- write instructions for looking after a bog baby
- draw and label a picture of a bog baby
- write a diary entry by one of the girls recording a day she took the bog baby to school
- write a short explanation text on how we need to care for and respect other living creatures.

Analysis

Look at the story in more detail focusing on how the bog baby is described. Discuss how the story starts in a magical setting and then moves to a familiar, non-magical setting followed by a return to the magical habitat. Focus on the descriptions of how the bog baby looks, moves and eats and what he likes doing at the magic pond. Discuss how some of the describing words and phrases such as 'round and blue' or 'ears like a mouse' help the reader imagine what the bog baby was like and how he was feeling.

Grammar: The prefix un- for changing adjectives.

Copy and cut out the adjective word cards for each child or pair of children to use. Hold up and read out the 'happy' card. Remind children that the bog baby was happy at first but then became unhappy. Hold up the other 'happy' card. Model writing 'un-' at the front of the word. Explain how adding un- to a describing word changes it to mean the opposite of the original meaning. Let the children continue reading their cards and adding un- to one of the pairs. They can then use them for a card game of opposite pairs, a simple sentence writing activity or for a drama activity.

Use Year 1, Vocabulary Unit 3 and Year 1, Spelling Unit 17 for more work on the prefix un-.

Phonics and spelling

Before the session, prepare a large blue piece of paper shaped like a pond with lily pad shaped word cards that can be added to the pond. Write the word 'baby' on one of the lily pad cards. Read the word out loud with the children. Underline the 'y' and ask the children to say the sound /ee/. Note that the /ee/ at the end of the word is spelled with a 'y'. List more -y words used from the book, for example: 'squelchy', 'boggy', 'spiky', 'jelly', 'angry', 'misty'. Read the words through with the children and ask them what letter they need to spell the /ee/ sound. Add the words to the pond. The children could work in groups to create their own magic pond -y words.

Use Year 1, Spelling Unit 13 for more work on spelling words ending -y.

Review of the Big Picture

At the end of this phase, discuss with the children what they have learned so far about the story and the main characters. Remind them that this is all working towards writing a set of descriptions of their own magical creature and why they love it.

Phase 2: Capture and organise

During Phase 2, children develop ideas for new content needed to write a description of a new magical creature to be presented as a little booklet. Working collaboratively, children decide on what their new magical creature is, what it is like, where it lives and why they love it. Phase 2 also includes work on adding -er and -est to adjectives where no change is needed to the root word.

Programmes of study: Year 1

Comprehension: Be encouraged to link what they read or hear read to their own experiences.

Comprehension: Discuss word meanings, linking new meanings to those already known.

Comprehension: Draw on what they already know or on background information and vocabulary provided by the teacher.

Comprehension: Participate in discussion about what is read to them, taking turns and listening to what others say.

Composition: Say out loud what they are going to write about.

Spelling: Add -er and -est to adjectives where no change is needed to the root word.

Introduction

Remind the children of the Big Picture. Re-read *The Bog Baby* with the children. Discuss the work the children have done to explore the story and the text in Phase 1.

Introduce the idea that the children are going to work together to create and describe a new magical creature and write a little booklet about it.

Discussing ideas

As a class, discuss and make decisions to create their new story setting and events for their class story. Record their ideas for Phase 3 and Phase 4.

Discuss the following with the children.

- What habitat will the creature live in? (for example desert, woodland, rock pools on beaches, cliffs, a rubbish tip, a compost heap, a cave)
- What words shall we use to describe the creature's habitat?
- What does the creature look like?
- What is the creature called?
- How does the creature move?
- What does the creature like to eat?
- What is the creature's favourite thing to do?
- What personality does the creature have?
- Has the creature got any magical powers? If so, what?
- Does the creature make a noise? If so, what?
- Why do you like the creature?

Drama and storytelling

Use a range of activities to allow the children to explore suggestions about their new magical creature and its habitat. Select the activities that would fit in with your lesson timing. Encourage mixed-ability grouping for the chosen activities.

- **Magical creature movements:** Have the children use their bodies, facial expressions and voice to help them explore their new magical creature. As well as the creature outlined in the discussion session, encourage the children to develop their own ideas for a new magical creature to use later for their own writing.
- **Magical creature questions:** In groups, children discuss questions they would like to ask the magical creature. Put two groups together and let them take turns to answer the questions in role as the creature.
- **Circle time:** Put small groups of children into a circle and remind them how the little girls in the story loved the bog baby. Ask each one why they would love their magical creature.

Incidental writing

Before you select any incidental writing, make sure the children are able to orally articulate the description of their magical creature and its habitat. Select activities that you think appropriate for the abilities and interests of your class. Children could:

- draw a picture with labels of the magical creature's habitat
- compile a list made by the magic creature of why it likes living in its habitat

- draw pictures and write sentences describing where the magical creature sleeps
- compile lists of adjective and verbs that could be used to describe of appearance and movements of the magical creature.

Organising the description into a structure

Once the children have thoroughly explored their ideas for their class description of a magical creature, bring them together and use their final suggestions to model how to plan the order of what to write for each page of their booklet. Show a blank version of the booklet. Model writing the front page, for example, 'This is a/an …' and add a picture of the creature. Look at the following six pages and create a page plan to show which description sections could go on which page, for example, one of the following topics per page: where it lives, what it looks like, how it moves, what it eats, its favourite pastime, why the children love it.

Phonics and spelling

Show an image of a duck to the children. Write the word, 'small' and place it underneath the picture. Then show a picture of a frog. Ask: 'Is the frog smaller or bigger?' (smaller) Write the word sum under the frog: 'small + er = smaller'. Note how -er can be added to the end with no change to the root word. Show a picture of a tadpole. Ask: 'Which is the smallest in the group?' Under the tadpole, write the word sum: 'small + est = smallest.' Note how -est can be added to the end with no change to the root word. Give the children a set of root adjectives. Have them create three pictures for each adjective illustrating the root word, the -er word and the -est word. Let them write the words under the pictures.

Use Year 1, Spelling Unit 12 and Year 1, Vocabulary Unit 2 for more work adding -er and -est to the ends of adjectives.

Review of the Big Picture

At the end of this phase, discuss with the children what they have achieved with their planning and ideas for their magical creature description booklet.

Phase 3: Collaborate and compose

Phase 3 has two writing lessons which support the children in writing their class description booklets. Each lesson starts with a short vocabulary, grammar and punctuation focus with links to the main text. The children then participate in a shared composition session, applying the VGP focus in context. Independent writing, with plenaries, follows. The VGP focuses are on joining words and clauses using 'and' and using capital letters and full stops in the correct places.

Programmes of study: Year 1

Composition: Say out loud what they are going to write about.

Composition: Compose a sentence orally before writing it.

Composition: Sequence sentences to form short narratives.

Composition: Discuss what they have written with the teacher or other pupils.

Vocabulary, grammar and punctuation: Join words and join clauses using 'and'.

Vocabulary, grammar and punctuation: Begin to punctuate sentences using a capital letter and a full stop, question mark or exclamation mark.

Introduction

Remind the children of the sequence's Big Picture. Explain that over several lessons the children are going to work as a class to draft and write their descriptions of their new magical creature. Use planning from Phase 2 to remind the children of their ideas.

Lesson 1

Joining words and phrases using 'and'

Write on the board, 'He had boggly eyes. He had a spiky tail'. Ask: 'Which two words are the same in the two sentences?' ('he had') 'How can we write a sentence without using 'he had' twice?' Work with the children to create the sentence, 'He had boggly eyes and a spiky tail.' Underline the joining word 'and' and note the change in punctuation. Ask children to think of a short phrase each, describing a magical creature's body part, for example, 'a purple nose'. In pairs, children join their phrases to create a sentence, for example, 'She had curly whiskers and a purple nose.' Let them share their sentences with the class.

Use Year 1, Grammar Unit 2 for more work on joining words and phrases with 'and'.

Shared writing

Use the children's work, and their content page plan for the booklet from Phase 2, to model writing the first three pages of the booklet. Note that you are not writing the sentences straight into the booklet. Aim for two or three sentences per booklet page. Use the Magical creature sentence starters resource sheet as support for sentence writing. Suggest some phrases or clauses and ask the children to suggest how they could be joined to make one sentence. Once written, collaboratively check that the sentences make sense and that sentence punctuation and spelling is correct.

Independent writing

The children can now write their first three descriptions of the magical creature with attention to joining words or clauses with 'and'. Make sure children can see or have a copy of 'Magical creature sentence starters' available to them to support their sentence writing. Depending on ability, they could aim to write from one to three sentences per description. Some children may benefit from guided group or peer-paired writing at this stage.

Plenary

Throughout the writing session, ask the children questions to help them focus on their progress and what they have created during that lesson, for example: 'What words have you used to describe where the magical creature lives?' 'What words or phrases have you used to describe what the magical creature looks like?' 'What verbs have you used to show how it moves?' 'Which words, phrases and/or short sentences can be joined using 'and'?' 'How will you check that each sentence makes sense?'

Lesson 2

Using full stops in sentences

Read out a small part of the text, pausing briefly after each full stop. Ask: 'What tells us when a sentence comes to an end?' (a full stop) 'What do you think would happen if the full stops were not put in?' Read through the same text again without pausing. Give groups of children a selection of texts that they can read easily that use mainly full stops at the ends of sentences. Have them explore their use by taking turns to read the texts, firstly with the full stops and then as if the full stops were not there.

Shared writing

Use the description page planner from Phase 2 to model writing the last two descriptions of the magical creature and the final page on why the class loves it. Aim for two to three sentences for the descriptions and one sentence for the final page. Use the 'Magical creature sentence starters' as support for sentence writing. Miss out a few full stops as you write. Read the sentences back to check that the children notice the omission. Once written, collaboratively check that sentences make sense and that spelling and punctuation is correct.

Independent writing

The children can now write their last two descriptions of the magical creature and the final page on why they love it, paying attention to full stops at the ends of sentences. Make sure that they can see or have a copy of 'Magical creature sentence starters' available for them as support for their sentence writing. Depending on the ability of the children, they could aim to write one to three sentences per description. Some children may benefit from guided group or peer-paired writing at this stage.

Plenary

Throughout the writing session, ask the children questions to help them focus on their progress and what they have created during that lesson, for example: 'What does the magic creature eat and how does it eat it?' 'What pastime or hobby does it have?' 'How have you described it?' 'Why would you love the magic creature? How will you write this in a sentence?' 'How will check to see if you have used a full stop at the end of sentences?'

Creating and sharing

Once the children have written their descriptions and they are happy with their work, encourage them to use their best handwriting skills to write their descriptions in the booklets along with illustrations. Have them copy the front page created in Phase 2: 'This is a …'. Encourage the children to share their work with each other.

Review of the Big Picture

Once you have completed all the lessons for this section, remind the children of the sequence's Big Picture. Discuss what they have learned so far.

Phase 4: Write independently

This final phase brings all the children's learning and writing skills together so that they can write their own booklet, containing the description of their own magical creature, independently. Through their writing, they will be able to utilise the different VGP focuses that they have been practising throughout previous phases.

Programmes of study: Year 1

Composition: Say out loud what they are going to write about.

Composition: Compose a sentence orally before writing it.

Composition: Sequence sentences to form short narratives.

Composition: Re-read what they have written to check that it makes sense.

Composition: Discuss what they have written with the teacher or other pupils.

Composition: Read aloud their writing clearly enough to be heard by their peers and the teacher.

Introduction

Introduce the phase by discussing what the children have learned in their planning and writing sessions and link it to the Big Picture. Emphasise the excitement of bringing all their learning together to write descriptions of their own magical creature and explaining why they would love it.

Use the work from Phase 2 to review the children's different ideas for magical creatures. Clarify that the planning and writing of a booklet that contains the descriptions of the magical creature will take place over several sessions.

Writing

Give each child a blank booklet, paper and Magical creature sentence starters. As they plan, draft and write each description section, encourage the children to compose their sentences orally before writing them down.

All the children should be encouraged to try to write independently to the best of their abilities. Ask open questions such as: 'What have you called your creature and why?' 'Why have you chosen that habitat for your magical creature?' 'What describing words have you used to describe how it looks?' 'What verbs have you used to describe how it moves?' 'How have you described its home?' 'How have you described its favourite hobby or pastime?' 'What does your creature eat?' 'Why would you love it?'

Make sure that the children have a chance to share their writing with others at appropriate points during each session.

Proofreading and redrafting

Encourage the children to read through their work at the end of each writing session with a partner. Ask them to check whether their writing makes sense. Proofreading and improvement without support means that the writing will happen over a few lessons. Offer the children the Proofreading sheet / My writing checklist, or create your own checklist with the assistance of the blank Proofreading sheet / My writing checklist.

Self- and peer-assessment

Encourage the children to take time to assess their own and others' writing. Make sure that they read out their writing clearly. Ask open questions to encourage self and peer-assessment such as: 'Does the magical creature's name give us some idea of where it lives?' 'What words have I used to describe where it lives?' 'What words have I used to describe what it looks like?' 'What words have I used to describe how it moves?' 'How have I described what it likes to do?' 'Why would I love it?' 'How have I checked that the sentences make sense and that the spellings are correct?'

Also encourage them to check their VGP focuses on using sentence punctuation correctly (especially full stops) and joining words and clauses with 'and' to check that they have been successfully applied throughout the texts.

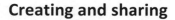

Creating and sharing

Once the children have written their descriptions, have a session where they can write them up in their booklets with illustrations for each page. Once completed, let the children swap their booklets to read, share and enjoy. Have a class feedback, about the different creatures and why they are loved. Discuss why it would be important not to take them away from their special habitat and the need to respect them.

Final review of the Big Picture

Individually or with partners, have children reflect on what they have learned from this sequence and what they will remember to do in future writing.

Sequence 12
Imaginary worlds

Approximate duration: Two weeks

Big Picture

Through this teaching sequence, children explore the story, structure and characters in, *Lollipop and Grandpa's Garden Safari*. By the end of the sequence, they will have written a new version of the imaginary safari story in a different setting.

Phase 1: Enjoy and immerse

Children become familiar with the story, structure and characters in the model text, *Lollipop and Grandpa's Garden Safari*.

Phase 2: Capture and organise

Children are supported in developing ideas for a new class version of *Lollipop and Grandpa's Garden Safari* within a different setting.

Phase 3: Collaborate and compose

Children undertake supported writing sessions to develop their own narrative writing of the class story.

Phase 4: Write independently

Children write, edit and read aloud their own version of the tale.

Main source text

Treasure House Anthology Sequence 12 text. *Lollipop and Grandpa's Garden Safari*, Penelope Harper, ISBN 978-1-90-791209-2

Background knowledge

Lollipop and Grandpa's Garden Safari is a perfect example of an imaginary adventure seen through the eyes of a child within an everyday setting. During Year 1, children can have very vivid imaginations and enjoy role-play and imaginary journeys and adventures. The story also shows how everyday things can turn into imaginary things or creatures.

In the storyline, the two main characters go on an imaginary safari around the garden, encountering imaginary African animals formed from everyday garden objects. The story has a rhythm and pattern in its repeated text and actions.

Spoken outcome

To perform their imaginary safari story to an audience

Writing outcome

To write a version of *Lollipop and Grandpa's Back Garden Safari* in a different setting

Prior knowledge

Check children's knowledge and understanding of:

- imaginary stories set in everyday situations
- safaris and the animals that can be seen on them
- nature trails or garden trails and what can be seen on them.

Diagnostic assessment options

Before starting the unit, you may wish to conduct an initial diagnostic assessment of the children's knowledge and understanding.

Ideas for initial diagnostic assessment options include:

- reviewing children's writing for correct sentence punctuation
- speaking and listening activities where children identify exclamations
- reviewing children's writing to check that they have correctly added -ing to verbs
- reviewing children's writing to check for correct sequencing of simple narratives
- spelling and speaking activities to test children on their ability to recognise words containing 'tch' with the /ch/ sound and compound words.

Cross-curricular links

KS1 Art and design

- Use drawing, painting and sculpture to develop and share their ideas, experiences and imagination.

KS1 Geography - Human and physical geography

- Refer to key physical features, including: beach, cliff, coast, forest, hill, mountain, sea, ocean, river, soil, valley, vegetation, season and weather.

Treasure House links

- Treasure House, Year 1, Punctuation Unit 1: Punctuating sentences
- Treasure House, Year 1, Spelling Unit 18: Spelling compound words
- Treasure House, Year 1, Spelling Unit 5: Spelling the /ch/ sound tch
- Treasure House, Year 1, Vocabulary Unit 2: Adding endings to root words (-ing, -ed, -er, -est)
- Treasure House, Year 1, Spelling Unit 9: Adding -ing to a root word

Resources

Props and percussion instruments for drama and storytelling activities (optional); a rucksack, a fictional or real map; binoculars; paper and writing materials for creating story maps

Source texts – see Anthologies; Safari writing frame; Safari sentences; Proofreading sheet / My writing checklist; Proofreading sheet / My writing checklist (blank)

Phase 1: Enjoy and immerse

In Phase 1, the children listen to the story, *Lollipop and Grandpa's Back Garden Safari*. Over several sessions, the children have opportunities to discuss the story and its characters through comprehension and discussion activities as well as exploring characters and story structure through drama, storytelling, writing and analysis of the text. Phase 1 also covers the vocabulary, grammar and punctuation focus on using exclamation marks in sentences and includes work on compound words.

Programmes of study: Year 1

Comprehension: Listen to and discuss a wide range of poems, stories and non-fiction at a level beyond that at which they can read independently.

Comprehension: Be encouraged to link what they read or hear read to their own experiences.

Comprehension: Discuss word meanings, linking new meanings to those already known.

Comprehension: Discuss the significance of the title and events.

Vocabulary, grammar and punctuation: Begin to punctuate sentences using a capital letter and a full stop, question mark or exclamation mark.

Spelling: Spell compound words.

Sparking interest

Show children a rucksack, a pair of binoculars and a map. Ask the children what they think you are planning to do. Explain that these belong to a girl called Lollipop and her Grandpa who are going on safari. Discuss what a safari is and what animals you may see on one. Explain that they are going on a make-believe safari in their garden. Encourage the children to share their own experiences of going on make-believe or imaginary adventures.

Reading and discussion

Read *Lollipop and Grandpa's Back Garden Safari* to the class using intonation where appropriate. Encourage the children to join in with the repetitions. Check the children understand the vocabulary. Stop at different parts of the story to discuss or ask questions to check children's understanding of the content and characters.

Discuss the following with the children.

- Why do you think Lollipop and Grandpa may need binoculars and a map for their back garden safari?
- What do you think they will see in the back garden?
- What is a 'Croco-logus'? (part log and part crocodile)
- What could the Croco-logus do to Lollipop?
- Why do Lollipop and Grandpa tiptoe past the object-creatures? (so as not to disturb them)
- Why would a Hippo-Potta-Compost be able to squish Lollipop flat? (it is very heavy)

- What animals are the chimpan-trees supposed to be like?
- Why do Grandpa and Lollipop run back to the house?
- What four action words are used when Grandpa and Lollipop race back? ('run', 'leap', 'dodge', 'spring')
- What do you think happens at the end of the story?

Drama and storytelling

Use a range of activities to reinforce children's understanding of the main story and investigate the main characters. Select the activities that fit in with your lesson timing. Encourage mixed-ability grouping for the chosen activities.

- **Storytelling:** Become a storyteller. The children could accompany your performance, either by using props for sound effects or by taking the roles of the characters.
- **Going on safari:** Ask the children to imagine they were also on the garden safari. Adapt the story and ask them to act it out as you narrate the journey through the garden and back. Let them join in with 'Sssh!' and 'Phew!'
- **Freeze-framing key moments:** Arrange the children into different scenes in the right story order. Use thought-tracking, asking each child in the freeze-frame what they are thinking at that particular moment.

- **Safari garden animals:** Use movement and drama to explore the different imaginary creatures in the book. Have them slowly change from the garden object into the African animal. Have them explore how they would use their bodies and voices to be both those things at the same time.

Incidental writing

Short writing activities enhance the children's understanding of the story and help to inform the teaching focuses in the collaborative composition phase. Children could:

- draw a map of the back garden safari
- write a diary or letter from Lollipop describing her adventure
- draw four labelled pictures of the safari creatures and write 'Look out, Lollipop!' with each one.

Analysis

Look at the story in more detail. Use the story map to record the different parts of the story. Note how the story starts with the characters getting ready, followed by their journey around the garden meeting the four different creatures. Encourage the children to discuss how the characters run back past the creatures into the house. Discuss the surprising end. Encourage the children to help you highlight the text for the repeated phrases and let them say the phrases again.

Grammar: Exclamation marks for the end of sentences

Write 'Look out, Lollipop' with a full stop and also with an exclamation mark. Say both the phrases using appropriate intonation for the statement and for the exclamation. Ask children which punctuation mark helps us know that the words should be exclaimed. Add the exclamation to the end of one of the sentences. Have the children work in pairs to think of other ways they could warn Lollipop, for example, 'Be careful, Lollipop!' Once the children have thought of an exclamation sentence, let them share it with the class. Write them on the board, and get all the children to draw the exclamation mark in the air as you add it on. Record their suggestions for Phase 2.

Use Year 1, Punctuation Unit 1 for more on exclamation marks.

Phonics and spelling

Write the word 'tiptoe' on the board. Ask: 'What does this word mean?' Let the children show you how to walk on 'tiptoe'. Write the two words 'tip' and 'toe' and explain that the word 'tiptoe' is made of two nouns. Tell children that when two words are joined together to make one word they are called compound words. Use the model text to look at the names of the creatures. Discuss how the author has made their names up using part of the object and part of the animal, for example, 'clothes-lion'. Have object word cards in one bag and animal word cards in another. Let the children take one from each and encourage them to create and write down a new fun compound words that describe creatures made of both items. Have them share their new words and keep them for Phase 2.

Use Year 1, Spelling Unit 18 for more work on compound words.

Review of the Big Picture

At the end of this phase, discuss with the children what they have learned so far about the story and the two main characters. Remind them that this is all working towards writing their own version of the story.

Phase 2: Capture and organise

During Phase 2, children start to develop ideas about content needed to create a new class version of *Lollipop and Grandpa's back Garden Safari*. Working collaboratively, children decide on where the new safari will be and what new creatures Lollipop and Grandpa will meet there. The chorus, 'Crumbs! We had better tiptoe past then. Sssh! Phew!' will be used again in the new story. Phase 2 also includes work on the /ch/ sound 'tch' when it comes after a single vowel letter.

Programmes of study: Year 1

Comprehension: Recognise and join in with predictable phrases.

Comprehension: Draw on what they already know or on background information and vocabulary provided by the teacher.

Comprehension: Make inferences on the basis of what is being said and done.

Comprehension: Participate in discussion about what is read to them, taking turns and listening to what others say.

Composition: Say out loud what they are going to write about.

Spelling: Spell the /tʃ/ sound 'tch' after a single vowel letter.

Introduction

Remind the children of the Big Picture and re-read *Lollipop and Grandpa's Back Garden Safari*. Discuss the work the children have done to explore the story and the text in Phase 1. Tell children they are going to work together to create a new version of the story where Lollipop and Grandpa will go somewhere else for a different safari and meet three new creatures.

Discussing ideas

As a class, discuss and make decisions to create their new story setting and events for their class story. Have their exclamation sentences and compound word animals from Phase 1 as well as the safari story map available to them. Record their ideas Phase 3 and Phase 4.

Discuss the following with the children.

- Where could Lollipop and Grandpa go for their new safari? (for example, a park, a school, a farm, a beach, a shopping centre, a castle)
- What three animals could they imagine seeing?
- What three objects could be the animals?
- Why does Lollipop need to be careful of each object-animal creature?
- Which of the object creatures will make Lollipop and Grandpa run home? Why?
- What type of ending shall we have? Will we have a surprise ending with one more creature?

Drama and storytelling

Use the drama and storytelling activities to allow the children to explore suggestions for their new story. Select the activities that fit in with your lesson timing. Encourage mixed-ability grouping for the chosen activities.

- **Safari object-creatures:** Have the children use their bodies, facial expressions and voices to create an object-creature. Ask: 'What would happen to Lollipop if she came too close?' They can use their own ideas or you could give them the cards used in the spelling focus in Phase 1.
- **Look out!** Ask the children to be an object-creature and to think of what they could do to an explorer. In a big space, have them stand as still as statues. Choose a child to be an explorer. Let them choose a child who turns into their creature and says 'Look out! You'll be in trouble if I...' The child playing the object-creature then has a turn as an explorer and the first child sits down.
- **Surprise endings:** Remind the children of the surprise ending. Put the children into threes and let them work together to act out their ending for the class story. Have them perform it to the other groups. Highlight that the end could just be one word, for example, 'tea!' or 'roar!'

Incidental writing

Before you select any incidental writing, make sure the children are able to orally articulate the main events. Select activities that you think appropriate for the abilities and interests of your class. Children could:

- draw and label a map of the new safari trail
- make a list of items to be taken on the safari
- draw and label pictures of the creatures including simple descriptive words and phrases, for example 'huge feet'
- make a 'Caution! Escaped creature!' poster for one of the creatures
- compile a list of running verbs that could be used for the run home at the end of the story.

Organising the new story into a structure

Once the children have thoroughly explored their ideas for their class story, bring them together and use their final suggestions to model how to plot the new story, using a story map, in picture and note form. Record the start of the story, encountering three creatures, the run home and the ending. Explain that they will be adding in new endings for the repeated phrases, 'You'll be in trouble if...' and 'I will have to ...' and they will be using the chorus response from Lollipop. Once recorded, go through the map and ask the children if they are happy with the plans for their class story.

Phonics and spelling

This activity works better with groups instead of a whole class activity. Use a long handled net. Write the word 'catch' on a word card. Ask the children to read it and then say each segment out loud with you. Underline 'tch' and circle the vowel before it 'a'. Explain that the letters 'tch' spell the /ch/ sound if they come after a short vowel like /a/. Add the word into the net. Create a trail 'tch' word cards around the classroom for the children to find. Once the words are collected, let children put them in the net, reinforcing the spelling rule with each card.

Use Year 1, Spelling Unit 5 for more work on words ending 'tch'.

Review of the Big Picture

At the end of this phase, discuss with the children what they have achieved with their planning and ideas for their new class story.

Phase 3: Collaborate and compose

Phase 3 has two writing lessons which support the children in the writing of their class version of *Lollipop and Grandpa's Back Garden Safari*. Each lesson starts with a short vocabulary, grammar and punctuation focus with links to the main text. The teacher then models writing in a shared composition session, applying the VGP focus in context. Independent writing, with plenaries, follows. The VGP focuses are on adding -ing to verb root words and sequencing sentences into a narrative.

Programmes of study: Year 1

Composition: Say out loud what they are going to write about.

Composition: Compose a sentence orally before writing it.

Composition: Re-read what they have written to check that it makes sense.

Composition: Discuss what they have written with the teacher or other pupils.

Vocabulary, grammar and punctuation: Use suffixes that can be added to verbs where no change is needed in the spelling of root words.

Vocabulary, grammar and punctuation: Sequence sentences to form short narratives.

Introduction

Remind the children about the sequence's Big Picture. Explain that over several lessons the children are going to work as a class to draft and write their new version of *Lollipop and Grandpa's Back Garden Safari*. Use the story map and other recorded plans from Phase 2 to remind the children of their ideas and final choice of the new safari setting and creatures.

Lesson 1

Adding -ing to verbs

Show *Lollipop and Grandpa's Back Garden Safari*. Highlight verbs ending -ing: 'whooping', 'howling', 'shrieking', 'swooping', 'leaping'. Underline the -ing. Discuss how these words describe movement and sound. Focus on one or more of the object-creatures in their class story and encourage children to create verb root words to show movement and sound. Work with the group to add -ing to the verbs or have the children individually copy the verbs out and add -ing to them. Keep the examples for use in the shared writing section.

Use digital Year 1, Vocabulary Unit 2 and Year 1, Spelling Unit 9 for more on the suffix -ing.

Shared writing

With the children, using their class story map from Phase 2, model writing the opening of the story and meeting three creatures, in the Safari adventure writing frame. Note the repeated phrases that are already in the frame. Model the oral composition of sentences before writing. Use the Safari writing frame to help with the story structure. Encourage the children to add -ing onto verbs. Once written, collaboratively check that sentences make sense and that sentence punctuation and spellings are correct.

Independent writing

The children can now write their own first part of the class story with attention to adding -ing to verb root words where appropriate. Make sure that the class safari story map is available for them to see. Give each child a Safari adventure writing frame to help with vocabulary, structure and phrasing. Some children may benefit from guided group or peer-paired writing at this stage.

Plenary

Throughout the writing session, ask the children questions to help them focus on their progress and what they have created during that lesson, for example: 'What have you written in the first sentence to show where the safari is?' 'What have you written for each repeating sentence to say why Lollipop has to be careful?' 'Which ends of words or sentences do you need to add an exclamation mark to?' 'Which -ing verbs have you used to show movement or sound?' 'How have you checked that each sentence makes sense?'

Lesson 2

Sequencing sentences into a narrative

Write out the following sentences on cards and show them in the wrong order: 'Look out, Lollipop!' 'The Snake-pipe will wrap himself around you.' 'Then he will squeeze you very tight.' Read the sentences with the children. Ask: 'What do we need to do for the sentences to make sense?' Have the children guide you into putting them in the right sequence. Give pairs of children the Safari sentences resource sheet to cut up sentences and stick them into the correct order.

Shared writing

Use the story map from Phase 2 to model writing the run home and the ending part of the story into the Safari adventure writing frame. Model the oral composition of the simple sentences before writing. Say and write a few sentences out of sequence. Encourage the children to help you put them in the correct logical sequence. Once written, collaboratively check the sentences make sense, and that sentence punctuation and spellings are correct.

Independent writing

The children can now write their own final part of the class story with attention to making sure their sentences are in the correct sequence. Make sure the class safari story map is available for them to see. Give each child a Safari adventure writing frame to help with vocabulary, structure and phrasing. Some children may benefit from guided group or peer-paired writing at this stage.

Plenary

Throughout the writing session, ask the children questions to help them focus on their progress and what they have created during that lesson, for example: 'How have you described which object-creature, Lollipop and Grandpa are running past?' 'Which different 'run' verbs have you used to show how Lollipop and Grandpa move?' 'What ending have you given the story?' 'What -ing words have you used?' 'How have you checked that each sentence makes sense and is in the correct order?'

Presenting and performing

Once the children have written their story, encourage them to retell it either as storytellers or by creating a performance. Take feedback on what they particularly liked about the stories they have heard.

Review of the Big Picture

Once you have completed all the lessons for this section, remind the children of the sequence's Big Picture. Discuss what they have learned so far.

Phase 4: Write independently

This final phase brings all the children's learning and writing skills together so that they can write their own version of a new Lollipop and Grandpa safari adventure independently. Through their writing, they will be able to utilise the different VGP focuses that they have been practising throughout previous phases.

Programmes of study: Year 1

Composition: Say out loud what they are going to write about.

Composition: Compose a sentence orally before writing it.

Composition: Sequence sentences to form short narratives.

Composition: Re-read what they have written to check that it makes sense.

Composition: Discuss what they have written with the teacher or other pupils.

Composition: Read aloud their writing clearly enough to be heard by their peers and the teacher.

Introduction

Introduce the phase by discussing what the children have learned in their planning and writing sessions and link it to the Big Picture. Emphasise the excitement of bringing all their learning together to write their own new Lollipop and Grandpa Safari adventure.

Review the children's different suggestions for the new safari setting and the three new object-creatures from Phase 2. Clarify that the planning and writing of their own story will take place over several sessions.

Writing

Give each child paper to create their own story map and a Safari adventure writing frame. As they plan, draft and write each section of the story, encourage the children to compose their sentences orally before writing them down. Possibly, have children draw a picture to illustrate each section.

All the children should be encouraged to try to write independently to the best of their abilities. Ask open questions such as 'Why have you chosen your safari setting?' 'Which object-creatures have you created for the safari?' 'How could they be of danger to Lollipop?' 'Why would Grandpa have to take Lollipop home? Is she attacked?' 'What sound word have you used to make Lollipop run back?' 'Which verb words have you used for the race home?' 'How have you ended your story?' 'What do you like about your story?'

Make sure that the children have a chance to share their writing with others at appropriate points during each session.

Proofreading and redrafting

Encourage the children to read through their work at the end of each writing session with a partner. Ask them to check whether their writing makes sense. Proofreading and improvement without support means that the writing will happen over a few lessons. Offer the children the Proofreading sheet / My writing checklist, or create your own checklist with the assistance of the blank Proofreading sheet / My writing checklist.

Self- and peer-assessment

Encourage the children to take time to assess their own and others' writing. Make sure that they read out their writing clearly. Ask open questions to encourage self- and peer-assessment such as: 'How similar or different is this story to the original?' 'How does the opening of the story tell us where the safari is set?' 'What words have I combined to make names for the object-creatures?' 'What could each creature do to Lollipop?' 'Why does Grandpa need to send her home?' 'What 'run' verbs have I used to describe the run back?' 'How have I ended the story?' 'How have I checked that the sentences make sense and that the spellings are correct?'

Also encourage them to check their VGP focuses on using exclamation marks, sequencing sentences in the correct order and adding -ing to root verbs to see whether they have been successfully applied throughout the texts.

Presenting and performing

Once the children have written their stories encourage them to retell it either as storytellers or by creating a performance. Take feedback on what they particularly liked about the stories they have heard. Encourage the children to use intonation to highlight exclamations and voices of the different characters.

Final review of the Big Picture

Individually or with partners, have children reflect on what they have learned from this sequence and what they will remember to do in future writing.

Sequence 13
Fairy tales

Approximate duration: Two weeks

Big Picture

Through this teaching sequence, children explore the story, structure and characters of the fairy tale, 'The Frog Prince'. By the end of the sequence, they will have written a new version of the tale in the same setting with a new animal character, a new character from the castle and one new promise.

Phase 1: Enjoy and immerse

Children become familiar with the story, structure and characters in, 'The Frog Prince'.

Phase 2: Capture and organise

Children are supported in developing ideas for a new version of the tale of the 'Frog Prince'.

Phase 3: Collaborate and compose

Children undertake supported writing sessions to develop their own narrative of the class tale.

Phase 4: Writing independently

Children write, edit and read aloud their own version of the tale.

Main source text

Treasure House Anthology Sequence 13 text.
'The Frog Prince', *First Fairy Tales*, Margaret Mayo,
ISBN 978-1-84-362400-4

Background knowledge

'The Frog Prince' was originally an old German fairy tale recorded by the Brothers Grimm in their fairy tale collection in 1812. The story has many of the typical elements of the fairy tale genre: a setting long ago, magic, a prince and a princess, a badly behaved character who does the right thing in the end and is rewarded for it, a series of three characters, events, or things (the three promises), and a happy ending.

In other versions of the tale, the frog is an enchanted princess and the prince was the one who released her from the spell.

Spoken outcome

To read or perform their story version of the 'The Frog Prince'

Writing outcome

To write a different version of 'The Frog Prince' with new characters and new promises

Prior knowledge

Check children's knowledge and understanding of:

- fairy tales
- the typical characteristics of fairy tales, in particular, magical transformations, and enchanted animals
- the story of 'The Frog Prince' (including its other variations)
- how fairy tales have been passed down orally.

Year 1, Sequence 13
Fairy tales

Diagnostic assessment options

Before starting the unit, you may wish to conduct an initial diagnostic assessment of the children's knowledge and understanding.

Ideas for initial diagnostic assessment options include:

- reviewing children's writing for correct sentence punctuation
- speaking and listening activities where children identify exclamations
- reviewing children's writing to check that suffixes have been added to words correctly
- reviewing children's writing to check for use of joining simples sentences with 'and'
- spelling and speaking activities to test their recognition of words with the sounds, /k/, /l/, /s/, /f/, /z/.

Cross-curricular links

KS1 Art and design

- Use drawing, painting and sculpture to develop and share their ideas, experiences and imagination.

KS1 Science – Animals, including humans

- Identify and name a variety of common animals including fish, amphibians, reptiles, birds and mammals.

Treasure House links

- Treasure House, Year 1, Punctuation Unit 2: Capital letter for names and 'I'
- Treasure House, Year 1, Spelling Unit 1: Spelling ff, ll, ss and zz
- Treasure House, Year 1, Spelling Unit 16: Spelling words with k
- Treasure House, Year 1, Vocabulary Unit 2: Adding endings to root words (-ing, -ed, -er, -est)
- Treasure House, Year 1, Spelling Unit 9: Adding -ing to a root word
- Treasure House, Year 1, Spelling Unit 11: Adding -ed to a root word
- Treasure House, Year 1, Punctuation Unit 1: Punctuating sentences
- Treasure House, Year 1, Grammar Unit 2: Building sentences using 'and'

Resources

Props and percussion instruments for drama and storytelling activities (optional); images of frogs and castles; information on who lived in castles

Source texts – see Anthologies; Fairy-tale story map; Proofreading sheet / My writing checklist; Proofreading sheet / My writing checklist (blank)

Phase 1: Enjoy and immerse

In Phase 1, the children listen to the fairy tale, 'The Frog Prince'. Over several sessions, the children have opportunities to discuss the story and its characters through comprehension and discussion activities as well as exploring characters and story structure through drama, storytelling, writing and analysis of the text. Phase 1 also covers the vocabulary, grammar and punctuation focus on using capital letters for names and work on spelling the /k/ sound 'k'.

Programmes of study: Year 1

Comprehension: Become very familiar with key stories, fairy stories and traditional tales, retelling them and considering their particular characteristics.

Comprehension: Recognise and join in with predictable phrases.

Comprehension: Discuss the significance of the title and events.

Comprehension: Predict what might happen on the basis of what has been read so far.

Vocabulary, grammar and punctuation: Use a capital letter for names of people, places, the days of the week, and the personal pronoun 'I'.

Spelling: Use 'k' for the /k/ sound.

Sparking interest

Show the children a picture of a frog. Ask the children what they would do or say if they met the frog and it talked to them. Ask: 'What would you ask this frog, if it could understand you?' Explain that you are going to read them a fairy tale about a princess who meets a talking frog.

Reading and discussion

Read the story to the class and check children's understanding of the vocabulary. Stop at different parts of the story to discuss or ask questions to check children's understanding of the content and characters.

Discuss the following with the children.

- Why did the princess play in the garden on her own?
- What promise did she need to make to get her ball back? Do you think she was going to keep it?
- Why did the princess not like the frog?
- What did the frog want her to promise?
- What did the king and the frog say when the princess tried to get out of her promise? (remember your promise)
- Why is it important to keep promises?
- Why was the princess upset?
- Who was the frog?
- What lesson do you think the princess learned from the frog prince?

Drama and storytelling

Use a range of activities to reinforce children's understanding of the main story and investigate the main characters. Select the activities that fit with your lesson timing. Encourage mixed-ability grouping for the chosen activities.

- **Class Performance:** Organise a drama performance of the story with children taking on different roles and making props, musical instruments and costumes.
- **Freeze-framing key moments:** Put the children into different scenes in the right story order. Use thought-tracking, asking each child in the freeze-frame what they are thinking at that particular moment.
- **Transformations:** Have a movement class where the children use their bodies and faces to gradually change from being a human into a frog. Have them move and hop around as a frog. Let them slowly change back again.
- **Hot-seating:** Put children into groups of four. Let one pair role-play the princess and a servant who explain why they don't like frogs. The other pair role-play the king and a gardener who explain why they like frogs.
- **Promises:** Have a circle game where the children can choose a fairy tale or fantasy character and make one promise relating to their story, for example, Goldilocks: 'I promise not to eat porridge without asking first.'

Incidental writing

Short writing activities enhance the children's understanding of the story and help to inform the teaching focuses in the collaborative composition phase. Children could:

- write a tea or supper menu for the frog
- design the prince and princess' wedding invitation with a frog theme
- research information about frogs
- write a letter of apology from the princess to the frog.

Analysis

Look at the story in more detail. Note the typical fairy tale opening, 'There was once a …' Discuss other starting sentences such as, 'Once upon a time …'. Show the Fairy-tale story map to the children. With the children, record the beginning, middle and the end of the story. Note the recurring phrases, 'Remember your promise' and 'Ugh!' Discuss the typical fairy tale final phrase, '… lived happily ever after!'

Grammar: Using capital letters for names

Remind the children that capital letters are used for the first letters of names, place names and days of the week. Highlight that the king in 'The Frog Prince' named the frog, 'Mr Croaky Water-splasher'. Write the name on the board and underline the capital letters. Note that Mr and Mrs also start with a capital letter. Discuss why the king used that name for the frog. Suggest that the children come up with more fun names for other animals that describe how they look or act. Let them work in pairs to draw the animal and write the name underneath. Check that they use capital letters in the right place.

Use Year 1, Punctuation Unit 2 for more on capital letters for names.

Phonics and spelling

Ask the children to help you spell the word, 'king'. Write the word out as they say each segment of the word. Underline the 'k' and emphasize the /k/ sound. Explain that the /k/ sound is spelled 'k' if it comes before the letters 'e', 'i' or 'y'. Create a table on the board with the column headings 'ke', 'ki' and 'ky'. Have the children suggest words that follow the spelling rule and write them in the correct columns of the table, for example, 'kiss', 'keep', 'frisky'.

Use Year 1, Spelling Unit 16 for more work on spelling words with k.

Review of the Big Picture

At the end of this phase, discuss with the children what they have learned so far about the tale and the main characters. Remind them that this is all working towards writing their own stories.

Phase 2: Capture and organise

During Phase 2, children develop ideas for content to create a new class version of 'The Frog Prince'. Working collaboratively, children decide on the two new main characters and the new events. Phase 2 also includes work on the sounds /f/, /l/, /s/ and /z/ spelled 'ff', 'll', 'ss', and 'zz'.

Programmes of study: Year 1

Comprehension: Draw on what they already know or on background information and vocabulary provided by the teacher.

Comprehension: Make inferences on the basis of what is being said and done.

Comprehension: Participate in discussion about what is read to them, taking turns and listening to what others say.

Comprehension: Explain clearly their understanding of what is read to them.

Composition: Say out loud what they are going to write about.

Spelling: Spell the /f/, /l/, /s/, /z/ and /k/ sounds ff, ll, ss, zz and ck.

Introduction

Remind the children of the Big Picture. Reread 'The Frog Prince' and discuss the work that the children have done to explore the story in Phase 1.

Tell children they are going to work together to create a new version of the story with a new enchanted animal, a new human character and a new promise that character has to keep.

Discussing ideas

As a class, discuss and make decisions to create their new class story. Record their ideas for Phase 3 and Phase 4.

Discuss the following with the children.

- Where will the story be set? (for example, another castle, a modern school, a village)
- What characters will live in the new setting? (for example, monarchs and servants, teachers and students, villagers)
- Who will the main human character be?
- What animal will the enchanted character be? Who were they before they were enchanted? Why were they enchanted?
- How will the two main characters meet?
- How will the enchanted animal character help the human character? What promises will the human character have to keep in return?
- How and why will the human character try to get out of keeping the promises?

- How will the human character help reverse the enchantment?
- How will the story end? (for example, the main characters get married or become best friends)

Drama and storytelling

Use a range of activities to allow the children to explore suggestions for their new tale.

- **Hot-seating characters:** Have children choose one of the new characters (main or peripheral). In role as their character have them discuss their daily life, likes, dislikes and opinions with other children who can ask them questions. If hot-seating the enchanted animal character, ask them what they miss most about being human.
- **Animal movements:** Have the children use their bodies and facial expressions to change from a given animal into a human. Explore different animals.
- **Animal sounds:** Have the children mimic animal sounds and then work out how to write them down potentially to use in the story.
- **Freeze-framing key moments:** Once the structure of the story is created, try out the different scenes in the right sequence. Use thought-tracking, asking each child in the freeze-frame what they are thinking at that moment of the story.

Incidental writing

Before you select any incidental writing, make sure the children are able to orally articulate the main events. Select activities that you think appropriate for the abilities and interests of your class. Children could:

- draw and label pictures of the two new main characters
- write the promises out on special paper with fun fonts
- write a diary entry by the main human character describing meeting the animal or vice versa.

Organising the new fairy tale into a structure

Once the children have thoroughly explored their ideas for their class tale, bring them together and use their final suggestions to model plotting the new story onto the Fairy-tale story map. Discuss the start of the story, the middle section and the happy ending. Add in key words or phrases that might be needed. Once recorded, go through the planner and ask the children if they are happy with the tale.

Phonics and spelling

Create four castle word wall shapes with spaces for word cards that can be placed within the walls. At the top of each wall, have a flag with /f/, /l/, /s/ or /z/ written on them.

Point to the /s/ flag castle wall and write the word 'princess' on a word card. Place it in the wall shape. Underline 'ss' and highlight that 'ss' stands for the /s/ sound. Ask the children for more examples to add to the wall, for example: 'dress', 'kiss', 'toss', 'class'. Repeat the process for the other sounds. Let the children add more words over the sessions.

Use Year 1, Spelling Unit 1 for more work on the four sounds.

Review of the Big Picture

At the end of this phase, discuss with the children what they have achieved with their planning and ideas for their new class tale.

Phase 3: Collaborate and compose

Phase 3 has three writing lessons which support the children in writing their class version of 'The Frog Prince'. Each lesson starts with a vocabulary, grammar and punctuation focus with links to the main text. The children then participate in a shared composition session, applying the VGP focus in context. Independent writing, with plenaries, follows. The VGP focuses are on adding -ing, and -ed to root verbs, punctuating sentences with exclamation marks and joining words and clauses using 'and'.

Programmes of study: Year 1

Composition: Say out loud what they are going to write about.

Composition: Compose a sentence orally before writing it.

Composition: Re-read what they have written to check that it makes sense.

Composition: Discuss what they have written with the teacher or other pupils.

Vocabulary, grammar and punctuation: Add the endings -ing, -ed and -er to verbs where no change is needed to the root word.

Vocabulary, grammar and punctuation: Begin to punctuate sentences using a capital letter and a full stop, question mark or exclamation mark.

Vocabulary, grammar and punctuation: Join words and join clauses using 'and'.

Introduction

Remind the children about the sequence's Big Picture. Explain that over several lessons the children are going to work as a class to draft and write a different version of 'The Frog Prince' involving new characters and new promises. Use the story map from Phase 2 to remind the children of their story plan and final choices on new characters and events.

Lesson 1

Adding -ing, and -ed to root verbs

Write: 'The princess went to play in the garden'. Ask: 'What did she do there?' Write: 'She was playing with her ball.' and 'She played 'catch.' Underline the root verb, 'play', in the same colour in each of the three sentences. Use another colour to underline 'ing' and 'ed' and discuss how they can be added to the ends of some verbs. Write a list of root verbs and ask the children to write them twice, the first time adding 'ing' to each of them and the second time adding 'ed'.

Use Year 1, Vocabulary Unit 2 and Year 1, Spelling Units 9 and 11 for more work on the suffixes -ing and -ed.

Shared writing

Use the story map from Phase 2 to model writing the opening of the story. Model the oral composition of sentences before writing. Discuss the opening sentence and the sentences in each section of the story. Aim for two or three sentences per section. Note either of the suffixes -ing or -ed added to the ends of root verbs. Once written, collaboratively check the sentences make sense and that sentence punctuation and spelling is correct.

Independent writing

The children can now write their own first part of the class tale, focusing on using verbs ending -ing or -ed. Make sure that the class Fairy-tale story map is available to them to help with vocabulary and structure. Some children may benefit from guided group or peer-paired writing at this stage. Highlight that they need only write two or three sentences for each section.

Plenary

Throughout the writing session, ask the children questions to help them focus on their progress and what they have created during that lesson, for example: 'What sentence have you used to start your story?' 'How does the human character meet the enchanted animal?' 'What promises must the main human character make and keep?' 'Have you used any words that end in -ing or -ed?' 'If so, what are they?' 'How have you checked that each sentence makes sense?'

Lesson 2

Using exclamation marks

Write on a board the three punctuation marks: a full stop, a question mark and an exclamation mark. Ask the children what each one is called. Write out some exclamation phrases from 'The Frog Prince' without the exclamation marks. Explain that a punctuation mark is missing and you need the children to help you decide which one. Say the phrases with exclamation, for example, 'Ugh! No, I won't!' 'There was the frog!' 'Ker-plump!' 'Let me in!' 'Thank you little princess!' Ask the children which punctuation mark is needed and ask them to explain why. Think of some exclamation phrases that could be used in the class story and record them.

Use Year 1, Punctuation Unit 1 for more work on exclamation marks.

Shared writing

Use the Fairy-tale story map from Phase 2 to model writing the middle part of the story. Model the oral composition of sentences before writing. Aim for two or three words per section. Include any exclamation phrases and use recurring phrases for each story section, for example: 'Remember your promise!' 'I won't do it!' Once written, collaboratively check that the sentences make sense and that sentence punctuation and spelling is correct.

Independent writing

The children can now write their own middle part of the class tale, focusing on using exclamation marks and making sure to include the recurring phrases. Make sure that the class Fairy-tale story map is available to them to help with vocabulary and structure. Some children may benefit from guided group or peer-paired writing at this stage. Highlight that they need only write two or three sentences for each section.

Plenary

Throughout the writing session, ask the children questions to help them focus on their progress and what they have created during that lesson, for example: 'What same sentences have you used for each promise?' 'Where have you put the exclamation marks?' 'What word have you used to show that the main character is not happy?' 'How have you checked that each sentence makes sense?' 'How have you checked your spellings?'

Lesson 3

Joining sentences using 'and'

Remind the children that short sentences or words can be joined together to make one longer sentence using the word 'and'. Write: 'The princess and prince married. They lived happily ever after.' With the children's help, join the sentences into one: 'The prince and princess married and lived happily ever after'. Note that 'they' and the full stop have been removed. Ask the children to work in pairs or small groups to compose sentences that could end '... lived happily ever after'. Write their ideas on the board for the class to discuss.

Use Year 1 Grammar Unit 2 for more work on joining sentences using 'and'.

Shared writing

Use the Fairy-tale story map from Phase 2 to model writing the final part of the story. Model the oral composition of the simple sentences before writing. Look at sentences that could be joined with 'and' including the last sentence of the story. Once written, collaboratively check that the sentences make sense and that sentence punctuation and spelling is correct.

Independent writing

The children can now write their own final part of the class tale focusing on joining sentences using 'and'. Make sure that the class story map is available to them to help with vocabulary and structure. Some children may benefit from guided group or peer-paired writing at this stage. Highlight that they need only write two or three sentences for each section.

Plenary

Throughout the writing session, ask the children questions to help them focus on their progress and what they have created during that lesson, for example: 'Have you shown how the enchanted animal becomes human again?' 'How does the story end?' 'Have you joined up two simple sentences using 'and'?' 'If so, which ones?' 'What sentence punctuation marks have you used?' 'How have you checked that each sentence makes sense?' 'How have you checked your spellings?'

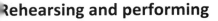

Rehearsing and performing

Once the children have written their tale, encourage them to retell it either as storytellers or by creating a performance. Take feedback on what they particularly liked about the tales they have heard.

Review of the Big Picture

Once you have completed all the lessons for this section, remind the children of the sequence's Big Picture. Discuss what they have learned so far.

Phase 4: Write independently

This final phase brings all the children's learning and writing skills together so that they can write their own version of 'The Frog Prince' independently. Through their writing, they will be able to utilise the different VGP focuses that they have been practising throughout previous phases.

Programmes of study: Year 1

Composition: Say out loud what they are going to write about.

Composition: Compose a sentence orally before writing it.

Composition: Sequence sentences to form short narratives.

Composition: Re-read what they have written to check that it makes sense.

Composition: Discuss what they have written with the teacher or other pupils.

Composition: Read aloud their writing clearly enough to be heard by their peers and the teacher.

Introduction

Introduce the phase by discussing what the children have learned in their story planning and writing sessions and link it to the Big Picture. Emphasise the excitement of bringing all their learning together to write their own version of 'The Frog Prince'.

Review the children's different suggestions for the new characters, promises and events from Phase 2. Clarify that the planning and writing of their own tale will take place over several sessions.

Writing

Give each child a Fairy-tale story map. As they plan, draft and write each section of the story, encourage the children to compose their sentences orally before writing them down. Have children draw a picture to illustrate each section.

All the children should be encouraged to try to write independently to the best of their abilities. Ask open questions such as 'Who is your main human character?' 'What enchanted animal do they meet?' 'Why does the human character have to make a promise?' 'What promise or promises do they have to make?' 'How do they feel when they have to keep the promises?' 'How does the enchanted animal become human again?' 'How does the story end?'

Make sure that the children have a chance to share their writing with others at appropriate points during each session.

Proofreading and redrafting

Encourage the children to read through their work at the end of each writing session with a partner. Ask them to check whether their writing makes sense. Proofreading and improvement without support means that the writing will happen over a few lessons. Offer the children the Proofreading sheet / My writing checklist, or create your own checklist with the assistance of the blank Proofreading sheet / My writing checklist.

Self- and peer-assessment

Encourage the children to take time to assess their own and others' writing. Make sure that they read out their writing clearly. Ask open questions to encourage self- and peer-assessment such as: 'How similar or different is this story to the original?' 'How have I started the story?' 'What happens in the middle part of my story?' 'Have I got a good start to the story?' 'Have I got a middle part of the story?' 'What exclamation words or sentences have I used?' 'Am I happy with the way the story ends?' 'What final sentence have I used?' 'How have I checked that each sentence makes sense?'

Also encourage children to check their VGP focuses on -ed or -ing suffixes, joining two simple sentences using 'and', and exclamation marks for exclamation phrases to make sure they have been successfully applied throughout the texts.

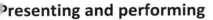

Presenting and performing

Once the children have written their tales, encourage them to retell it either as storytellers or by creating a performance. Take feedback on what they particularly liked about the tales they have heard. Encourage the children to use appropriate intonation for exclamations and different voices for the different characters.

Final review of the Big Picture

Individually or with partners, have children reflect on what they have learned from this sequence and what they will remember to do in future writing.

Sequence 14
Letters

Approximate duration: Two weeks

Through this teaching sequence, children explore the fictional letters written to and from well-known fairy tale characters to the Fairy Godmother in, *Dear Fairy Godmother*. By the end of the sequence, they will have written their own letters from a fairy tale character to the Fairy Godmother.

Phase 1: Enjoy and immerse

Children become familiar with the content, language and structure of *Dear Fairy Godmother*.

Phase 2: Capture and organise

Children are supported in developing ideas for a letter written by a fairy tale character and the reply from the Fairy Godmother.

Phase 3: Collaborate and compose

Children undertake supported writing sessions to develop their own writing based on the two class letters.

Phase 4: Write independently

Children write, edit and read aloud their own letter written by a fairy tale character and the reply from the Fairy Godmother.

Main source text

Treasure House Anthology Sequence 14 text. *Dear Fairy Godmother*, Michael Rosen, ISBN 978-1-40-633836-2

Background knowledge

During Year 1, children should be able to plan and write simple letters within a frame. They should be able to identify that a letter starts with an address and a date, a greeting such as 'Dear…' with the recipient's name followed by the letter content and finished with a sign-off and the writer's name.

In *Dear Fairy Godmother* there is a wide variety of letters to read and study from nine well-known fairy tale characters. Each one has written a letter to the Fairy Godmother detailing a problem that relates to their story or their character. Acting as an agony aunt, the Fairy Godmother writes each character a letter back with suggestions on how to solve the problem.

Spoken outcome

To read out their fairy tale character letter and the Fairy Godmother's response

Writing outcome

To write two letters: one from and one to a well-known fairy tale character

Prior knowledge

Check children's knowledge and understanding of:

- well-known fairy tale characters and their stories, especially those featured in *Dear Fairy Godmother*
- who the Fairy Godmother is and her role in 'Cinderella'
- what a fairy tale is and its common characteristics
- writing and receiving letters.

Diagnostic assessment options

Before starting the unit, you may wish to conduct an initial diagnostic assessment of the children's knowledge and understanding.

Ideas for initial diagnostic assessment options include:

- reviewing children's writing for correct use of capital letters for proper names
- speaking and listening activities where children listen to and identify correct sequences of sentences.
- reviewing children's writing to check that they have used 'and' to join words or clauses
- spelling and sorting activities putting objects or labelled images into alphabetical order.

Cross-curricular links

KS1 Art and design

- Use drawing, painting and sculpture to develop and share their ideas, experiences and imagination.

KS1 Music

- Use their voices expressively and creatively by singing songs and speaking chants and rhymes.
- Play tuned and untuned instruments musically.

Treasure House links

- Treasure House, Year 1, Punctuation Unit 2: Capital letter for names and 'I'
- Treasure House, Year 1, Spelling Unit 6: Spelling words that end in a /v/ sound
- Treasure House, Year 1, Grammar Unit 2: Building sentences using 'and'

Resources

Props and percussion instruments for drama and storytelling activities (optional); a short letter in an envelope from the Fairy Godmother (Phase 1); fairy tale problem cards (Phase 1); a range of fairy tales linked to the characters in the book; fairy land post office role-play area

Source texts – see Anthologies; Fairy-tale letter writing frame; Who sits where?; Proofreading sheet / My writing checklist; Proofreading sheet / My writing checklist (blank)

Phase 1: Enjoy and immerse

In Phase 1, the children listen to and read a range of letters from *Dear Fairy Godmother*. Over several sessions, the children have opportunities to discuss the language and structure of the letters through comprehension and discussion activities as well as exploring the contents of the letters through drama, performance, writing and analysis of the text. Phase 1 also covers the vocabulary, grammar and punctuation focus on using capital letters for people and places and includes work on naming the letters of the alphabet in order.

Programmes of study: Year 1

Comprehension: Listen to and discuss a wide range of poems, stories and non-fiction at a level beyond that at which they can read independently.

Comprehension: Make inferences on the basis of what is being said and done.

Comprehension: Predict what might happen on the basis of what has been read so far.

Comprehension: Explain clearly their understanding of what is read to them.

Vocabulary, grammar and punctuation: Use a capital letter for names of people, places, the days of the week, and the personal pronoun 'I'.

Spelling: Name the letters of the alphabet in order.

Sparking interest

Write a short letter to the children from The Fairy Godmother, inviting them to listen to a set of letters from fairy tale characters and her answers. Put the letter in an envelope with an address to the classroom. Show the envelope and ask: 'What is this?' 'What do you think is inside it?' Open up the letter and read it to the class. Discuss who the Fairy Godmother is and what she did in 'Cinderella'. Encourage the children to share their experiences of getting or sending letters or postcards.

Reading and discussion

Read *Dear Fairy Godmother* to the children. Before reading the Fairy Godmother's response to each letter, ask the children what advice they think she will offer. Lead discussion to check their understanding of the letters and story.

Discuss the following with the children.

- Why do the fairy tale characters ask the Fairy Godmother for help and advice?
- What is each character's problem?
- Do you agree with the Fairy Godmother's advice?
- What, in your opinion, is the best piece of advice the Fairy Godmother has given? Why?
- Which is your favourite letter?

- Which fairy tale characters, do you think will not like the Fairy Godmother's advice? (the wolf, Goldilocks, the Gingerbread Man chasers)

Drama and storytelling

Use a range of activities to reinforce children's understanding of the story and individual letters. Select the activities that fit in with your lesson timing. Encourage mixed-ability grouping for the chosen activities.

- **Class performance:** In groups, have the children create before and after scenes for each fairy tale scenario, for example, a scene in which the Gingerbread Man is being chased and a scene in which he puts on aftershave. Have some of the children narrate and read out the letters.
- **Match the letters:** Put children into small groups. Give half the groups a card each with a fairy tale problem on each. Give the other half cards with the solutions. Have children find and match the problems and solutions. Read out the letters that go with each group.
- **Fairy Godmother rap:** Put the children into groups to represent each of the different fairy tale characters. Have them work together to come up with two or three raps for a Fairy Godmother thank you song. Let them perform it to a drum beat and record it.

Incidental writing

Short writing activities enhance the children's understanding of the letters and story and help to inform the teaching focuses in the collaborative composition phase. Children could:

- design a thank you card from one of the fairy tale characters
- practise their handwriting by neatly writing out one of the letters on special paper
- write a letter from the Wolf or Goldilocks, moaning about being treated badly
- draw a comic strip based on one of the letters to show a different story ending, for example, the giant and Jack becoming friends
- write an invitation from a fairy queen for the Fairy Godmother to accept an award for her good work.

Analysis

Focus on two letters from a fairy tale character and the Fairy Godmother. Point to the addresses at the top of the page and read them out. Ask: 'What are these?' 'Why is it a good idea to have your address on a letter?' (So the recipient can send a reply.) Highlight the starting phrase of the letter, 'Dear…' and discuss how all the letters start in the same way. Let the children practise saying the phrase using each other's names. Look at the content of the fairy tale character's letters. Note how most of the characters explain what their problem is and then ask for help. Note how the Fairy Godmother writes just two short sentences of advice. Ask: 'Why have the characters written their names at the bottom of the letter?' (To inform the recipient of the letter who wrote it.)

Grammar: Using a capital letter for names and places

Display one of the letters. Highlight the names at the bottom of the page and read them out with the children. Ask: 'Why do the words start with a capital letter?' Use the book or extracts to look for, highlight and discuss more examples of proper names and their capitals. Explain how most animal characters in fairy tales are given their animal name as their proper name. Provide examples of this such as 'Ugly Duckling!' and 'Here comes Tortoise!'

Use Year 1, Punctuation Unit 2 for more work on capital letters for names.

Phonics and spelling

Explain that, at the Fairy Godmother's party, the fairy tale characters need to sit at the table in a special order. To do this, each first letter of their names must be put in the right alphabetical order. With the children, say the alphabet and write it out on the board as you say it. Give the children the alphabetical character cut-out names from 'Who sits where?'. Working individually or in pairs, let them put the names into alphabetical order using the first name letter (in bold). Once they have checked the order, let them stick the names onto a long piece of paper. They can then draw a party table underneath the names.

Review of the Big Picture

At the end of this phase, discuss with the children what they have learned so far about the letters and story, *Dear Fairy Godmother*. Remind them that this is all working towards writing their own fairy tale character's letter to the Fairy Godmother and her letter back.

Phase 2: Capture and organise

During Phase 2, children develop ideas about the content needed for their class letters for a new fairy tale character and the Fairy Godmother's response. Working collaboratively, children decide on the words and phrases they could use in the new letters. Phase 2 also includes work on spelling words ending 've'.

Programmes of study: Year 1

Comprehension: Become very familiar with key stories, fairy stories and traditional tales, retelling them and considering their particular characteristics.

Comprehension: Be encouraged to link what they read or hear read to their own experiences.

Comprehension: Draw on what they already know or on background information and vocabulary provided by the teacher.

Comprehension: Participate in discussion about what is read to them, taking turns and listening to what others say.

Composition: Say out loud what they are going to write about.

Spelling: Spell the /v/ sound at the end of words.

Introduction

Remind the children of the Big Picture. Re-read *Dear Fairy Godmother* and encourage children to join in with you on a repeat performance. Discuss the work children have done to explore the letters and story.

Tell children they are going to work together to write another letter from a different fairy tale character and write the Fairy Godmother's response.

Discussing ideas

As a class, discuss and make decisions to create their new letters. Record their ideas for Phase 3 and Phase 4.

Discuss the following with the children.

- What other well-known fairy tale characters can we think of? (list no more than 5-6 characters)
- What problem could each of these characters have?
- How could the problems be solved?
- How would the Fairy Godmother's help make a difference to the characters?
- Do you think the fairy tale characters would/could follow the advice?

Drama and storytelling

Use a range of activities to reinforce children's understanding of the poem. Select the activities that fit in with your lesson timing. Encourage mixed-ability grouping for the chosen activities.

- **Post office writing corner:** Set up a role-playing area: the 'Fairy tale Land Post Office'. Provide envelopes, paper or postcards, pretend stamps, and a post-box. Deliveries could be made from and to different fairy tale characters.
- **Can you help me?** Working in pairs, let the children take turns to role-play a fairy tale character who is visiting the Fairy Godmother's to tell her about their problem and role-play the Fairy Godmother giving advice.

Incidental writing

Before you select any incidental writing, make sure the children are able to orally articulate the main events. Select activities that you think appropriate for the abilities and interests of your class. Children could:

- draw and label pictures of a fairy tale character
- draw before and after pictures, with captions, showing the problem and the advice taken (as in the illustration design of the book)
- create an address for a new character and practise writing it on an envelope with correct capital letter punctuation
- design and write a postcard from one of the characters, for example, Cinderella on a holiday.

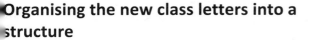

Organising the new class letters into a structure

Once the children have thoroughly explored their ideas for their class letters, bring them together and make a final decision on the content. Recap letter structure: a letter starts with an address and a date, a greeting such as 'Dear…' with the recipient's name followed by the letter content and finished with a sign-off and the writer's name. Also review the correct layout of letters. Record the final decision on content. Once recorded, go through the plans and ask the children if they are happy with the letter ideas.

Phonics and spelling

Highlight to the children how the fairy tale characters at the end of *Dear Fairy Godmother* gave the Fairy Godmother a party. Write the word, 'gave' on the board and say each segment of the word. Underline 've' and ask the children what sound the letters stand for (/v/). Explain that words that end with the /v/ sound end with the letters 've'. Put the children into small groups. Give each group an envelope containing a mix of words: some ending in 've' and some other words. Ask them to sort the words into two groups: those with 've' at the end and those without. Once the cards are sorted, encourage them to write a few sentences using some of the words ending 've'.

Review of the Big Picture

At the end of this phase, discuss with the children what they have achieved with their planning and ideas for their class fairy tale letters.

Phase 3: Collaborate and compose

Phase 3 has two writing lessons which support the children in writing their two new fairy tale letters. Each lesson starts with a vocabulary, grammar and punctuation focus with links to the main text. The children then participate in a shared composition session, applying the VGP focus in context. Independent writing, with plenaries, follows. The VGP focuses are on joining sentences using 'and' and sequencing sentences into a narrative.

Programmes of study: Year 1

Composition: Say out loud what they are going to write about.

Composition: Compose a sentence orally before writing it.

Composition: Sequence sentences to form short narratives.

Composition: Discuss what they have written with the teacher or other pupils.

Vocabulary, grammar and punctuation: Join words and join clauses using 'and'.

Introduction

Remind the children about the sequence's Big Picture. Tell children they are going to start work as a class to draft and write a letter from a new well-known fairy tale character and write a response from the Fairy Godmother. Use the recorded information from Phase 2 to remind the children of their letter ideas and content.

Lesson 1

Sequencing sentences to form short narratives

Copy out the individual sentences from Little Bear's letter in 'Dear Fairy Godmother' onto strips of paper or card. Hold up the sentences in the wrong order. Explain that the letter has got ripped up in the post and needs putting back together again. Read out each sentence with the children. Work with them to decide which is the first sentence, which is the middle sentence, and which is the last sentence. Read out the complete letter. Discuss why it was important to have the sentences in the right order. Do the same activity using the Gingerbread Man's letter.

Shared writing

Remind the children that, in this lesson, they will be writing a letter to the Fairy Godmother from their chosen fairy tale character. Revise why the character needs help. Display the Fairy-tale letter writing frame. Use the structure to model writing the first letter, starting with the address and then the greeting 'Dear …'. Model the oral composition of the sentences that the children want to use for their letter before writing them down. Once written, ask the children if the sentences are in the right order. Change them if not.

Model writing the name of the character at the end of the letter, emphasising the capital letters. Once written, collaboratively check that the sentences make sense, and there is accurate sentence punctuation and correct spelling.

Independent writing

The children can now write their own version of the class letter, focusing on sequencing sentences into a narrative. Make sure that the class plans are available for them to see. Give each child a copy of the Fairy tale letter writing frame to help with the phrasing and structure. Some children may benefit from guided group or peer-paired writing at this stage.

Plenary

Throughout the writing session, ask the children questions to help them focus on their progress and what they have created during that lesson, for example: 'What address have you written?' 'Where have you written the address?' 'What greeting have you used?' 'How does the middle of your letter make it clear what the problem is?' 'Have you used a question to ask for help?' 'If so, what question have you used?' 'What name have you put at the bottom of your letter?' 'Does the name start with a capital letter?' 'How have you checked that your sentences make sense?' 'How have you checked they in the right order?'

Lesson 2

Joining words and joining clauses using 'and'

Write: 'My brother is a big swan. He is very beautiful'. Read out the two sentences. Remind the children of previous work they have done joining sentences using 'and'. Ask: 'Which two words would you lose to join the sentences up?' 'Where should you place 'and'?' 'What punctuation marks do we lose?' Discuss and write out their different suggestions.

Write two more sentences: 'Take up a hobby. Be a good singer.' Have the children work in pairs, to join the two sentences using 'and' and write the sentence out.

Use Year 1, Grammar: Unit 1 for more work on joining words and clauses using 'and'.

Shared writing

Remind the children that, in this lesson, they will be writing a letter from the Fairy Godmother in answer to the letter written in the last lesson. Display the Fairy-tale letter writing frame. Model the oral composition of sentences that the children want to use for their letter before writing them down. Write two simple sentences and ask the children how they can be joined into one longer sentence. Once written, collaboratively check that sentences make sense, and there is accurate sentence punctuation and correct spelling.

Independent writing

The children can now write their own version of the class letter, focusing on joining sentences using 'and'. Make sure the class plans are available for them to see. Give each child a copy of the Fairy-tale letter writing frame to help with the phrasing and structure. Some children may benefit from guided group or peer-paired writing at this stage.

Plenary

Throughout the writing session, ask the children questions to help them focus on their progress and what they have created during that lesson, for example: 'What address have you written?' 'Where have you written the address?' 'What greeting have you used?' 'How does the middle of your letter make it clear what the problem is?' 'Have you used a question to ask for help?' 'If so, what question have you used?' 'What name have you put at the bottom of your letter?' 'Does the name start with a capital letter?' 'How have you checked that your sentences make sense?' 'How have you checked they in the right order?' 'Where have you used 'and' to join words, phrases or sentences?'

Presenting and performing

Once the children have written their letters let them read them out and share them within a group or as a pair. Encourage the children to offer feedback on what they particularly liked about the verses they have heard.

Review of the Big Picture

Once you have completed all the lessons for this section, remind the children of the sequence's Big Picture. Discuss what they have learned so far.

Phase 4: Write independently

This final phase brings all the children's learning and writing skills together so that they can write their own fairy tale letters. Through their writing, they will be able to utilise the different VGP focuses that they have been practising throughout previous phases.

Programmes of study: Year 1

Composition: Say out loud what they are going to write about.

Composition: Compose a sentence orally before writing it.

Composition: Sequence sentences to form short narratives.

Composition: Re-read what they have written to check that it makes sense.

Composition: Discuss what they have written with the teacher or other pupils.

Composition: Read aloud their writing clearly enough to be heard by their peers and the teacher.

Introduction

Introduce the phase by discussing what the children have learned in their planning and writing sessions and link it to the Big Picture. Emphasise the excitement of bringing all their learning together to write their own letter from a fairy tale character and the reply letter from the Fairy Godmother.

Review the children's suggestions of different fairy tale characters and their problems as well as the possible suggestions from the Fairy Godmother from Phase 2. Clarify that the planning and writing of their letters will take place over several sessions.

Writing

Give each child two Fairy-tale writing frames. As they plan, draft and write their letters encourage the children to compose their words and phrases orally before writing them down.

All the children should be encouraged to try to write independently to the best of their abilities. Ask open questions such as 'Which fairy tale character will you use?' 'Why do they need help?' 'What will they ask the Fairy Godmother?' 'What advice could she give them?'

Make sure that the children have a chance to share their writing with others at appropriate points during each session.

Proofreading and redrafting

Encourage the children to read through their work at the end of each writing session with a partner. Ask them to check whether their writing makes sense. Proofreading and improvement without support means that the writing will happen over a few lessons. Offer the children the Proofreading sheet / My writing checklist, or create your own checklist with the assistance of the blank Proofreading sheet / My writing checklist.

Self- and peer-assessment

Encourage the children to take time to assess their own and others' writing. Make sure that they read out their writing clearly. Ask open questions to encourage self- and peer-assessment such as: 'What addresses have I written?' 'Where on my letters have I written the addresses?' 'What greetings have I used at the starts of my letters?' 'Have I used capital letters at the beginnings of names?' 'How have I made it clear what problem my fairy tale character has?' 'What advice does the Fairy Godmother give them?' 'Where have I written the names of both letter writers?' 'Do my letters make sense?' 'How have I made my letters fun to read?'

Also encourage them to check their VGP focuses on capital letters for names of people, the sequencing of sentences to form a narrative and linking two sentences using 'and'.

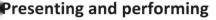

Presenting and performing

Once the children have written their letters, encourage them to share them with the class or within groups. Have the listeners try to predict what the Fairy Godmother would suggest before the child reads out the reply. Have a feedback session from the children on the letters and the content.

Let the children use fun, coloured envelopes to put their letters in. Encourage them to add the address. Post them in the fairy tale class post box.

Final review of the Big Picture

Individually or with partners, have children reflect on what they have learned from this sequence and what they will remember to do in future writing.

Sequence 15
Information texts

Approximate duration: Two weeks

Big Picture

Through this teaching sequence, children look at the structure, content and language of the information text, *The Fantastic Flying Squirrel*. By the end of the sequence, each child will have written an information booklet about another nocturnal animal.

Phase 1: Enjoy and immerse

Children will become familiar with the content, language and structure of the information text, *The Fantastic Flying Squirrel*.

Phase 2: Capture and organise

Children are supported in developing ideas to write an information booklet about another nocturnal creature.

Phase 3: Collaborate and compose

Children undertake supported writing sessions to develop their own writing based on the class information text.

Phase 4: Write independently

Children write, edit and read aloud their own information booklet about another nocturnal creature.

Main source text

Treasure House Anthology Sequence 15 text. *The Fantastic Flying Squirrel*, Nic Bishop, ISBN 978-0-00-718583-2

Extra source text

Spines, Stings and Teeth, Andy and Angie Belcher, ISBN 978-0-00-718589-4, pp.10–15

Background knowledge

An information text provides information on a subject in order to help the reader understand more about it. During Year 1, children begin to develop their ability to recognise the characteristics of a simple information text and use them to write their own information writing for a range of cross-curricular subjects. Common characteristics of information texts include a short introduction, simple, informative sentences, use of topic specific vocabulary and captioned or labelled pictures or diagrams. Children's work can be presented in a variety of interesting and stimulating ways such as attractive class displays, posters, within cut-out shapes and as booklets.

Spoken outcome

To show and tell their information booklets to other children

Writing outcome

To write an information booklet about a nocturnal animal

Prior knowledge

Check children's knowledge and understanding of:

- simple information texts covering a wide range of subjects
- the characteristics of a simple information text
- how some animals/creatures have adapted unusual characteristics to survive.

Diagnostic assessment options

Before starting the unit, you may wish to conduct an initial diagnostic assessment of the children's knowledge and understanding.

Ideas for initial diagnostic assessment options include:

- reviewing children's writing for the ability to write their words with a suitable space between them
- speaking and listening activities where children listen to and recognise the /oo/ sound spelled 'oo' and the /igh/ sound spelled 'igh'
- reviewing children's writing to check that they are beginning to join words and clauses using 'and'
- listening activities and writing activities to check that children can hear and write verbs with the -ing suffix.

Cross-curricular links

KS1 Art and design

- Use drawing, painting and sculpture to develop and share their ideas, experiences and imagination.

KS1 Science - Animals, including humans

- Identify and name a variety of common animals including fish, amphibians, reptiles, birds and mammals.
- Describe and compare the structure of a variety of common animals (fish, amphibians, reptiles, birds and mammals, including pets).

Treasure House links

- Treasure House, Year 1, Vocabulary Unit 2: Adding endings to root words (-ing, -ed, -er, -est)
- Treasure House, Year 1, Spelling Unit 9: Adding -ing to a root word
- Treasure House, Year 1, Grammar Unit 2: Building sentences using 'and'

Resources

Props and percussion instruments for drama and storytelling activities (optional); information on flying squirrels; information, audio-visual resources, sound recordings and images on UK nocturnal creatures; information about owls; booklets for the children made from two folded A4 pieces of a paper.

Nocturnal animals wall display: display materials to create a nocturnal animal habitat wall display. Include a tree with branches that leaf shapes with 'igh' words can be added to. Also include a moon shape for an activity on 'oo' words. Have star shapes for writing words on that can be added to the display. Images of nocturnal animals can also be added to the display.

Source texts – see Anthologies; 'Making -ing words'; 'igh' word leaves; Proofreading sheet / My writing checklist; Proofreading sheet / My writing checklist (blank)

Phase 1: Enjoy and immerse

In Phase 1, the children listen to and read *The Fantastic Flying Squirrel*. Over several sessions, the children have opportunities to discuss the language and structure of the information text through comprehension and discussion activities as well as exploring the content through activities, writing and analysis of the text. Phase 1 also covers the vocabulary, grammar and punctuation focus on adding -ing to root verbs and includes work on spelling the /igh/ sound 'igh'.

Programmes of study: Year 1

Comprehension: Listen to and discuss a wide range of poems, stories and non-fiction at a level beyond that at which they can read independently.

Comprehension: Discuss word meanings, linking new meanings to those already known.

Comprehension: Check that the text makes sense to them as they read and correct inaccurate reading.

Comprehension: Explain clearly their understanding of what is read to them.

Vocabulary, grammar and punctuation: Use suffixes that can be added to verbs where no change is needed in the spelling of root words.

Spelling: Spell words with the trigraph 'igh'.

Sparking interest

Show the children the front cover of, *The Fantastic Flying Squirrel* or another information book such as *Spines, Stings and Teeth*. Briefly show the pages to the children without reading the text. Ask: 'What kind of book do you think this is?' Explain that it is called an information book. Ask: 'What information do you think this book is giving us?' Highlight that the children will be looking at an information book in more detail so that they can write their own information booklets.

Reading and discussion

Read *The Fantastic Flying Squirrel* with the children. Check children understand the vocabulary. Stop at different parts of the text to discuss, ask questions and check children's understanding of the content.

Discuss the following with the children.

- What sentence tells us when the flying squirrel is awake and where it lives?
- What does the flying squirrel need when it wakes up?
- What words tell us how the flying squirrel moves?
- What can the flying squirrel and the owl hear?
- What word is used to describe the sound of the flying squirrel eating?
- Look at the flying squirrel. Why do you think it has large ears and big eyes? (to hear very quiet sounds and to see in the dark)

Drama and storytelling

Use a range of activities to reinforce children's understanding of the information text. Select the activities that fit in with your lesson timing. Encourage mixed-ability grouping for the chosen activities.

- **Flying squirrels:** Have the children act out the flying squirrel's movements in the sequence outlined in the book: wakes, climbs, looks, listens, jumps, glides, eats, jumps, glides, eats, jumps, glides, climbs, sleeps.
- **Presentation:** Have the children take turns at reading out or memorising the sentences of the information book and use it for a class presentation. Use visual aids and sound effects if possible.
- **Listen!** Let the children listen to audio recordings of night creatures and tree sounds. Remind them how both the squirrel and the owl are very still as they listen for other creatures they could eat. Once the children have listened, ask them what they think they heard.

Incidental writing

Short writing activities enhance the children's understanding of the information text and help to inform the teaching focuses in the collaborative composition phase. Children could:

- compile a list of facts about the flying squirrel
- compile a list of words to describe flying and write them in flying squirrel shapes
- design an information poster about a flying squirrel
- draw and label a picture of a flying squirrel to show different features
- design a flow chart of the flying squirrel's hunt for food.

Analysis

Look at how the information book, *The Fantastic Flying Squirrel*, has been put together. Note the title. Ask: 'Why is it a good name for an information book?' (It says what it's about, it sounds exciting, it alliterates.) Discuss how the sentences are in the right sequence to show how the squirrel gets her food. List key words and topic specific vocabulary used in the book, for example: 'flying', 'squirrel', 'glides', 'hungry', 'listens', 'crunch', 'grasshopper', 'nocturnal'. Discuss the photographs and images and how the captions at the end of the book help the reader.

Use the extract text, *Spines, Stings and Teeth* for another example of an information text.

Grammar: Adding -ing to root verbs

Show a photograph of a flying squirrel to the children. Ask: 'Why do you think it is called a flying squirrel?' Write the word 'fly' on the board. Ask: 'What do we need to add to the end of the word to turn it into 'flying'?' Encourage a volunteer to come up and add 'ing' to the end. Remind the children how we can add 'ing' to the ends of some doing words. Give each child a copy of the resource sheet 'Making -ing words'. Children add -ing to root verbs to complete simple sentences. There is also an opportunity to write a sentence using a verb ending in 'ing'.

Use Year 1 Vocabulary Unit 2 and Year 1, Spelling Unit 9 for more consolidation work on the suffix -ing.

Phonics and spelling

Focus the children on the nocturnal animals wall display (see resources for details). Explain that animals such as the flying squirrel, that are awake mostly during the night, are called 'nocturnal' animals. Write the word, 'night' on a leaf shape and say each segment of the word. Underline 'igh' and ask the children to say the sound. Add the leaf to the tree and add 'igh' in the circle of the trunk. Give out copies of 'igh word leaves' for the children to complete by adding in the missing 'igh' to the words. Stick them onto the branches and say each word with the children.

Review of the Big Picture

At the end of this phase, discuss with the children what they have learned so far about the information book, *The Fantastic Flying Squirrel*. Remind them that this is all working towards writing their own information booklets about other night creatures.

Phase 2: Capture and organise

During Phase 2, children develop ideas about the content needed for a new class information booklet about another nocturnal animal. Working collaboratively, children decide on the words and layout they could use in the booklet. Phase 2 also includes work on spelling the /oo/ sound 'oo'.

Programmes of study: Year 1

Comprehension: Discuss word meanings, linking new meanings to those already known.

Comprehension: Draw on what they already know or on background information and vocabulary provided by the teacher.

Comprehension: Participate in discussion about what is read to them, taking turns and listening to what others say.

Comprehension: Explain clearly their understanding of what is read to them.

Composition: Say out loud what they are going to write about.

Spelling: Spell words with the digraph 'oo' (/u:/).

Introduction

Remind the children of the Big Picture. Reread or discuss the model information text, *The Fantastic Flying Squirrel*. Discuss the work that the children have done to explore the book and its information.

Tell children they are going to work together to create a new information booklet about another nocturnal animal: the owl. Remind the children what 'nocturnal' means. Show a blank booklet so that the children have some idea of what it looks like (see Resources).

Discussing ideas

As a class, discuss and make decisions to create their new class information booklet on an owl. Have information on owls available for the children to look at and read. Record their ideas for Phase 3 and Phase 4.

Discuss the following with the children.

- How many different types of owls are there?
- Where do owls live?
- What do owls eat? How do owls hunt?
- What special features do owls have?
- What information about owls shall we include in the booklet? What topic headings shall we use?
- What key words will we need to use?
- What features shall we use to present and organise our writing? (for example, headings, subheadings, sentences, lists, pictures, captions, diagrams)
- What shall we call the booklet?

Drama and storytelling

Use a range of activities to reinforce children's information text ideas. Select the activities that fit in with your lesson timing. Encourage mixed-ability grouping for the chosen activities.

- **Being an owl:** Let the children act out the movements of an owl from sitting on a tree to catching its prey.
- **Nature films:** Let the children watch a nature film about owls followed by a discussion.
- **Owl narration:** Either use a film of an owl or have children acting as an owl with other children giving a documentary-style narration.
- **Listen to owl sounds:** Have the children create owl sounds or use percussion instruments for the sound. Discuss how the sound could be written down.
- **Owl visitor:** Have someone who keeps owls come in to talk about owls or show them owls. Alternatively, visit an owl sanctuary or similar.

Incidental writing

Before you select any incidental writing, make sure the children are able to orally articulate the main parts to the information text. Select activities that you think appropriate for the abilities and interests of your class. Children could:

- compile a list of words to describe an owl hunting
- design a flowchart to show the owl catching prey
- compile a list of interesting facts about owls
- draw and label pictures of different types of owls. Add these to the 'Nocturnal animals' display.

Organising the new booklet into a structure

Once the children have thoroughly explored their ideas for their class information booklet, bring them together and make a final decision on the content using their final suggestions. List keywords and any other features, for example lists, diagrams. Decide on the name of the booklet. Once recorded, go through all the information and ask the children if they are happy with their information booklet plan.

Phonics and spelling

Point to the moon on the nocturnal animals wall display (see Resources for details). Ask the children what it is and then say each segment of the word. Ask: 'What sound does 'oo' stand for?' (/oo/) Encourage the children to make the sound again as you write, 'oo' in the moon with the word 'moon' underneath. With the children, think of other words with the /oo/ sound. For each one, let the children spell out the word with emphasis on the /oo/ and then have a volunteer write the word in a star shape. Put the stars onto the display and then read them all out again.

Review of the Big Picture

At the end of this phase, discuss with the children what they have achieved with their planning and ideas for their new class information booklet on owls.

Phase 3: Collaborate and compose

Phase 3 has two writing lessons which support the children in writing their class information booklet. Each lesson starts with a vocabulary, grammar and punctuation focus with links to the main text. The children then participate in a shared composition session, applying the VGP focus in context. Independent writing, with plenaries, follows. The VGP focuses are on joining words and joining clauses using 'and', and separating words with spaces.

Programmes of study: Year 1

Composition: Say out loud what they are going to write about.

Composition: Compose a sentence orally before writing it.

Composition: Re-read what they have written to check that it makes sense.

Composition: Discuss what they have written with the teacher or other pupils.

Handwriting: Begin to form lower-case letters in the correct direction, starting and finishing in the right place.

Handwriting: Form capital letters.

Vocabulary, grammar and punctuation: Join words and join clauses using 'and'.

Vocabulary, grammar and punctuation: Leave spaces between words.

Introduction

Remind the children about the sequence's Big Picture. Tell children they are going to work as a class to draft and write their information texts. Use the recorded information from Phase 2 to remind the children of their ideas.

Lesson 1

Joining words and joining clauses using 'and'

Using *The Fantastic Flying Squirrel*, show examples of sentences joined by 'and'. Write: 'The owl is hungry. The owl wants food.' Letting the children guide you, join the two sentences together: 'The owl is hungry and wants food.' Note how the second 'The owl' is removed as well as the full stop. Give the children a couple more information sentences to join. Let them work with another child to explain how to join them. Walk around to listen to their discussion.

Use Year 1, Grammar Unit 2 on words and phrases joined with 'and'.

Shared writing

With the children, model writing the class information text. With the children's input, model writing the heading and the first two lines for the introduction. Use the planner to help the children orally compose their information sentences for each part of the text. Check that they are using some of the key words listed in the previous phase. Note simple

sentences that could be combined into one using 'and'. Once written, collaboratively check that the sentences make sense, the information is clear and that sentence punctuation and spellings are correct.

Independent writing

The children can now write their own version of the class information text focusing on joining words or clauses using 'and'. Make sure that the class plans and word lists are available for them to see. Some children may benefit from guided group or peer-paired writing at this stage.

Plenary

Throughout the writing session, ask the children questions to help them focus on their progress and what they have created during that lesson, for example: 'What title have you written for the information?' 'How have you started your information text?' 'What will the reader find out about the owl?' 'What verbs ending in -ing have you used?' 'Which sentences have you joined using 'and'?' 'Which key words have you used?' 'How have you checked to see if your sentences make sense?' 'How have you checked that your information is in the right order?'

Lesson 2

Separating words with spaces

Highlight how important it is for captions and two or three word labels to be clear to read. Add a picture of an owl to the nocturnal animals wall display and write a caption that has no spaces between the words: 'Theowleatsmice'. Tell the children what it says. Ask: 'What is wrong with the caption?' There are no spaces. Encourage them to help you write it out with spaces. Write another caption: 'Themoonisfull'. Let the children use their whiteboards to write the sentence out with spaces between the words.

Use Year 1, Punctuation Unit 1 for more on punctuating sentences.

Shared writing

Remind the children that the class information text is now going to be rewritten as a booklet. Using a blank booklet, write out the information text. Write the sentences on the lines provided. Remind the children for the need to leave spaces between words to make their sentences clear to read. Highlight how the children can add pictures in the booklet above the sentences. Write the title on the front cover, highlighting the use of capital letters. Once written, collaboratively check through the work, especially for accurate use of sentence punctuation and spellings.

Independent writing

The children can now write out their own class information texts into booklets. Have resources available for the children to draw pictures of the owls or use images they can stick into their booklets. Encourage them to design their front covers and create flow charts or simple diagrams if needed. Some children may benefit from guided group or peer-paired writing at this stage.

Plenary

Throughout the writing session, ask the children questions to help them focus on their progress and what they have created during that lesson, for example: 'How have you made sure that you have left spaces between your words?' 'What punctuation marks have you used at the ends of your sentences?' 'What does the first letter of your sentences need to start with?' 'In what way, is your writing easy to read?'

Presentation and feedback

Once the children have written and illustrated their booklets, have a class show and tell to read and look at the information. Encourage the children to discuss what they learned about owls and what else they would like to find out about owls. Add any drawings or images and captions to the nocturnal animals wall display.

Review of the Big Picture

Once you have completed all the lessons for this section, remind the children of the sequence's Big Picture. Discuss what they have learned so far.

Phase 4: Write independently

This final phase brings all the children's learning and writing skills together so that they can write their own information text for another nocturnal animal. The children will work in groups to research information about a nocturnal animal before using it to write their own booklets about that animal individually. Through their writing, they will be able to utilise the different VGP focuses that they have been practising throughout previous phases.

Programmes of study: Year 1

Composition: Say out loud what they are going to write about.

Composition: Compose a sentence orally before writing it.

Composition: Sequence sentences to form short narratives.

Composition: Re-read what they have written to check that it makes sense.

Composition: Discuss what they have written with the teacher or other pupils.

Composition: Read aloud their writing clearly enough to be heard by their peers and the teacher.

Introduction

Introduce the phase by discussing what the children have learned in their information planning and writing sessions and link it to the Big Picture. Emphasise the excitement of bringing all their learning together to write their own information booklet about another nocturnal animal. Clarify that the planning and writing of their information text will take place over several sessions.

Planning

Put the children into groups and give each group a nocturnal animal to find out about and use for their information booklet. Provide information resources for the children to use. If needed, focus the information on one area such as feeding and hunting.

Writing

As the children draft and write their information, encourage the children to compose their words and sentences orally before writing them down.

All the children should be encouraged to try to write independently to the best of their abilities. Ask open questions such as 'What information about your animal are you writing about?' 'What do you want the reader of your booklet to know about your animal?' 'What key words are you using in some of your sentences?' 'Which information sentences do you think can be joined with 'and'?' 'Are you using labels or captions in your booklet?' 'If so, what will they be and how are they connected to the animal?'

Make sure that the children have a chance to share their writing with others at appropriate points during each session.

Proofreading and redrafting

Encourage the children to read through their work at the end of each writing session with a partner. Ask them to check whether their writing makes sense. Proofreading and improvement without support means that the writing will happen over a few lessons. Offer the children the Proofreading sheet / My writing checklist, or create your own checklist with the assistance of the blank Proofreading sheet / My writing checklist.

Self- and peer-assessment

Encourage the children to take time to assess their own and others' writing. Make sure that they read out their writing clearly. Ask open questions to encourage self- and peer-assessment such as: 'What title have I given my information booklet?' 'How do my first sentences introduce the animal?' 'How are my sentences easy to understand?' 'What key words have I used for the reader?' 'Which sentences have I joined up with 'and' and why?' 'How can I check that my information is in the right order?' 'What else could I add to my information text to make it interesting for the reader?'

Also encourage them to check their VGP focuses on using verbs ending in -ing, joining sentences using 'and' and leaving spaces between words.

Presenting and performing

Once the children have written their information text on their writing frames, have an extra session set aside for them to spend time writing their information into the booklets. Encourage the use of labelled pictures and check that they leave space between words. Have a show and tell session for the children to share their booklets with each other.

Add pictures and captions of the nocturnal animals to the nocturnal animals wall display. Put the booklets under the display for the children to read.

Final review of the Big Picture

Individually or with partners, have children reflect on what they have learned from this sequence and what they will remember to do in future writing.

Use this template to plan your own teaching sequence.

Sequence title

Approximate duration:

Big Picture

Phase 1: Enjoy and immerse

Phase 2: Capture and organise

Phase 3: Collaborate and compose

Phase 4: Write independently

Main source text

Spoken outcome

Extra source texts

Writing outcome

Background knowledge

Prior knowledge

Diagnostic assessment options

Treasure House links

Cross-curricular links

Resources

Phase 1: Enjoy and immerse

Programmes of study: Year 5
- Comprehension:

- Comprehension:

- Comprehension:

- Comprehension:

- Composition:

- Vocabulary, grammar and punctuation:

- Spelling:

Sparking interest

Drama and storytelling

Reading and discussion

Incidental writing

Phonics and spelling

Analyse

Review of the Big Picture

Grammar

Phase 2: Capture and organise

Programmes of study: Year 5
- Comprehension:

- Comprehension:

- Composition:

- Composition:

- Spelling:

Introduction   **Drama and storytelling**

Discussing ideas

Incidental writing

Phonics and spelling

Organising into a structure

Review of the Big Picture

Phase 3: Collaborate and compose

Programmes of study: Year 5

- Composition:

- Composition:

- Composition:

- Composition:

- Composition:

Introduction   Independent writing

Lesson 1

Starter (VGP focus)

Daily plenary

Shared writing

Lesson 2

Starter (VGP focus)

Shared writing

Independent writing

Daily plenary

Lesson 3

Starter (VGP focus)

Shared writing

Independent writing

Daily plenary

Lesson 4

Starter (VGP focus)

Rehearsing and performing

Shared writing

Review of the Big Picture

Independent writing

Daily plenary

Phase 4: Independent writing

Programmes of study: Year 5
• Composition:
• Composition:
• Composition:
• Composition:
• Composition:

Introduction

Self- and peer-assessment

Writing

Rehearsing and performing

Proofreading and redrafting

Final reflection on learning

Proofreading sheet / My writing checklist

Name: _____

Title: _____

	✓	✗
I have planned and written a story.		
I have planned and written a poem.		
I have planned and written non-fiction, for example recount diary, information report, explanation, instructions.		
Writing checklist	✓	✗
I said out loud what I am going to write about.		
I have composed a sentence orally before writing it.		
I can sequence sentences to form short narratives.		
I have re-read what I have written to check it makes sense.		
I have discussed what I have written with others.		
I have read aloud my writing clearly to others.		
I have left spaces between words.		
I have joined words and clauses with 'and'.		
I have used full stops, capital letters, exclamation marks and question marks correctly.		
I have used capital letters for names of people, places, days of the week and 'I'.		
I have checked that my words are spelt correctly.		

Proofreading sheet / My writing checklist (blank)

Name: _____

Title: _____

	✓	✗
I have planned and written a story.		
I have planned and written a poem.		
I have planned and written non-fiction, for example recount diary, information report, explanation, instructions.		
Writing checklist	✓	✗

Percy's story planner

Beginning: Where Percy was in the park. What the weather was like.

Animal	Why were they unhappy?

What was Percy's problem with all the animals?

How did Percy sort out the problem?

Phrases and words:

Knock! Knock! Now who can that be?

Can I come in? I can't get to sleep!

It is too (hot, cold, windy).

Oh dear. This won't do at all.

Fairy-tale planner

New 'bad' character	New setting

Keywords and phrases we could use:

Once upon a time …;   Once there lived …

… and they lived happily ever after.

Beginning: Hansel and Gretel get lost

Middle: Tricked and trapped by the bad character

Middle: Escaping from the bad character

Happy ending: Hansel and Gretel get home

Hansel and Gretel sentence cards

Cut out the sentences for the children to join with 'and'.

Hansel took the cake.	Hansel put it in his pocket.
Gretel walked into the woods.	Gretel picked up sticks.
Gretel sat down.	Gretel cried.
The birds saw the cake crumbs.	The birds ate the cake crumbs.
The granny smiled.	The granny waved at them.
I am going to cook you.	I am going to eat you.
Gretel pulled her hair.	Gretel pushed her into the cauldron.
They unlocked the gate.	They ran away.
The birds flew down.	The birds helped them.
The woodman ran out of his hut.	The woodman gave them a hug.

Making food sentences

Complete the sentences by adding in words from the word boxes.

'doing' words (verbs)			Food items (nouns)		
baking	eating	sipping	cakes	eggs	soup
licking	cooking	boiling	lollipops	pasta	curry

Hansel likes eating muffins.

Gretel likes _____ _____ .

Hansel likes _____ _____ .

Gretel likes _____ _____ .

Hansel likes _____ _____ .

Write two more sentences to say what you and a friend like to eat.

1. _____

_____

2. _____

_____

Mixed-up sentences

is magic This my paintbrush.

I can paint a of food. big pot

white fan. Shen painted a

warm blankets. need We

I want tree. on golden coins a

deep river. I paint will a

large Shen dragon. painted a

ran away. The Emperor

drums and flutes. painted Shen

fun had a The villagers party.

Traditional tale map

Good characters	Bad characters

Keywords and phrases

1. Beginning

2. Middle

3. Middle: sort out problem

4. End: Happy ending

Animal poem planner

Title: _____

Opening phrase:

Cats _____

_____

8 examples:

1. _____

2. _____

3. _____

4. _____

5. _____

6. _____

7. _____

8. _____

Last phrase:

_____

_____

Repeat top phrase:

_____

_____

Sorting 'ck' words

Read all the 'ck' words and sound-talk them out.
Listen to the short vowel sounds before the 'ck'.
Write the words into their right groups in the chart below.

back   lick   sock   neck   duck

deck   lock   suck   pack   tick

brick   sack   speck   clock   stuck

Jack   truck   pick   peck   rock

ack	eck	ick	ock	uck

Add one or two more 'ck' words to the chart.

'Busy Day' poem writing frame

_____

_____

_____

_____

_____

can't stop

got to _____

_____ where?

_____ what?

well

I've got to

_____

_____

_____

_____

_____

can't stop

got to _____

Investigating sounds and spellings

Some words have the same sound but different spellings.

Read out the words in the boxes. Add more words to each box.

/ou/

ou	ow
out	now
cloud	down
about	town

/oa/

oa	oe	ow	o-e
boat	toe	grow	bone
goal	hoe	snow	pole
road	Joe	blow	home

/or/

or	ore
for	more
horse	wore
born	tore

/air/

air	ear	are
fair	bear	rare
chair	pear	care
hair	tear	dare

Long vowel /oo/ or /yoo/

ue	ew	u-e
blue	new	June
glue	few	use
true	grew	tube

© HarperCollins *Publishers* 2015

'On some other planet' verse planner / Writing frame

My plan

On some other planet

(where?) _____

_____

Who or what lives there? _____

_____

_____

_____

My verse

On some other planet

_____

_____

_____

_____

_____

_____

Instructions writing frame

(heading) _____

What you need:

_____

_____

_____

_____

What you do:

1. _____

_____

2. _____

_____

3. _____

_____

4. _____

_____

_____

_____

Diary storyboard

Friday	Saturday	Sunday

Wednesday	Thursday	Friday

Saturday	Sunday	Monday

Match the 'ph' labels

All the words in the box below have 'ph'.
Use the words to write labels for the pictures.

dolphin	elephant	photograph
telephone	microphone	alphabet

a b c d e f g h i j
k l m n o p q r s
t u v w x y z

_____

_____

_____

_____

_____

_____

Dinosaur report writing frame

Introduction sentence:

_____

_____

Name of dinosaur: _____

(how to say the name) _____

Picture of the dinosaur

Information (three sentences to describe it):

_____

_____

_____

_____

_____

_____

Dinosaur information sheet

Triceratops

(tri-cera-tops)

- Three horns
- Large backwards-pointing frill
- 400–800 teeth
- Plant eater (herbivore)

Pteranodon

(teh-ran-owe-don)

- Winged lizard
- Wing span as long as a hang-glider
- Wings are leathery and not feathered
- Fish eater

Giganotosaurus

(gee-gah-no-toe-sor-us)

- As heavy as two elephants
- Very small brain (as small as a cucumber)
- Long tail for balance
- Meat eater (carnivore)

Iguanodon

(ig-wah-na-don)

- Two strong legs
- Hands with four fingers and a cone-shaped spike for a thumb
- As heavy as one van
- Plant eater

Spinosaurus

(spin-o-sor-us)

- Long snout / mouth
- Sail-shape spine on the back
- Very big
- Meat and fish eater

Diplodocus

(dip-lod-ic-uss)

- Long neck and long tail
- Four sturdy legs
- As heavy as one truck
- Largest ever dinosaur
- Plant eater

Making 'au' pairs

Add in 'au' to make the words. Then cut out the word squares.
Use the words to play "Pairs".

✂

dinos_____r	astron_____t	_____gust
_____thor	s_____ce	dinos_____r
_____gust	h_____nt	_____thor
h_____nt	s_____ce	astron_____t

Matty's storyboard

Keywords and phrases:

Beginning:

Middle:

End:

Split vowel digraph, i-e

Add the missing i-e to the words below, for example p ___ p ___ = p i p e

r ___ d ___

f ___ v ___

s m ___ l ___

d ___ n ___

d ___ v ___

k ___ t ___

sl ___ d ___

h ___ k ___

l ___ n ___

Underline the 'i-e' words in this sentence.

I like to ride my bike.

Add in the right 'i-e' word to the sentence.

I went to the park to fly my _____.

Adjective word cards

Copy and cut out the words.

happy	happy
fair	fair
wise	wise
funny	funny
fussy	fussy
selfish	selfish
well	well
lucky	lucky
kind	kind

Magical creature sentence starters

We found a _____

It was _____

It was the size of a _____

It had _____

It looked like _____

It had _____ like a _____

It moved _____

It liked to eat _____

It liked to _____

Its favourite thing was _____

I loved it because _____

Safari writing frame

Beginning

_____

_____

_____

1st creature

_____

_____

_____

"Look out, Lollipop!" says Grandpa.

"You'll be in trouble if _____

_____

I will have to take you home _____

_____

"Crumbs!" says Lollipop.

"We had better tiptoe past them."

Sssh!

Phew!

2nd creature

_____

_____

_____

"Look out, Lollipop!" says Grandpa.

"You'll be in trouble if _____

_____

I will have to take you home _____

_____

"Crumbs!" says Lollipop.

"We had better tiptoe past them."

Sssh!

Phew!

3rd creature

_____

_____

_____

"Look out, Lollipop!" says Grandpa.

"You'll be in trouble if _____

_____

I will have to take you home _____

_____

"Crumbs!" says Lollipop.

"We had better tiptoe past them."

Sssh!

Phew!

End

_____

_____

_____

Safari sentences

Cut out the sentences and put them in the right order.

✂ -

At the shops, we found a stripy pair of SOCK-OR-US.

- -

We were glad to get home and have our tea.

- -

Gran and I went on a shopping safari.

- -

After the shops, Gran and I went into a CAFÉ-I-TUS.

- -

On the way home, we rode on a WOBBLE-TRAM.

- -

We packed our bags, a shopping list and a bottle of water.

- -

Gran and I caught a big red BUS-O-LOCUS.

- -

Fairy-tale story map

New 'frog' character:	New 'castle' character:

Keywords and phrases we could use:

Once upon a time ...; Once there lived ...

... and they lived happily ever after.

Beginning:

Middle:

Happy ending:

Fairy-tale letter writing frame

_____

_____

Dear _____

_____

_____

_____

_____

_____

_____

_____

Who sits where?

Copy and cut out the name tags.

Gingerbread Man	Hare
Three Little Pigs	Slow Tortoise
Jack	Red Riding Hood
Beanstalk Giant	Pinocchio
Ugly Duckling	Fairy Godmother
Little Bear	Troll

'igh' word leaves

- Add in the missing 'igh' to the words in the leaves.
- Cut out the leaves.

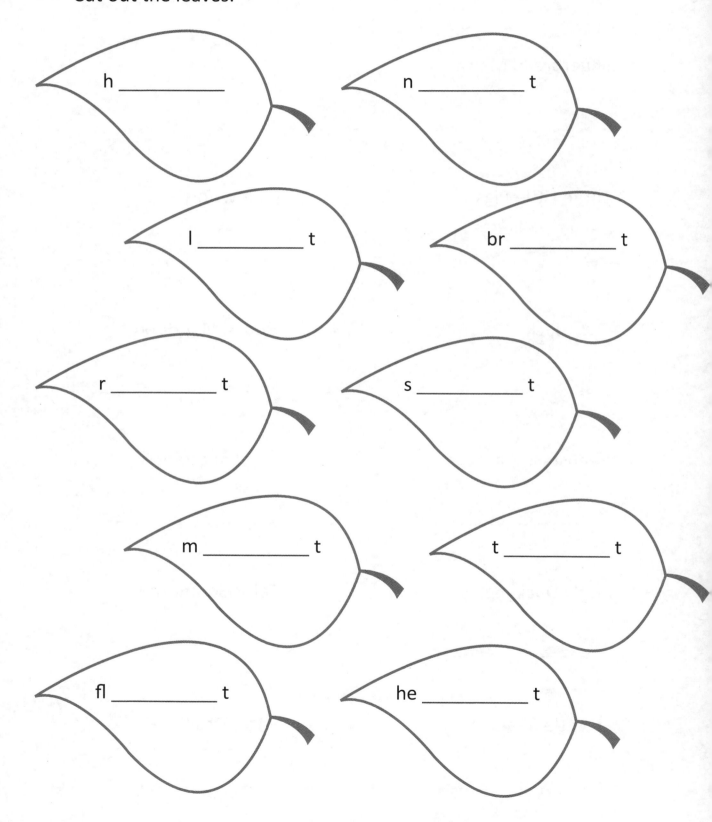

h _____

n _____ t

l _____ t

br _____ t

r _____ t

s _____ t

m _____ t

t _____ t

fl _____ t

he _____ t

Making -ing words

Add -ing to the end of the words.

1. I can hear an owl hoot_____ in the wood.

2. The flying squirrel is jump_____ from a tree.

3. A fox likes hunt_____ at night.

4. A hedgehog is roll_____ into a ball.

5. The frog is jump_____ over the leaves.

6. That snake is hiss_____ in the bushes.

Use the -ing words to make two sentences about night animals.

| climbing | jumping | walking | flying | calling | sniffing |
| glowing | howling | hunting | catching | playing | rolling |

1. _____

_____

2. _____

_____

Comprehension

These Challenge questions can be used in conjunction with the Treasure House Pupil Book units. They provide an additional activity to stretch children and give them the opportunity to apply their learning in a more challenging context.

Unit 1

Draw and label all the things Percy puts on to keep warm. With a partner, add other things he could wear.

Unit 2

Draw and label Hansel and Gretel when they are left in the woods. With a partner, plan what they can do next. Add a sentence to your picture to explain what their plan is.

Unit 3

Draw a picture of the fox and the tiger in the forest. With a partner, think of what they will say next. Add speech bubbles to show what they will say.

Unit 4

As a class, say the poem aloud. Repeat the poem and try to remember the words when your teacher pauses. Then write down the pairs of words that sound the same. Read the pairs of words aloud to a partner. With your partner, add other words that sound like them.

Unit 5

As a class, say the poem aloud. Repeat the poem and try to remember the words when your teacher pauses. With a partner, list things that make you want to spend your money. Draw a poster to remind you and the bear to 'Save, Don't Spend!'.

Unit 6

As a class, say the poem aloud. Repeat the poem and try to remember the words when your teacher pauses. Draw a picture of the snowman after the bunny has taken his carrot nose. With a partner, think about what happens next. Add a sentence to your picture to explain what happens next.

Unit 7

With a partner, do this test. Write a sentence about what you found out.

Unit 8

Draw a picture of yourself eating breakfast. What are you eating? Add a sentence to your picture to explain what you are eating. With a partner, talk about what else you do in the morning. Add one more sentence to your picture to explain what else you do in the morning.

Unit 9

Look at your eye in a mirror. Draw and label a picture of an eye. With a partner, think of two facts about eyes and add them to your picture.

Composition

Some of these Challenge questions appear at the end of 'Now try these' in the Treasure House Pupil Book units. They provide an additional activity to stretch children and give them the opportunity to apply their learning in a more challenging context.

Unit 1
Write a sentence about Mr Bear looking for somewhere to sleep.

Unit 2
Write a sentence about the miller telling the king a lie.

Unit 3
Write a sentence about the party games Arthur wants to play.

Unit 4
Write a sentence about noises you can hear at night.

Unit 5
Write a sentence to the boy in the poem to tell him his mom will still love him even when she has a new baby.

Unit 6
Write a sentence about creatures under the sea.

Unit 7
Write four instructions that would help a new child in your class know what to do in the mornings when they get to school.

Unit 8
Write a sentence about birds in winter.

Unit 9
Write a sentence about something your friend did yesterday.

Spelling

These Challenge questions can be used in conjunction with the Treasure House Pupil Book units. They provide an additional activity to stretch children and give them the opportunity to apply their learning in a more challenging context.

Unit 1

Write a sentence using the word dress.

Unit 2

Practise spelling the words **pocket**, **rocket** and **chicken.**

Unit 3

Practise spelling the words donkey and monkey.

Unit 4

Write the words crocodile and kangaroo. These words have three syllables. Draw lines to split them into syllables

Unit 5

Sort these words into two groups: words spelled **tch** and words spelled **ch**.

much, notch, which, stretch, switch, chin

Unit 6

Write sentences using the words starve, curve and active.

Unit 7

Some nouns do not take an s to make them plural. Instead, the whole word changes. Here are some for you to learn to spell.

child → **children**

man → **men**

mouse → **mice**

Unit 8

How many more plural nouns can you think of? Write them down and learn their spellings.

Unit 9

Write words that end with -**ing** to complete each sentence. Use your own ideas.

1. The children are _____ in the playground.
2. I like _____ and _____.

Unit 10

Write sentences using the words **harder**, **faster** and **longer**.

Unit 11

Write these sentences as if they happened in the past.

1. I want a new bike.
2. We pass the park.
3. The people crowd into the party.

Unit 12

Adjectives with **-er** at the end are called **comparative** adjectives. Adjectives with **-est** at the end are called **superlative** adjectives. Sort these adjectives into two groups: **comparative** and **superlative**.

highest, faster, duller, dullest, slowest, deeper, greener, brighter, brightest, calmest

Unit 13

Write a sentence using as many words ending in **y** as you can.

Unit 14

Practise spelling the words **microphone**, **telephone** and **photograph**

Unit 15

Sometimes the **/h/** sound is spelled **wh**. Practise spelling the words **who**, **whose** and **whole**. What do these words mean?

Unit 16

The **/k/** sound is also usually spelled **k** if it is at the end of a word. For example: **tank**. How many words can you think of that end with **k**? Make a list and learn the spellings.

Unit 17

How many words beginning with **un** can you think of? Write a list and learn the spellings.

Unit 18

How many more compound words can you think of? Write a list and learn the spellings.

Unit 19

1. Write the two days of the week with an **/er/** sound.
2. Write the day of the week with an **/oo/** sound.

Vocabulary, Grammar and Punctuation

These Challenge questions can be used in conjunction with the Treasure House Pupil Book units. They provide an additional activity to stretch children and give them the opportunity to apply their learning in a more challenging context.

Vocabulary Unit 1

Write some sentences about going for a walk in the woods. Imagine you saw more than one of these things: **fox**, **rabbit**, **tree**, **flower**, **bush**. Use the correct suffix, **-s** or **-es**, to write about the things you saw.

Vocabulary Unit 2

Write at least three sentences using as many **-ing** words as you can. How many can you find?

Vocabulary Unit 3

Write at least three sentences using as many words with the prefix **un-** as you can. How many can you find?

Grammar Unit 1

Write three sentences about your classroom. Use capital letters at the start of each sentence. Use full stops at the end of each sentence. Check your sentences make sense.

Grammar Unit 2

Write two sentences about your favourite toys. Then join them with **and**.

For example: **They are big. They are soft. They are big and they are soft.**

Punctuation Unit 1

Ask a friend about their weekend. Can you write down your question using a question mark? Answer your friend's question with a shocking sentence. Can you write down your answer using an exclamation mark? Remember to put capital letters at the start of your sentences.

Punctuation Unit 2

Write two sentences about you and your friends. Remember to use capital letters to start their names and for the word **I**.

Punctuation Unit 3

Write two sentences about places you have visited or would like to see. Remember to use a capital letter at the start of place names.

Comprehension

Unit 1
Open-ended question: Look for discussions and at least one additional item (e.g. gloves, jumper, ear muffs).

Unit 2
Open-ended question: Look for features including Hansel and Gretel in a woodland setting, discussions and at least one idea for a plan.

Unit 3
Open-ended question: Look for features including the fox and the tiger in a forest setting, discussions and at least one speech bubble containing words that would make sense coming next in the extract.

Unit 4
Read the poem out loud with the children. Then repeat it, pausing before the rhyming words ('chair', 'edge', 'do', 'frocks' and 'anywhere'). Prompt the children to remember the words, using the rhyme to help.

The rhyming pairs are anywhere/chair, ledge/edge, shoe/do, box/frocks, care/anywhere.

Open-ended question: Look for discussions, reading skills, confident performances and at least one additional rhyme (e.g. there / hedge / new / fox / pair).

Unit 5
Read the poem out loud with the children. Then repeat it, pausing before the rhyming words ('save', 'money', 'pound' and 'honey'). Prompt the children to remember the words, using the rhyme to help.

Unit 6
Read the poem out loud with the children. Then repeat it, pausing before the rhyming words ('suppose' and 'crunch'). Prompt the children to remember the words, using the rhyme to help. Then draw attention to the lines in which appear, and ask the children to say the lines. Repeat the poem again, prompting the children to try to say these two lines from memory.

Open-ended question: Look for features including a chubby snowman without a carrot nose, discussion and a sentence that offers a reasonable idea (e.g. 'The rabbit says sorry.' / 'The snowman is sad.' / 'The rabbit finds the snowman a new nose.').

Unit 7
Open-ended question: Look for discussion, co-operation and ability to follow the instructions. In the sentences, look for a reasonable summary of the findings of the test (e.g. 'I could tell the foods better when I did not hold my nose.' / 'Smelling the foods helped me to tell what they were').

Unit 8
Open-ended question: Look for features such as the child eating breakfast, discussion and sentences that offer reasonable descriptions of what the child eats for breakfast and does in the morning (e.g. 'I eat toast for breakfast. I brush my teeth.' / 'I have a bowl of cornflakes for breakfast. I leave for school on the bus.).

Unit 9
Open-ended question: Look for labelled features including eyelashes, eyelids and (possibly) a pupil, and two reasonable ideas for facts (e.g. 'people have two eyes', 'eyes are covered by eyelids', 'eyelids have eyelashes at the ends', 'eyes let you see things', 'eyes can be different colours', 'eyes have a white and a pupil'.

Composition

Unit 1
Open ended. Less confident children might like to copy some or all of a sentence from the story. More confident children can construct their own sentence, saying it first then writing it. The sentence should show attempts to use a capital letter and full stop and the content should relate to the context.

Unit 2
Open ended. Less confident children might like to copy some or all of a sentence from the story. More confident children can construct their own sentence, saying it first then writing it. The sentence should show attempts to use a capital letter and full stop and the content should relate to the context.

Unit 3
Open ended. Less confident children might like to copy some or all of a sentence that an adult has scripted. More confident children can construct their own sentence, saying it first then writing it. The sentence should show attempts to use a capital letter and full stop and the content should relate to the context.

Unit 4

Open ended. Less confident children might like to copy some or all of a sentence from the poem. More confident children can construct their own sentence, saying it first then writing it. The sentence should show attempts to use a capital letter and full stop and the content should relate to the context.

Unit 5

Open ended. Less confident children might like to copy some or all of a sentence scribed by an adult. More confident children can construct their own sentence, saying it first then writing it. The sentence should show attempts to use a capital letter and full stop and the content should relate to the context.

Unit 6

Open ended. Less confident children might like to copy some or all of a sentence that an adult has scripted. More confident children can construct their own sentence, saying it first then writing it. The sentence should show attempts to use a capital letter and full stop and the content should relate to the context.

Unit 7

Open ended. Less confident children might like to copy some or all sentences from those scribed with an adult. More confident children can construct their own sentence, saying it first then writing it. The sentence should show attempts to use a capital letter and full stop and the content should relate to the context, including using imperative verbs where appropriate.

Unit 8

Open ended. Less confident children might like to copy some or all of a sentence scripted with an adult. More confident children can construct their own sentence, saying it first then writing it. The sentence should show attempts to use a capital letter and full stop and the content should relate to the context.

Unit 9

Open ended. Less confident children might like to copy some or all of a sentence scripted with an adult. More confident children can construct their own sentence, saying it first then writing it. The sentence should show attempts to use a capital letter and full stop and the content should relate to the context using the past tense.

Spelling

Unit 1

Accept any sentence where **dress** is spelled correctly.

Unit 2

Children learn to spell the words pocket, rocket and chicken.

Unit 3

Children learn to spell the words **donkey** and **monkey**.

Unit 4

croc/o/dile   kang/a/roo

Unit 5

Tch: notch; stretch; switch

Ch: much; chin; which

Unit 6

Accept any sentences where **starve**, **curve** and **active** are spelled correctly.

Unit 7

Children learn to spell the following.

child → **children**

man → **men**

mouse → **mice**

Unit 8

Children write as many plural nouns as they can think of and learn their spellings.

Unit 9

Children use their own ideas to complete the sentences. Accept any correctly spelled verbs ending in **-ing**.

Unit 10

Children write sentences using the words **harder**, **faster** and **longer**.

Unit 11

1. I wanted a new bike.
2. We passed the park.
3. The people crowded into the party.

Unit 12

Comparative: faster; duller; deeper; greener; brighter

Superlative: highest; dullest; slowest; brightest; calmest; dullest

Unit 13

Children write sentences using as many words ending in **y** as they can. Award 1 mark per correctly spelled target word.

Unit 14

Children learn to spell the words **microphone**, **telephone** and **photograph.**

Unit 15

Children learn to spell the words **who**, **whose** and **whole**.

Unit 16

Children make a list of words that end with **k** and learn the spellings.

Unit 17

Children think of words beginning with **un** and learn the spellings.

Unit 18

Children think of compound words and learn the spellings.

Unit 19

1. Thursday, Saturday
2. Tuesday

Vocabulary, Grammar and Punctuation

Vocabulary Unit 1

Accept any appropriate sentences that include the correct suffix **–s** or **–es**.

Vocabulary Unit 2

Accept any appropriate sentences incorporating **–ing** words.

Vocabulary Unit 3

Accept any appropriate sentences incorporating words with the prefix **un-**.

Grammar Unit 1

Accept any appropriate sentences, using capital letters and full stop.

Grammar Unit 2

Accept any appropriate sentences incorporating the word and.

Punctuation Unit 1

Accept any appropriate sentences, using question marks and exclamations marks, as well as capital letters.

Punctuation Unit 2

Accept any appropriate sentences using capital letters for names and the word I.

Punctuation Unit 3

Accept any appropriate sentences using capital letters for place names and the word For example: My friend Marie is from France.

Comprehension

Unit 1

Get started

1. winter [1 mark]
2. Percy [1 mark]
3. fresh [1 mark]
4. middle [1 mark]

Try these

Accept appropriate answers, e.g.:

1. A park keeper [1 mark]
2. In the hut / In the park [1 mark]
3. Wellington boots / Two pairs of woolly socks [1 mark]
4. Cosy and warm [1 mark]

Now try these

Open-ended questions.

1. Look for any appropriate description of a park in summer, e.g. 'warm', 'sunny', 'full of flowers'. [2 marks max]
2. Look for relevant objects in the drawing, e.g. Percy's coat and scarf, a small cosy hut. [2 marks max]
3. Look for features relevant to the description 'cosy and warm', e.g. a fire, a comfy chair. [2 marks max]

Unit 2

Get started

1. food [1 mark]
2. eat [1 mark]
3. Gretel [1 mark]
4. cake [1 mark]

Try these

Accept appropriate answers, e.g.:

1. The woodman, his wife, Hansel and Gretel. [1 mark]
2. There is no food. [1 mark]
3. Into the Brown Wood. [1 mark]
4. He gave them cake to eat. [1 mark]

Now try these

Accept appropriate answers, e.g.:

1. To show the way home. [1 mark]
2. Look for features in the drawing including Hansel and the cake, and possibly the wood, Gretel and the woodman. [2 marks max]
3. Look for features in the drawing including Hansel and Gretel, and possibly the wood and the woodman. Look for appropriate plans, e.g. 'follow the trail of cake' and 'find their way out of the wood'. [3 marks max]

Unit 3

Get started

1. fox [1 mark]
2. leapt [1 mark]
3. idea [1 mark]
4. bows [1 mark]

Try these

Accept appropriate answers, e.g.:

1. Having a nap [1 mark]
2. He trembled (and then had an idea) [1 mark]
3. The king of the forest [1 mark]
4. The lion [1 mark]

Now try these

Open-ended questions.

1. Look for an appropriate reason, e.g. 'Yes, because the tiger is interested' / 'No, because the fox is not the king of the forest'. [2 marks max]
2. Look for features in the drawing including the fox sleeping, and possibly the forest and the tiger. [2 marks max]
3. Look for features in the drawing including the fox and the tiger in the forest. Look for appropriate responses, e.g. 'tiger says "I don't believe you", fox says "I'll prove that I'm the king"' [2 marks max]

Unit 4

Get started

1. anywhere [1 mark]
2. chair [1 mark]
3. lap [1 mark]
4. cardboard [1 mark]

Try these

1. Look for appropriate ideas, e.g. 'Your frocks / A cardboard box' [2 marks max]
2. Look for appropriate ideas, e.g. 'In the middle or on the edge' [2 marks max]
3. Answers should list three of these places: table, chair, piano, window-ledge, drawer, shoe, lap, cardboard box, cupboard. [3 marks]
4. edge [1 mark]

Now try these

Open-ended questions.

1. Look for appropriate ideas, e.g. 'Because cats aren't fussy' / 'Because cats are lazy' / 'Because fur makes cats comfy anywhere'. [2 marks max]
2. Look for features in the drawing including a cat sleeping inside a shoe. [2 marks max]
3. Guide the class to read the poem out loud together, pause in appropriate places. Pairs list rhyming words:

anywhere / chair, ledge / edge, shoe / do, box / frocks, anywhere / care /anywhere. Monitor pairs as they suggest further rhyming words. [3 marks max]

Unit 5

Get started

1. bear [1 mark]
2. love [1 mark]
3. money [1 mark]
4. saved [1 mark]

Try these

Accept appropriate answers, e.g.:

1. honey [1 mark]
2. two pence [1 mark]
3. red and round [1 mark]
4. pound [1 mark]

Now try these

Open-ended questions.

1. Look for any reasonable ideas, e.g. 'Because he kept spending his money on honey'. [2 marks max]
2. Look for features in the drawing including a bear eating honey, and possibly the cave setting or a red, round money box. [2 marks max]
3. Guide the class to read the poem out loud together, pause in appropriate places. Pairs list things that make them want to spend their money – look for appropriate ideas, e.g. toys, clothes, music. Monitor pairs as they draw a poster containing appropriate images related to saving money. [3 marks max]

Unit 6

Get started

1. snowman [1 mark]
2. carrot [1 mark]
3. hungry [1 mark]
4. nose [1 mark]

Try these

Accept appropriate answers, e.g.:

1. The snowman [1 mark]
2. The bunny [1 mark]
3. Ate his carrot nose [1 mark]
4. A bit fat. Assist children, if they ask for help, by discussing what they think the word might mean before providing an explanation of the vocabulary. [1 mark]

Now try these

Open-ended questions.

1. Look for appropriate ideas, e.g. 'hungry' before eating the carrot, and 'full', 'happy' or 'bad for taking the snowman's nose' after eating the carrot. [2 marks max]

2. Look for features in the drawing including a chubby snowman and a carrot nose. [2 marks max]
3. Guide the class to read the poem out loud together, pausing in appropriate places. Look for features in the drawing including a snowman without a nose. Monitor pairs as they suggest further appropriate next actions, e.g. 'the snowman cries' or 'the rabbits says sorry'. [3 marks max]

Unit 7

Get started

1. blindfold [1 mark]
2. spoonful [1 mark]
3. food [1 mark]
4. holding [1 mark]

Try these

Accept appropriate answers, e.g.:

1. A blindfold, grated apple, grated pear, grated carrot and three bowls [1 mark]
2. Three [1 mark]
3. Put on the blindfold and hold your nose. [1 mark]
4. Look at the numbers. [1 mark]

Now try these

Open-ended questions.

1. Look for clear labels on the drawing and features including two children, one wearing a blindfold and one feeding them a spoonful of food. [2 marks max]
2. Monitor pairs as they carry out the test. Look for appropriate sentences, e.g. 'it is difficult to tell which food is which when you cannot see it'. [2 marks max]

Unit 8

Get started

1. morning [1 mark]
2. breakfast [1 mark]
3. buy [1 mark]
4. work [1 mark]

Try these

Accept appropriate answers, e.g.:

1. Wakes up / Has a cup of tea [1 mark]
2. A newspaper [1 mark]
3. Chocolate toffees [1 mark]
4. On the moon [1 mark]

Now try these

Open-ended questions.

1. Look for attempts to explain Bob's feelings, e.g. 'I think he is excited as space is amazing'. [2 marks max]

2. Look for features in the drawing including Bob sat at the breakfast table with a cup of tea and two eggs. [2 marks max]

3. Look for appropriate features in the drawing, e.g. a child eating breakfast cereal, and an appropriate description. Monitor pairs as they discuss their morning routine, and write appropriate sentences, e.g. 'I brush my teeth'.

Unit 9

Get started

1. nose [1 mark]
2. top [1 mark]
3. hurts [1 mark]
4. nostrils [1 mark]

Try these

Accept appropriate answers, e.g.:

1. On the front of your face [1 mark]
2. Big or small [1 mark]
3. The end [1 mark]
4. Hairs and snot/wetness [2 marks]

Now try these

Open-ended questions.

1. Look for appropriate reasons, e.g. 'to smell things' / 'to breathe'. [2 marks max]
2. Look for labelled features on the drawing including hardness on top and softness at the end, two nostrils, hairs in the nostrils and snot. [2 marks max]
3. Look for appropriate drawings of eyes. Monitor pairs as they suggest facts about eyes, e.g. 'eyes have eyelashes' and 'eyes have a black dot in the middle' [2 marks max]

Composition

Unit 1

Get started

1. park [1 mark]
2. rabbit [1 mark]
3. snow [1 mark]
4. mice [1 mark]
5. house [1 mark]

Try these

Accept appropriate answers, e.g.:

1. upset [1 mark]
2. happy/helpful [1 mark]
3. playing/naughty [1 mark]
4. snowy/cold [1 mark]
5. warm/cosy [1 mark]

Now try these

Open-ended questions.

1. Look for features in the drawing such as snow, trees, etc. [2 marks max]
2. Look for features in the drawing that suggest a warm, cosy home with a rabbit in it. [2 marks max]
3. Look for appropriate speech, such as "we are having fun!" or "it's nice and warm in here!". [2 marks max]

Unit 2

Get started

1. upon [1 mark]
2. foolish [1 mark]
3. daughter [1 mark]
4. wanted [1 mark]
5. king's [1 mark]]

Try these

Accept appropriate answers, e.g.:

1. poor, silly [1 mark]
2. greedy [1 mark]
3. normal, ordinary [1 mark]
4. big, grand [1 mark]
5. yellow, dry [1 mark]

Now try these

Open-ended questions.

1. Look for features in the drawing such as the miller inside/nearby a cottage style house. [1 mark]
2. Look for features in the drawing such as the king and palace looking grand to contrast with the miller. [1 mark]
3. Look for appropriate speech, such as "she can weave straw into gold" [1 mark]
4. Look for sentences that refer to the miller telling a lie, because his daughter cannot spin straw into gold. [1 mark]

Unit 3

Get started

Open-ended questions.

1. Look for a labelled drawing of Arthur. [1 mark]
2. Look for a labelled drawing of Flora. [1 mark]
3. Look for a labelled drawing of three pigs. [1 mark]
4. Look for a labelled drawing of the wolf. [1 mark]
5. Look for a labelled drawing of the bears. [1 mark]

Try these

Accept appropriate answers, e.g.:

1. "I am excited about my party" [1 mark]
2. "It will be fun if lots of animals come to the party" [1 mark]
3. "Thanks for inviting us" [1 mark]

4. "I love parties" [1 mark]

5. "Yes we'll come to the party too" [1 mark]

Now try these

Open-ended questions.

1. Look for invented characters that are characterful and well described. [1 mark]

2. Look for speech that is appropriate to the character. [1 mark]

3. Look for details such as who the recipient is, when and where the party is, etc. [3 marks]

4. Look for sentences that include descriptions of the games. [2 marks]

Unit 4

Get started

Accept appropriate answers, e.g.:

1. twit-ta-woo/hoot [1 mark]

2. tick tock [1 mark]

3. screech/growl [1 mark]

4. squeak/eek [1 mark]

5. flap/squeak [1 mark]

Try these

Accept appropriate answers, e.g.:

1. bed [1 mark]

2. owls hooting [1 mark]

3. books on the shelf [1 mark]

4. soap from my bath [1 mark]

5. sleepy [1 mark]

Now try these

Open-ended questions.

1. Look for drawings that show it is night time in the bedroom. [1 mark]

2. Look for drawings that show night time features such as the moon and nocturnal animals. [1 mark]

3. Look for labels on the details such as nocturnal animals. [1 mark]

4. Talk about what could be making a noise during the night and about how our senses are often heightened when we are in the dark. Discuss senses and reassure children who say they feel afraid at night. Say sentences out loud before writing them and remind children to use a capital letter and full stop. [3 marks]

Unit 5

Get started

Open-ended questions. Accept appropriate answers, e.g.:

1. I'm a cheeky monkey [1 mark]

2. I'm a sweetie [1 mark]

3. I'm a rumbletum [1 mark]

4. I'm a sleepy bunny [1 mark]

5. I'm a grouch [1 mark]

Try these

Open-ended questions. Accept appropriate answers, e.g.:

1. a good boy/girl [1 mark]

2. a funny boy/girl [1 mark]

3. a superstar [1 mark]

4. fun to play with [1 mark]

5. wonderful [1 mark]

Now try these

Open-ended questions.

1. Look for drawings which show the boy in the poem looking worried about his mom's pregnant belly. [1 mark]

2. Children could copy the speech shown in the poem or create their own speech. It should be relevant to the storyline of the boy feeling anxious about his mom's feelings for him once the new baby comes. [1 mark]

3. Look for details in the drawing such as facial expression and clothing. [1 mark]

4. Look for appropriate speech that reflects the relationship between the two people.

5. Look for sentences that are correctly formed, with capital letters and full stops and which show appropriate reassurance.

Unit 6

Get started

1. Crabs [1 mark]

2. Octopuses, Otters [1 mark]

3. Weevers, Walruses, Whales [1 mark]

4. Starfish, Seals, Sea lions, Shrimps [1 mark]

Try these

Open-ended questions. Accept appropriate answers, e.g.:

1. Starfish have lots of pointy arms like a star. [1 mark]

2. Dolphins are grey and friendly. [1 mark]

3. Jellyfish are soft and squishy. [1 mark]

4. Turtles have patterned shells on their backs. [1 mark]

Now try these

Open-ended questions. Accept appropriate answers, e.g.:

1. boats, shipwrecks, caves, rocks, seaweed, coral, sand [1 mark]

2. Encourage children to use the poem to select six sea creatures to include in their drawing. [1 mark]

3. "Did you see that huge boat?" "Yes, the humans are fishing again." [1 mark]

Unit 7

Get started
1. yes [1 mark]
2. no [1 mark]
3. yes [1 mark]
4. no [1 mark]
5. yes [1 mark]

Try these
1. Get [1 mark]
2. Put [1 mark]
3. Place [1 mark]
4. Add [1 mark]
5. Pat [1 mark]

Now try these
Open-ended questions.
1. Sentence needs to make sense and use an imperative verb. [1 mark]
2. Encourage children to think about how far apart the people in their picture should stand and how the hands of the people in the picture should be positioned. Labels should indicate features such as 'Take it in turns'. [1 mark]
3. Children should write sentences that make sense, are relevant to buttering bread and use imperative verbs. [1 mark]
4. Less confident children might like to copy some or all sentences from those scribed with an adult. More confident children can construct their own sentence, saying it first then writing it. The sentence should show attempts to use a capital letter and full stop and the content should be relative to the context, including using imperative verbs where appropriate. [3 marks]

Unit 8

Get started
1. red [1 mark]
2. fatter [1 mark]
3. warm [1 mark]
4. lovely [1 mark]
5. fierce [1 mark]

Try these
Accept appropriate answers, e.g.:
1. feathery [1 mark]
2. spindly [1 mark]
3. small, sharp [1 mark]
4. wiggly [1 mark]
5. beady [1 mark]

Now try these
Open-ended questions.

1. Encourage children to use the information in the report to inform their picture e.g. bright red face and breast. [1 mark]
2. Encourage children to talk about robins and with support use books or the internet to find a new fact about robins. [1 mark]
3. Children could write about any bird that they know of; birds that they see in their garden or at school; what birds like to eat or do in general. This will stimulate opportunities to relate the text to children's own experiences. [1 mark]
4. Less confident children might like to copy some or all of a sentence scripted with an adult. More confident children can construct their own sentence, saying it first then writing it. The sentence should show attempts to use a capital letter and full stop and the content should be relative to the context. [3 marks]

Unit 9

Get started
Accept appropriate answers, e.g.:
1. scratched [1 mark]
2. flapped [1 mark]
3. scrabbled [1 mark]
4. pecked [1 mark]
5. rested [1 mark]

Try these
Accept appropriate answers in the past tense, e.g.:
1. I brushed my teeth. [1 mark]
2. I watched TV. [1 mark]
3. I played football. [1 mark]
4. I went to the beach. [1 mark]
5. I crawled everywhere. [1 mark]

Now try these
Open-ended questions.
1. Encourage children to show the chick pecking in a farmyard. Discuss the appearance of a chick. [1 mark]
2. Encourage children to show themselves as a baby. Discuss how different they would have looked then, e.g. smaller, sitting or crawling, clothing, hair, etc. [1 mark]
3. Encourage children to remember how they celebrated their last birthday. Did they have a party? Did they have a family meal? Did they get any gifts? Did they feel different getting older? [1 mark]
4. Less confident children might like to copy some or all of a sentence scripted with an adult. More confident children can construct their own sentence, saying it first then writing it. The sentence should show attempts to use a capital letter and full stop and the content should be relative to the context using the past tense. [3 marks]

Spelling

Unit 1

Get started

1. she**ll** [example]
2. fu**ss** [1 mark]
3. o**ff** [1 mark]
4. pre**ss** [1 mark]
5. i**ll** [1 mark]
6. tro**ll** [1 mark]
7. gla**ss** [1 mark]
8. cli**ff** [1 mark]

Try these

1. doll [example]
2. smell [1 mark]
3. buzz [1 mark]
4. fluff [1 mark]
5. mess [1 mark]

Now try these

1. Jill has a doll. [example]
2. Ring the doorbell. [1 mark]
3. Cut the grass. [1 mark]
4. Do not miss the bus. [1 mark]
5. Roll down the hill. [1 mark]

Unit 2

Get started

1. sho**ck** [example]
2. ti**ck** [1 mark]
3. li**ck** [1 mark]
4. ro**ck** [1 mark]
5. lu**ck** [1 mark]

Try these

1. a back pack [example]
2. truck [1 mark]
3. a black dog [1 mark]
4. a stack of blocks/bricks [2 marks]

Now try these

1. The duck went quack. [example]
2. The wall is made of brick. [1 mark]
3. The cat is black. [1 mark]
4. The dog did a trick. [1 mark]
5. The clock tells the time. [1 mark]

Unit 3

Get started

1. dri**nk** [example]
2. pi**nk** [1 mark]
3. pla**nk** [1 mark]
4. i**nk** [1 mark]
5. su**nk** [1 mark]
6. clu**nk** [1 mark]
7. thi**nk** [1 mark]
8. bla**nk** [1 mark]

Try these

1. stink [example]
2. bunk [1 mark]
3. junk [1 mark]
4. blink [1 mark]
5. bank [1 mark]

Now try these

1. trunk [example]
2. sink [1 mark]
3. thank [1 mark]
4. wink [1 mark]
5. bunk [1 mark]

Unit 4

Get started

One syllable: frog [example]; bed [1 mark]

Two syllables: carrot [1 mark]; chicken [1 mark]; pocket [1 mark]

Try these

1. seahorse [example]
2. kitten [1 mark]
3. zebra [1 mark]
4. parrot [1 mark]
5. hamster [1 mark]

Now try these

1. The spotty dog has two puppies. [example]
2. I wear my jumper to keep warm. [1 mark]
3. I eat bread and butter. [1 mark]
4. I saw monkeys at the zoo. [1 mark]
5. Daisies are white and yellow flowers. [3 marks]

Unit 5

Get started

1. ca**tch** [example]
2. pi**tch** [1 mark]
3. cru**tch** [1 mark]
4. sna**tch** [1 mark]

5. la**tch** [1 mark]
6. ha**tch** [1 mark]
7. wa**tch** [1 mark]
8. ke**tch**up [1 mark]
9. ske**tch** [1 mark]
10. ki**tch**en [1 mark]

Try these

1. My dog ~~feches~~ **fetches** sticks. [example]
2. My rabbit lives in a ~~huch~~ **hutch**. [1 mark]
3. I like to ~~wach~~ **watch** television. [1 mark]
4. The pirate has an eye ~~pach~~ **patch**. [1 mark]
5. Measles make you ~~ich~~ **itch** and ~~scrach~~ **scratch**. [1 mark]

Now try these

Spelt tch: notch [1 mark]; stretch [1 mark]; switch [1 mark]

Spelt ch: much [1 mark]; chin [1 mark]; which [1 mark]

Unit 6

Get started

1. glo**ve** [example]
2. capti**ve** [1 mark]
3. dissol**ve** [1 mark]
4. oli**ve** [1 mark]
5. ser**ve** [1 mark]
6. ha**ve** [1 mark]
7. remo**ve** [1 mark]
8. mo**ve** [1 mark]
9. wa**ve** [1 mark]

Try these

1. carve [example]
2. love [1 mark]
3. starve [1 mark]
4. curve [1 mark]
5. solve [1 mark]

Now try these

1. On birthdays people _give_ presents. [example]
2. It is good to be _active_. [1 mark]
3. I _have_ a pet _dove_. [2 marks]
4. Blue whales are _massive_! [1 mark]
5. I _live_ in a flat _above_ a shop. [2 marks]

Unit 7

Get started

1. two rabbits [example]
2. a banana [1 mark]
3. many hands [1 mark]
4. one log [1 mark]
5. one hundred books [1 mark]

Try these

1. he drinks [example]
2. I run [1 mark]
3. she hops [1 mark]
4. you rock [1 mark]
5. it sucks [1 mark]

Now try these

1. The chicken has laid two eggs. [example]
2. I can see two **cows** in the field. [1 mark]
3. Rashid **kicks** the ball. [1 mark]
4. Harriet **eats** a lot of fresh fruit. [1 mark]
5. I have two **pens** and one **pencil**. [2 marks]

Unit 8

Get started

1. a fox [example]
2. some dishes [1 mark]
3. three wishes [1 mark]
4. lots of matches [1 mark]
5. one cross [1 mark]

Try these

1. Tim brushes [example]
2. I fetch [1 mark]
3. it switches [1 mark]
4. We watch [1 mark]
5. She catches [1 mark]

Now try these

1. My hat **matches** my gloves! [example]
2. My brother **plays** the piano. [1 mark]
3. My dog **bites** and **scratches**. [2 marks]
4. Henri **reads** a lot of **books**. [2 marks]
5. My aunt gives me lots of **hugs** and **kisses**. [2 marks]

Unit 9

Get started

1. sleeping [example]
2. dressing [1 mark]
3. buzzing [1 mark]
4. fizzing [1 mark]
5. hunting [1 mark]
6. cleaning [1 mark]
7. jumping [1 mark]
8. eating [1 mark]

Try these

-ing words	root words
blinking	blink [example]
sinking	sink [1 mark]
licking	lick [1 mark]
snowing	snow [1 mark]
drying	dry [1 mark]

Now try these

1. We are **playing** with toys. [example]
2. The eggs are **hatching**. [1 mark]
3. We are **watching** the school play. [1 mark]
4. Mena is **kicking** the ball. [1 mark]
5. Outside it is **raining**. [1 mark]

Unit 10

Get started

1. rower [example]
2. hunter [1 mark]
3. printer [1 mark]
4. reader [1 mark]
5. thinker [1 mark]
6. cleaner [1 mark]
7. sweeper [1 mark]
8. cooker [1 mark]

Try these

-er words	root words
singer	sing [example]
helper	help [1 mark]
worker	work [1 mark]
caller	call [1 mark]
mixer	mix [1 mark]

Now try these

1. Jose is a fantastic football player. [example]
2. The gardener cut the grass. [1 mark]
3. The builder is building a house. [1 mark]
4. Mrs Brown is my teacher. [1 mark]
5. Billy has always been a dreamer. [1 mark]

Unit 11

Get started

1. dressed [example]
2. fizzed [1 mark]
3. played [1 mark]
4. sorted [1 mark]
5. snowed [1 mark]
6. cooked [1 mark]

Try these

-ed words	root words
kicked	kick [example]
parked	park [1 mark]
itched	itch [1 mark]
blinked	blink [1 mark]
pulled	pull [1 mark]

Now try these

1. Joel **painted** a picture. [example]
2. Last night it **snowed**. [1 mark]
3. The dog **panted** in the heat. [1 mark]
4. Jack **cleaned** his bedroom. [1 mark]
5. Dad **cooked** dinner last night. [1 mark

Unit 12

Get started

1. small   smaller   smallest   [example]
2. kind   kinder   kindest   [2 marks]
3. cold   colder   coldest   [2 marks]
4. clean   cleaner   cleanest   [2 marks]
5. pink   pinker   pinkest   [2 marks]
6. dark   darker   darkest   [2 marks]
7. neat   neater   neatest   [2 marks]

Try these

1. greener [example]
2. longest [1 mark]
3. faster [1 mark]
4. nearest / earnest [1 mark]
5. fuller [1 mark]

Now try these

1. Giraffes are the **tallest** animals on Earth. [example]
2. Feathers are **softer** than stones. [1 mark]
3. Africa is **warmer** than Iceland. [1 mark]
4. My dad is the **shortest** man I know. [1 mark]
5. My brother is strong. I am even **stronger**. But my mum is the **strongest**. [2 marks]

Unit 13

Get started

1. tasty [example]
2. party [1 mark]
3. family [1 mark]
4. hurry [1 mark]
5. bendy [1 mark]
6. fizzy [1 mark]
7. messy [1 mark]
8. angry [1 mark]
9. yummy [1 mark]

Try these

1. crazy [example]
2. lucky [1 mark]
3. jolly [1 mark]
4. mucky [1 mark]
5. crunchy [1 mark]

Now try these

1. The **silly** clown fell over his big shoes. [example]
2. I went on a **scary** ride at the fair. [1 mark]
3. Josh felt **sleepy** after swimming. [1 mark]
4. It was a **very windy** day. [2 marks]
5. I ride my **pony every** day. [2 marks]

Unit 14

Get started

1. dol**ph**in [example]
2. **ph**antom [1 mark]
3. **ph**onics [1 mark]
4. telegra**ph** [1 mark]
5. micro**ph**one [1 mark]
6. ele**ph**ant [1 mark]
7. gra**ph** [1 mark]
8. **ph**otogra**ph** [2 marks]
9. ne**ph**ew [1 mark]

Try these

1. phrase [example]
2. telephone [1 mark]
3. microphone [1 mark]
4. graph [1 mark]
5. orphan [1 mark]

Now try these

1. **Elephants** are very big animals.
2. I can say the **alphabet** backwards.
3. My mother's **nephew** is my cousin.
4. **Megaphones** make your voice louder.
5. Make a **photocopy** of this page.

Unit 15

Get started

1. **wh**ale [example]
2. **wh**at [1 mark]
3. **wh**ere [1 mark]
4. **wh**eel [1 mark]
5. **wh**isper [1 mark]
6. **wh**eeze [1 mark]
7. **wh**ine [1 mark]
8. **wh**ite [1 mark]
9. **wh**at [1 mark]

Try these

1. whisk [example]
2. when [1 mark]
3. which [1 mark]
4. white [1 mark]
5. why [1 mark]

Now try these

1. I keep a **white** rabbit as a pet. [example]
2. I wonder **why** the sky is blue. [1 mark]
3. **When** will it be your birthday? [1 mark]
4. Please tell me **what** your name is. [1 mark]
5. I use a **wheelchair** to get around. [1 mark]

Unit 16

Get started

1. b**ike** [example]
2. str**ike** [1 mark]
3. str**oke** [1 mark]
4. b**ake** [1 mark]
5. f**ake** [1 mark]
6. br**oke** [1 mark]
7. h**ike** [1 mark]

Try these

k before e: kettle [example]; kennel [1 mark]

k before i: skin [1 mark]; kid [1 mark]

k before y: frisky [1 mark]

Now try these

1. I like to fly my <u>kite</u> on windy days. [example]
2. Dirty socks smell <u>stinky</u>. [1 mark]
3. I like watching clouds in the <u>sky</u>. [1 mark]
4. The <u>king</u> rules over this land. [1 mark]
5. I like to bake <u>cakes</u> in the <u>kitchen</u>. [2 marks]

Unit 17

Get started

1. unwrap [example]
2. unzip [1 mark]
3. unlucky [1 mark]
4. undo [1 mark]
5. unsafe [1 mark]
6. unplug [1 mark]
7. unlock [1 mark]

Try these

1. brave: <u>unafraid</u> [example]
2. messy: <u>untidy</u> [1 mark]
3. not fair: <u>unjust</u> [1 mark]

4. take out: <u>unpack</u> [1 mark]

5. sad: <u>unhappy</u> [1 mark]

Now try these

1. Tommy **undressed** before having a bath.

2. To open the door you must **unlock** it first.

3. The sink is blocked. We need to **unplug** it.

4. That nasty boy is very **unkind**.

5. My muddy boots are very **unclean**.

Unit 18

Get started

1. foot   ball [example]

2. bed   room [1 mark]

3. black   berry [1 mark]

4. pop   corn [1 mark]

5. after   noon [1 mark]

6. sun   flower [1 mark]

7. snow   man [1 mark]

8. gold   fish [1 mark]

Try these

1. grandmother [example]

2. thunderstorm [1 mark]

3. starfish [1 mark]

4. farmyard [1 mark]

5. sunshine [1 mark]

Now try these

1. I do not want to be stung by a <u>jellyfish</u>. [example]

2. Tilly brushed her hair with a <u>hairbrush</u>. [1 mark]

3. We took a bus to the <u>airport</u>. [1 mark]

4. Our feet left <u>footprints</u> in the sand. [1 mark]

5. I put a <u>bookmark</u> in my book. [1 mark]

Unit 19

Get started

1. <u>Sunday</u> [example]

2. <u>Monday</u> [2 marks]

3. <u>Tuesday</u> [2 marks]

4. <u>Wednesday</u> [2 marks]

5. <u>Thursday</u> [2 marks]

6. <u>Friday</u> [2 marks]

7. <u>Saturday</u> [2 marks]

Try these

1. Sunday [example]

2. Monday [1 mark]

3. Tuesday [1 mark]

4. Wednesday [1 mark]

5. Thursday [1 mark]

6. Friday [1 mark]

7. Saturday [1 mark]

Now try these

1. On <u>S</u>unday we fed the ducks. [example]

2. <u>Monday</u> is the first day of the week. [1 mark]

3. On <u>Tuesday</u> Saul goes karate. [1 mark]

4. Seb swims on <u>Wednesday</u>. [1 mark]

5. Granny is visiting on <u>Thursday</u>. [1 mark]

6. We are going on holiday on <u>Friday</u>. [1 mark]

7. Let's go to town on <u>Saturday</u>. [1 mark]

Vocabulary, Grammar and Punctuation

Vocabulary Unit 1

Get started

1. My cat<u>s</u> are black. [example]

2. We pack the box<u>es</u>. [1 mark]

3. I saw some chick<u>s</u> in a nest. [1 mark]

4. Look at those pink bus<u>es</u>! [1 mark]

5. The children sat on the bench<u>es</u>. [1 mark]

Try these

1. I put my <u>socks</u> on my feet. [example]

2. I have three paint <u>brushes</u>. [1 mark]

3. All my <u>pens</u> had run out. [1 mark]

4. The <u>foxes</u> were in the den. [1 mark]

5. I had six <u>books</u>. [1 mark]

Now try these

1. Open-ended question: accept any sentence that includes the word **gifts**. [2 marks]

2. Open-ended question: accept any sentence that includes the word **wishes**. [2 marks]

Vocabulary Unit 2

Get started

1. I add<u>ed</u> one extra sweet to the bag. [example]

2. Max is a teach<u>er</u> in the next town. [1 mark]

3. Samir need<u>ed</u> to finish his task. [1 mark]

4. Zak is the fast<u>est</u> boy in the race. [1 mark]

5. Dad was sleep<u>ing</u> in his chair. [1 mark]

Try these

1. I was <u>meeting</u> my pet for the first time. [example]

2. The <u>gardener</u> has green fingers. [1 mark]

3. Dad <u>painted</u> the wall. [1 mark]

4. Katya is <u>looking</u> at her book. [1 mark]

5. Raj is the <u>loudest</u> singer. [1 mark]

Now try these

1. Open-ended question: accept any sentence that includes the word **painting**. [2 marks]

2. Open-ended question: accept any sentence that includes the word **playing**. [2 marks]

Vocabulary Unit 3

Get started

1. Tom can not <u>un</u>do the box. [example]

2. Karam will <u>un</u>hook the gate for you. [1 mark]

3. Meena is <u>un</u>afraid of bugs. [1 mark]

4. Jen will <u>un</u>load her bags. [1 mark]

5. Marc did some <u>un</u>paid jobs. [1 mark]

Try these

1. The <u>un</u>lit room was dark. [example]

2. Eva can not <u>un</u>stick her teeth from the toffee! [1 mark]

3. Jayden will <u>un</u>block the sink for us. [1 mark]

4. When I go to bed, I <u>un</u>dress myself. [1 mark]

5. Dad is unfit as he likes burgers too much! [1 mark]

Now try these

1. Open-ended question: accept any appropriate sentence that uses the word **unfair**. [2 marks]

2. Open-ended question: accept any appropriate sentence that uses the words **unpack**. [2 marks]

Grammar Unit 1

Get started

1. The dog is barking. [example]

2. The pin drops. [1 mark]

3. Marvis likes jam. [1 mark]

4. Tim has the ball. [1 mark]

5. We look at him. [1 mark]

Try these

1. The fox <u>runs</u> in the wood. [example]

2. The little <u>bugs</u> dig down. [1 mark]

3. Sam is <u>in</u> the bath. [1 mark]

4. The sun is so <u>hot</u>. [1 mark]

5. I have socks on my <u>feet</u>. [1 mark]

Now try these

1. Open-ended questions: accept any properly formed sentence about the student's lunch that has a capital letter at the start and a full stop at the end. Award one mark for correct use of capital letter, one mark for correct use of full stop and one mark for relevant content. [3 marks max]

2. Open-ended questions: accept any properly formed sentence about the student's family that has a capital letter at the start and a full stop at the end. Award one mark for correct use of capital letter, one mark for correct

use of full stop and one mark for relevant content. [3 marks max]

Grammar Unit 2

Get started

1. She brushes her hair <u>and</u> she brushes her teeth. [example]

2. I can hop <u>and</u> you can jump. [1 mark]

3. I like bats <u>and</u> he likes hats. [1 mark]

4. I can swim <u>and</u> we can sail. [1 mark]

5. Jaz will sing <u>and</u> he will shout. [1 mark]

Try these

1. I can stomp <u>and</u> you can stamp. [example]

2. She hears bells <u>and</u> she hears horns. [1 mark]

3. I go to you <u>and</u> you come to me. [1 mark]

4. It is raining <u>and</u> we get wet. [1 mark]

5. It is winter <u>and</u> you have a chill. [1 mark]

Now try these

1. We see bees and we see flowers. / We see flowers and we see bees. [1 mark]

2. He likes swinging and she likes running. / He likes running and she likes swinging. [1 mark]

Punctuation Unit 1

Get started

1. Jamal went for a run. [example]

2. Jan had a trip and fell! [2 marks]

3. There was a black bird in the garden. [2 marks]

4. What did my cat do? [2 marks]

5. My cat sat on a car. [2 marks]

Try these

1. I went to see a film. [example]

2. What was it like? [1 mark]

3. It was good. [1 mark]

4. What happened in it? [1 mark]

5. There was a funny clown! [1 mark]

Now try these

1. Can you skip? [2 marks]

2. I like books. [2 marks]

3. A shark is in my pond! [2 marks]

Punctuation Unit 2

Get started

1. <u>We</u> got the book for <u>Mark</u>. [example]

2. <u>She</u> did art with <u>Jorge</u>. [2 marks]

3. <u>After</u> this, <u>I</u> will go swimming. [2 marks]

4. <u>Then</u> <u>I</u> can see <u>Kim</u>. [2 marks]

5. <u>Jon</u> and <u>I</u> did maths with <u>Klaus</u>. [3 marks]

Try these

1. Now Carol has a doll. [example]
2. It is a fact that I like frogs. [2 marks]
3. Did you see how Eva can run? [2 marks]
4. Mum said that I sing like a pop star. [2 marks]
5. The cat is called Matt. [2 marks]

Now try these

1. Open-ended question: accept any three names that correctly use capital letters. [3 marks]
2. Open-ended question: accept any three words that correctly do not use capital letters. [3 marks]

Punctuation Unit 3

Get started

1. I live in Liverpool. [example]
2. We got the bus to London. [2 marks]
3. I went to Oxford. [2 marks]
4. We will have fun on Sunday. [2 marks]
5. On Monday we will be in the town of Bognor. [3 marks]

Try these

1. I think Robin lives in Ashford. [example]
2. We have a big day on Tuesday. [2 marks]
3. It is a fact that Friday is the day after Thursday. [3 marks]
4. The town of Elgin is in Scotland. [3 marks]
5. We go to Paris on Saturday. [3 marks]

Now try these

1. Open-ended question: accept any three place names that correctly use capital letters. [3 marks]
2. Open-ended question: accept any two sentences that correctly use capital letters, and accurately introduce the child and where he or she lives. Award one mark for each correctly used capital letter: for the child's name, for the place name, for the 'I', and at the beginnings of the sentences. [4 marks]